TRAVIS ELBOROUGH

Travis Elborough is the author of four acclaimed books: *The Bus We Loved*, a history of the Routemaster bus; *The Long Player Goodbye*, a hymn to vinyl records; *Wish You Were Here*, a survey of the British beside the seaside; and *London Bridge in America*, which tells the transatlantic story of the sale of the world's largest antique. From 2014 to 2015, he was the artist in residence at Victoria Park in East London.

TRAVIS ELBOROUGH

A Walk in the Park

Park

The Life and Times of a People's Institution

VINTAGE

1 3 5 7 9 10 8 6 4 2

Vintage
20 Vauxhall Bridge Road,
London SW1V 2SA

Vintage is part of the Penguin Random House group of companies whose
addresses can be found at global.penguinrandomhouse.com

Penguin
Random House
UK

Copyright © Travis Elborough 2016
Afterword © Travis Elborough 2017

Travis Elborough has asserted his right to be identified as the author of this
Work in accordance with the Copyright, Designs and Patents Act 1988

First published by Vintage in 2017
First published by Jonathan Cape in 2016

penguin.co.uk/vintage

A CIP catalogue record for this book is available from the British Library

ISBN 9780099593829

Printed and bound by Clays Ltd, St Ives Plc

Penguin Random House is committed to a sustainable future
for our business, our readers and our planet. This book is made
from Forest Stewardship Council® certified paper.

MIX
Paper from
responsible sources
FSC
www.fsc.org   FSC® C018179

For my parents and in
reminiscence of afternoons
spent on Sompting Rec

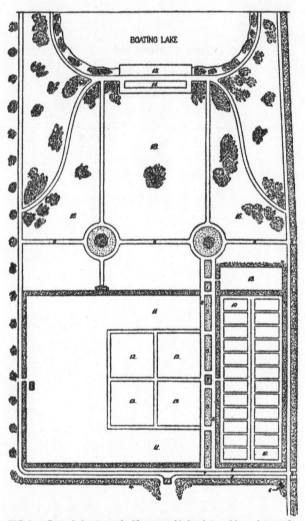

BOATING LAKE

FIG. 1a.—Ground plan (part of a 90-acre park) showing positions of games for which charges are made. 1, Public shelters ; 2, Bowls and Tennis Pavilion ; 3, Beds of ornamental shrubs and herbaceous plants ; 4, Shrubberies ; 5, Wide grass border ; 6, Public convenience ; 7, A 15-ft. walk ; 8, 10-ft. walks ; 9, Entrances from public highway ; 10, Tennis courts ; 11, Putting greens ; 12, Bowling greens ; 13, Croquet lawns ; 14, Boat house ; 15, Boating stage ; 16, Babies' lawns ; 17, Putting green ticket box ; 18, Grass sward for use of picnickers

CONTENTS

Introduction

The Swiss author Robert Walser once argued that it always feels like a Sunday in a park. Like Sundays, parks certainly occupy a unique temporal zone. For their visitors at least, they seem at one remove from workaday life. Time within them can be wasted, parks supplying the ideal location when we've nothing else to do. Or desperately want to do nothing in particular, and as languorously as possible. And yet they are also hives of activity – albeit of a leisurely, if athletic, kind.

When Walser spoke of Sundays, though, it was because, for him, these public spaces were imbued with the same melancholy as the interminable Sundays you only ever experience as a small child. Perhaps Walser's melancholy is unique, but the park, for many of us, is surely infused with childhood memories: of lazy sun-dappled afternoons, of swings and roundabouts, and mud-stained knees on the local playing fields, the aroma of freshly mown grass and the cloying scent of brightly coloured geraniums. Nearly all of us first encounter parks as small children. And, in due course, take our own children to parks. So maybe some of us do share Walser's melancholy – perhaps these spaces remind us of lost innocence and the passing of the years.

When it comes to space rather than time, the limits of the majority of public parks remain clearly demarcated by fences and gates. Such barriers are seemingly there to protect the park from the noise and mess of the town or city. Or vice versa, with the metropolis quite possibly fearing contamination from too much exposure to plants and grass, much like a small child forever nudging uneaten vegetables to the edge of their dinner plate. But these barriers also create an aura of expectation, crowning the park as a precious destination in its own right, one that takes us out of the humdrum streets surrounding it, and out of ourselves. For grander public parks, there are postcards to send and collect, as if they were far-flung and exotic locations. To orientate ourselves in these places we consult their maps as eagerly as sailors, back in the day, staved off scurvy with sauerkraut and peered at the horizon with a sextant in hope of land. And like other newly discovered worlds, their founding principles were on occasion utopian, if, in retrospect, no less naive, misguided, presumptuous and plain wrong.

And this is a crucial point. Public parks were indeed 'founded', or – to escape the metaphor, and put it plainly – *invented*. General access to tended green spaces and the ability to enjoy them at relative leisure are comparatively modern and hard-fought developments, and the roots of even the humblest neighbourhood park or recreation ground lie in age-old battles over land and liberty. In Britain and much of the developed world, historically very little land was ever truly public. Under feudal systems, all land was essentially the property of the King, and access to it granted directly by the Crown or via feudal lords. 'Common law' in Britain meant that there were such things as commons, where the public might, for instance, graze cattle. But this space was not at all sacred, and was frequently enclosed by royalty and landlords for their private pleasure.

This trend continued right up until the opening decades of the nineteenth century, as British monarchs remained unstinting in snaffling previously accessible land and adding it to their store of greenery. Charles I, for instance, had blocked off several local footpaths and removed acres of parish grazing ground when he walled in Richmond

Park in the 1630s. It was 1904 before the public got full access to the park again. And it was only the vigilance of Robert Walpole, Britain's de facto first Prime Minister, that prevented Queen Caroline from seizing the whole of St James's Park as her personal garden. While George IV's Regent's Park – which casually absorbed areas of smallholding farmland used to grow hay for London's horses – was developed as a money-making scheme for the Crown, with exclusive residential properties incorporated into what was a gated private park.

As we'll see, the creation of public parks wasn't a sudden thing. The first parks were private, and, more often than not, used as royal hunting grounds. But over time it became apparent to some enlightened souls that an unhappy, subjugated population would benefit from designated public green space. And so would their rulers. Indeed, many of the globe's most famous public parks were created in part to quell political unrest and prevent revolutions. Parks are, of course, tamed wilder-nesses. And as the world became farmed and then industrialised and consequently less wild, ecologically speaking, parks were widely deployed as tools to tame supposed wildness among the population, ease alienation and see off social discord.

But cultivated wildness can unexpectedly cultivate wildness, and much as rebellious peasants had once conspired to steal game from royal preserves, so disaffected urbanites would consistently use the park as a place to gather to misbehave, often disgracefully, a boon to doggers as much as democrats, and forcefully challenge authority.*

Parks are full of such fascinating contradictions: authoritarian yet liberating, public and communal yet private and solitary. This book aims to pick its way through them, exploring the park's place in history and parks as places where history has so often happened. It explores both the lives of the people who created landscapes that really have changed lives and the ordinary people who have used them.

But our cosy familiarity with public parks should not blind us to their increasing vulnerability in many countries around the world, and here in the UK too, for that matter. In a period when global economic conditions mean local authority budgets are being cut by central government, the upkeep and management of public parks is becoming ever harder to accomplish. Relief and support is being offered through outsourcing and private partnership, which, when it comes to a truly public resource, can be dangerous territory. In a world where almost anything, seemingly, can be converted into luxury flats, it's worth recalling that parks are a noticeable absence from the board game Monopoly.† As a character in Don DeLillo's 1973 novel

---

* One park ranger who led me on a tour of his particular park pointed out a copse seemingly popular with those cruising for gay sex, and said, entirely oblivious to the double entendre, 'As you can see, it's a heavily wooden area'.

† Though the world's largest permanent Monopoly board is to be found in a park in downtown San Jose, California.

Great Jones Street presciently observed, 'the whole secret of corporate structures' is to tell 'the enemy you'll plant some trees'. Protests such as those in 2013 in Istanbul against plans to redevelop Gezi Park in Taksim Square into a private shopping mall – protests which were violently suppressed by Turkish government forces – may become more familiar sights.

So many snippets of our own histories are bound up in the hours we've whiled away in parks. Days, if not weeks, of my own life have been spent in them. As I'm a city dweller with no garden, they are where I normally go to escape the desk and work. For the past three years, that was impossible. The local park served as an office, laboratory, a rebuke to procrastination and a place to talk to people about parks, all rolled into one. The resulting book then is a user's history of sorts, one informed by the odd field trip and underscored by my foibles and preoccupations.

Like a walk in any park, it probably strays off an already winding path on occasions. There are, no doubt, one or two intermittent, or unexpected, pauses to survey a scene or take in the flowers, or watch a football game along the way. But hopefully its overall passage is no less diverting for that. Most parks are, after all, largely peripatetic places, and part of their beauty is that we usually take them in at our own pace.

CHAPTER I

Killing Fields and Common Lands

In the photograph posted online, the goatskin looked purple. And less like a goat skin than a dried-out jellyfish. Or a pair of diseased lungs, of the kind cigarette manufacturers appear obliged to put on packets to dissuade smokers. The purple ranged from light violet to a thoroughly poisonous deadly nightshade. It was mottled with patches of white, the sickliness of its pigmentation brought sharply into focus by the green of the long grass on which it lay. 'This is not a goatskin rug', the poster advised. 'There is flesh still attached to it.' This grisly specimen had been found in Clissold Park in Stoke Newington in May 2015. Its discovery caused consternation among the Park User Group's Facebook page, and excitable column inches in the local and national press – 'Black magic fears as whole animal skin is found in Clissold Park' ran a not untypical headline. This is as appropriate a place as any to begin, as from the very outset parks have been concerned with slaughter.

The English word derives from the Old French *parc*, meaning 'an enclosed preserve for beasts of the chase', and the earliest known literary description of a park-type landscape appears in the ancient Sumerian tale *The Epic of Gilgamesh*. Believed to have been written around 2000 BC, it tells the story of two friends – Gilgamesh, ruler of Uruk, a third human and two-thirds deity; and Enkidu, a wild man of the woods previously given to consorting with animals – and their quest to discover the secret of immortality. The quest leads them to a sacred cedar forest, forbidden to mortals. Well-tended, with winding trails and beautiful flowers, tall trees, sweet-smelling plants and exotic beasts, it is a park, to all intents and purposes. It even has its own keeper, an ogre named Humbaba, whose 'breath' is said to be 'like fire ... and jaws like death'.

The poem was preserved on stone tablets from the Assyrian King Ashurbanipal's palace at Nineveh (near today's Mosul in Iraq). The Assyrian monarchy established garden hunting preserves across the Tigris–Euphrates Valley from around 1250 BC. Here native herbivores along with more colourful ostriches, lynx and lions roamed in sumptuous greenery, specially cultivated to enhance sporting pleasures. These were places to entertain as well as exterminate, with lodges for wining and dining honoured guests. Over time, other delights were added and horticultural diversions gradually grew in importance alongside the hunting. These early parks became a means, and sometimes on an epic scale, of expressing status and power. Such gardens were adopted, refined and further propagated by the Persians after they conquered Mesopotamia in 539 BC. Indeed, they were refined to such an extent that the parklands and walled gardens of ancient Iran, first encountered by the Israelites during their exile in Babylon between 597 BC and 538 BC, were known as *pairidaeza* – literally paradise. Such gardens are almost indisputably the source for the Judaeo-Christian concept of the Garden of Eden.

As for Britain, there is little in the way of evidence of parks before the Norman Conquest – though the Romans would certainly have had gardens and reserves for deer and other animals.

For a long time it was believed that once the Romans had left, the English landscape basically went to pot, rather as the home of an elderly widower whose wife had always done the cooking and cleaning might. And while the Saxons had a bit of a bash about, draining the odd marsh and clearing a forest or two and holding folkmoots to determine who got which parcel of land, 'vast areas remained in their natural state, awaiting the sound of a human voice', as W. G. Hoskins once put it. It was only with the arrival of the Normans that the real business of a medieval way of life got going with the strip fields, farmsteads, roads, villages and towns that persisted into Chaucer's day. More recent archaeological findings, however, clearly show that the Normans only intensified a process of urbanisation that had been under way since about the seventh century. But in inserting a fresh layer of government, and an attendant army of clerks to help rule and administer this new kingdom, the conquerors would leave far more comprehensive records than their Saxon predecessors; for example, the very first reference to a British park appears in a Saxon document dated 1045, but this is a haphazard mention in a personal will, rather than any official census or registry. It almost seems too much of a tabloid cliché to note that the Normans hailed from the land that eventually gave the world the word 'bureaucracy'.

Prior to the Norman Conquest, a manorial system had operated in Britain. The manor, essentially, was the most basic, and supposedly self-sufficient, collective agrarian unit – typified by a village settlement like that of Bruegel's painting *Summer*, with a church, cottages, hovels, working fields and hay meadows, a pond for ducks (and for dunking witches), and a manor house. Following the Norman Conquest, this system was formalised. One of the first laws enacted by William in January 1067 was to declare that all land in England belonged to the Crown. Accordingly, all manors now came under the monarch's gift, and more significant individuals from the state or Church might be granted the governance of more than one, their estate consisting of a variety of lands. The manor was then subdivided. One half was retained by the lord for 'his own support' and tended by serfs, the other

half 'parcelled out' in return for 'services'. William himself magnani-
mously dished out property as a reward to those who'd rendered service
in the invasion or at other points along the way.

There remained, nevertheless, certain civil rights under common law
that were recognised and supported by the Anglo-Norman courts.
Among the most confusing are the rights of the so-called 'commons'.

Contrary to widely held opinion, 'commons' did not *belong* to 'the
people'. Technically, all land in Norman England was subject to some
kingly edict and, under the manorial system, either owned, leased, lent or

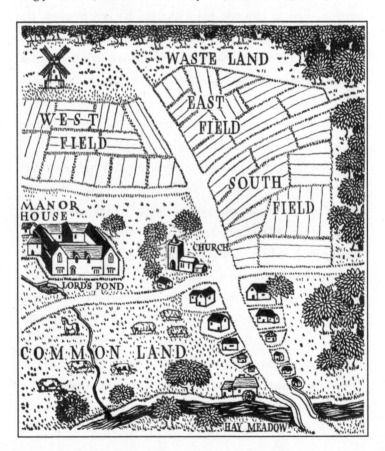

gifted for such time as was agreed. But often, in acknowledgement of long-standing traditions and arrangements under common law, local people had free access and use of fallow or perpetually 'waste' ground, for collecting firewood, grazing their animals, and for recreation. None of these were casual endeavours as such. Berries and plants foraged or animals reared and nurtured on the common might add to the wealth of the manor by providing subsistent serfs or tenant farmers with extra food or fuel, thus keeping them from freezing or starving to death, seeking charity or taking up poaching. Many of the sports undertaken on these 'waste grounds', archery particularly, were encouraged for their potential military benefits when the time came to raise an army. It was to that end that an Act of Parliament in Shakespeare's day was to rule that it was not

> lawful to any person or persons to inclose or take in any parte of the Commons or Waste Groundes scituate lienge or beinge within three Myles of any gates of the ... Cittie of London ... heretofore used for trayninge and musteringe of Souldiers ... and for the use and exercise of Archerie ...

For now, though, commons could be used freely by the common people. Until, that is, their manorial lords sought to indulge in their favourite pastime, at which point commons and the people's freedom to roam on previously open land would be radically reduced.

While they were certainly keen pen-pushers and expert bureaucrats, the Normans also prided themselves on being an elite warrior caste. These were, after all, the same 'north men' who only a couple of generations earlier had sailed south from Scandinavia with the flaming of villages on their minds. Hunting was the proving ground of such a caste, and they had a particular obsession with the sport. On horseback. With dogs. With hawks. With a bow and arrow. With a sword. You name it: beast, bird, fish or disobedient Saxon fellow – if it could be hunted, Normans needed only the flimsiest of pretexts to be after it with something sharp.

But it wasn't just a question of satisfying a certain bloodlust. For teaching horsemanship, instilling discipline, courage and a reverence for the land, learning to hunt was considered an essential part of any nobleman's education, and would remain so for centuries to come. In an anonymous letter of 1517, a friend of Richard Pace, Cardinal Wolsey's secretary, wrote that: 'It behoves the sons of gentlemen to blow horn calls correctly, to hunt skilfully, to train a hawk well and carry it elegantly.' And as late as 1653, Izaak Walton similarly commended its pedagogical qualities for the upper crust, in his book *The Compleat Angler*, writing:

> Hunting trains up the younger nobility to the use of manly exercise
> in their riper age. What more manly exercise than hunting the
> Wild Boar, the Stag, the Buck, the Fox or the Hare? How doth
> it preserve health, and increase strength and activity.

Walton's stress on manliness rather ignores the fact that many aristocratic women – Queen Elizabeth I and her mother Anne Boleyn, to name but two – were no less avid hunters. Though Privy Purse accounts record that Boleyn only succeeded in bagging a cow on one deer hunt.

In order to satisfy this elite desire to hunt during the Middle Ages, a process of emparkment began, as more and more nobles and churchmen sought royal licences to set aside areas of their estates for game reserves, and even enclosed so-called commons for the purpose. With the passing of William the Conqueror's 1079 Forest Law, which allowed the granting of these licences, the public lost any access they may have had to the land.

This stipulated that only the King and his court, and those granted the privilege to do so, were allowed to hunt deer and 'other beasts of the chase'. The penalties for breaking the law were severe, with anyone caught slaying 'a hart or hind' blinded. The law also covered the trees and herbage that the deer fed on, hereby criminalising the gathering of timber or allowing your own pigs to stray into the woods to feast on scrub and acorns.* An understandably unpopular law with the people, its abolition would be one of the conditions demanded by King John's disgruntled barons in the Magna Carta. Perhaps there was some justice when the Conqueror's son and England's second Norman king, William Rufus, was felled by a stray arrow while out hunting in Hampshire's New Forest – a forest that was 'new' precisely because his father had recently emparked it under the law.

* Under the 1390 Statute of the Realm, Richard II would go even further, restricting gaming itself to the aristocratic sphere, decreeing that hunting with hounds, ferrets and snares was prohibited to those who lacked 'lands and tenements to the value of 40s a year, or any priest or clerk if he had not preferment of £10'.

The new enclosures were far from simple 'killingscapes'. Their creation made a pleasant change from fruitlessly wading after game through the country's then endless woods and forests. But such predictability, that you could count on a kill – the whole point of all these parks, essentially – also allowed greater displays of pageantry and ritual to creep into hunts. Hunting, as it were, became more refined for the elite. The savagery of the slaughter of beasts, like men in battle for that matter, came to be ruled by a code of chivalry that by definition rendered it noble. If no one batted an eyelid at fox-tossing (the game of lobbing a live fox up and down, trampoline-style, on a sheet or blanket until it expired), killing a beast of the chase 'falsely' was a grave offence to the spirit of hunting.

But in time, treatises on its etiquette like William Twiti's *The Noble Art of Venery* of 1314, and Gaston Phoebus's *Le Livre de chasse* of 1387, would offer advice for novice sportsmen. Phoebus, whose book included tips on how to trap a wild boar (most likely already extinct in England by that time), added a spiritual dimension to the sport. Equating hunting with godliness, he wrote, 'Good hunters live long and happily, when they die, they go to Paradise.'

On a practical level, the parks also served as meat counters for hungry manorial lords and their kith, kin and dependants. Monarchs too. Henry II's park at Havering in Essex yielded over forty fallow deer a year for his banqueting tables. This royal menu of turf and more turf was regularly augmented by the monks who ran the Priory Park in Somerset (founded in 1090) with surf in the form of fish from their ponds and wine from their vineyards. The medieval deer parks seemed to function, as the landscape historian Susan Lasdun has written, 'as a kind of auxiliary farm'. As the Middle Ages progressed, however, grazing animals such as sheep were fast becoming too profitable an addition for many park owners to ignore entirely in favour of deer.

In any event, the private parks boomed. Only thirty-one parks were recorded in the Domesday Book in 1087, but over 1,900 were counted a century and a half later and it is estimated that by 1300 there were already some 3,200 parks in Britain. Two centuries on from that Polydore Vergil, the Archdeacon of Wells, maintained that up to a third of the country was under parkland and stated that 'almost everywhere a man may see clausures and parks paled and enclosed'. Like the sacred garden of *Gilgamesh*, this land remained forbidden to the mere mortal that was the common man.

For ease of enclosing and to save on the cost of fencing and paling, most parks were circular or oval in shape. Some were surrounded by a bank or deep ditch, sometimes filled with water not unlike a castle's moat. In 1129, Henry I went as far as to have seven miles of stone wall erected around Woodstock, 'favourite seat of his retirement and privacy' in Oxfordshire. Here, aside from a hunting lodge and the usual park fare, he kept the first royal menagerie, with lions, leopards, lynxes, camels and England's first porcupine, a gift from William of Montpellier, which was later removed to the Tower of London.

Another structure at Woodstock gave rise to the legend of 'Fair Rosamond', a mythic tale of regal adultery, queen-on-concubine murder, mazes and yarn. Henry II – the first of the Plantagenets, whose request to be rid of 'this turbulent priest' led to the martyrdom of Thomas Becket – had his mistress Rosamond Clifford installed in a cloistered garden apartment, a bower 'of stone and timber strong', in the recesses of the park. This love-nest-cum-hideaway, known as 'Everswell', was a complex of rooms, courtyards and ornamental pools centred around a spring. According to the story, for extra protection it was concealed deep within a labyrinth that only the King knew how to navigate. Unfortunately for Rosamond, the King's wife was Eleanor of Aquitaine, a formidable adversary by any standards. And by following the trail of a silken thread allegedly snagged on one of Henry's spurs Eleanor succeeded in gaining entry to the bower, where she forced her rival to drink a draught of poison. Immortalised in courtly romances and medieval ballads, it later proved a particular favourite with the Pre-Raphaelites, for whom the chance to paint what is effectively a maiden-on-maiden catfight with some embroidery thrown in proved peculiarly irresistible.

Rosamond ponds or pools, such as one in St James's Park until the 1770s, dedicated to her memory, or the juiciness of her murder, became a popular addition to many parks. Sadly, though, there is nothing to support the poisoning rumour. Rosamond died peacefully in 1176 at a convent to which she'd voluntarily withdrawn. Everswell, though, did exist. Royal accounts from 1166 record a payment for the upkeep or installation of the spring or pool: '£26 9s. 4d *in operatione fontis*'. In 1239, Henry III had a herbarium put up around one of the pools and twenty-five years later ordered a hundred pear trees to be planted around the garden.

In the seventeenth century, by which point Everswell had fallen into ruins, the antiquarian John Aubrey, whose nurse sang him to sleep with verses about Rosamond as a child, visited Woodstock and sketched the remains of three pools. From his drawings, garden historians have surmised that Everswell was most probably modelled on the walled water gardens of Moorish Spain, reports of which would have reached England in the wake of the successive Crusades; or, more likely still, on similar Islamic gardens in Sicily, which the Norman king Roger I was busy conquering between 1070 and 1090. The presence of a garden such as Everswell within a larger hunting park indicates an attention to horticultural aesthetics that would start to take hold in the Middle Ages, and was to continue in country house estates and parks for centuries.

In the latter half of the Middle Ages, Europe was knocked sideways by the Black Death, which first appeared at Messina in Sicily in 1347. Counter-intuitively, perhaps, this would not be all bad for parks. As the population diminished, idle agricultural land was sometimes colonised for deer and other game. Indeed, as the historian Emma Griffin observes in her history of hunting, *Blood Sport*: 'The century following the Black Death is widely regarded as something of a golden age in the history of hunting, the reduction in population creating a straightforward increase in hunting opportunities.' In Shropshire, for example, eleven new parks were laid out between 1350 and 1370, and in Northamptonshire deserted villages were turned into private parks, though lack of labour meant the enclosures there were not fenced but banked. Traces of ridge and furrow beneath the surface were the only indication of the land's earlier use.

But the Black Death also brought about a subtle recalibration of the park towards breeding and feeding a much wider range of animals than before, and some would even be turned over almost entirely to grazing. With pigeons a reliable source of all-year-round meat, dovecotes flourished in manorial parklands following the Black Death, as surplus grain previously devoted to humans could now feed birds. Rabbits also thrived. The Romans probably first brought the animal to these shores, but the Normans bred them more assiduously; Henry III was credited in 1241 with owning one of the earliest purpose-built warrens in Guildford, Surrey. Peter des Roches, Bishop of Winchester to Henry III and before that to King John, who had grown accustomed to eating rabbit in his native Poitou, was seemingly the major catalyst for the conspicuous consumption of this French delicacy among the high-born and the High Church in England in this period. After the Plague, warrens spread in the acres of land left spare or that were too difficult to farm for lack of hands. While the sheer numbers of rabbits soon meant their meat ceased to be an expensive luxury, their skins proved a viable commercial product. Cultivated on manorial estates and in parkland, they also made for easy sport, satisfying the basic need for a kill whenever deer or larger prey were proving more elusive. Elsewhere, hunting-ground fishponds were leased to peasants in search of food and livelihood, and at Pinner Park, under the Archbishop of Canterbury's Manor of Harrow, the local peasants were given leave to feed their pigs in the deer park during these grim years.

This act of generosity, however, was not enough to stop peasants plundering the park and the manor in the revolt of 1381, an early example of a park – at this point the very emblem of authority – as the site of protest against social injustice and the powers that be. It was far from the first example, of course: royal parks and forests had been raided at the death of William the Conqueror back in 1087. Indeed, the road to parkdom was not always smooth for the landed gentry, and there had been some encouraging victories for the common(-ish) people over high-handed emparkment. In 1292, Edward I granted a licence to the Bishop of London, Richard de Gravesend, to enclose and fence part of his land at Bow and stock it with deer to use as a personal game park. But in an era not short of baronial rebellions, the licence was successfully revoked, after the Aldermen of the City protested that:

> from time when no memory is extant, they, the citizens of London, had used to take and hunt in the said woods and without, hares, conies, foxes and other beasts. And they pray that this Bishop may

hold his woods in the form and manner as his predecessors have held them. And they will not consent that he enclose them, nor will they grant him any warren.

But with the English Reformation and the dissolution of the monasteries, a select few laymen even found themselves in possession of their own parks. Henry VIII's seizure of the Church's substantial lands, which included plenty of deer parks, orchards and gardens, and the subsequent dispersal of two-thirds of them through grace-and-favour gifts and hard-cash sales, was to have wide-ranging consequences. Not least of which was an expanded and greatly enriched aristocracy, who in the long run would be far less dependent on either the Crown or the Church. Some of the aristocracy even found themselves with a surplus of land. The offloading of this surplus to richer merchants, or to those who'd risen to the gentry from yeomanry by industry, patronage or political intrigue (or all three), was to produce a new landed class.

For these nouveau riche, owning a country pile was a mark of having arrived – manors making the gentleman, as it were. They also knew that having a hunting park was essential to looking the part. In this, the lead had been taken by the monarch himself. A fanatical hunter, as a boy the young King Henry had lapped up *The Mayster of Game*, a primer by Edward, 2nd Duke of York. As king, he would enclose thousands of acres to indulge a love of blood sports and in his younger years he sometimes exhausted eight horses in a day at the saddle. One of his secretaries remarked that in respect of the animal Henry spared 'no pain to convert the sport of hunting into martyrdom'. Even whole villages, like Cuddington in Surrey, sacrificed for the park at Nonsuch Palace, were razed to make room for formal gardens and rolling hills where chase might be given to red and fallow deer. In London his new hunting parks – at Whitehall in 1532 (remade as St James's), Hyde in 1536, Richmond in 1637 and Marylebone in around 1640 (later subsumed into Regent's Park) – would ring the city, like a tourniquet. The conditions of exclusion of the general public, were, unsurprisingly, absolutist. The Hyde Park Edict of 1536, for example, records that: 'as the King's most royal majesty is desirous to have the games of hare, partridge and heron preserved, in and about the honour of his palace of Westminster, for his own disport and pastime, no person on pain of imprisonment of their bodies ... is to presume to hunt or hawk' in the preserve.

Henry's main London seat was Greenwich Palace, a site first emparked by Humphrey, Duke of Gloucester in 1433. Here he had a royal tiltyard, a 'real tennis' court and cockpit added to the grounds. It was at this tiltyard that a forty-four-year-old Henry would be crushed under his own armoured horse in a joust. The injuries the King received that day severely impaired his mobility and prevented him from ever competing in the sport again. They quite plausibly also contributed to a rapid decline in his physical and mental health, with the piling on of pounds and the turnover of wives stepping up in near unison from thereon in.

Despite, or perhaps because of, being maimed by his own horse, Henry was preoccupied with the quality of English mounts. On the Continent, the mounts of the British cavalry had cut a rather meagre picture against the steeds of the Dutch and as early as 1535, prior to his accident, the King had passed the Breed of Horses Act to improve what he judged to be the poor stature and shape of English nags. Another of his innovations was establishment of the Honourable Band of Gentlemen Pensioners, a corps of servants in the King's Household who furnished riding horses on royal occasions, among other duties. After the Dissolution, the corps was provided with the grants of several former monasterial parks on the understanding that they would promote 'the better breeding of horses'.

Henry is credited with being the first English king to race horses, having laid out a flat course at Cobham in Surrey. This future Sport of Kings, to a large part predicated on the idea of steeds chasing after, well, nothing really, was, in effect, hunting without a prey. Its development ran in parallel to the dwindling stocks of the most prized quarry: red deer. By 1539, their numbers in the Royal Game preserves of the north of England are calculated to have fallen to just 2,000. Emparked and purpose-bred fallow bucks were to make up the numbers, and coursing – running after hares with greyhounds – rose in popularity.

Along with breeding horses, Henry sponsored the cultivation of fresh strains of plants and fruits. At Richmond as early as 1501, his gardens were saluted for 'having many vines, seeds and strange fruit, right goodly beset, kept nourished with much labour and dignity'. In 1542 his head gardener imported the first 'apricock' from Italy. Orange groves were to follow and, in their ornamentation and the rigour of their planting, these were to advance the notion of the pleasure garden as a feature of all noble parks. Indeed, soon the private park was emerging as a much broader aristocratic theatre of play, one where hunting in all its forms would slowly start to take a back seat to horticulture.

In this era, whole new horizons were being opened up by maritime exploration, as lands were found to plug the gaps on existing maps. At home, woods and forests were felled to provide the timber needed for naval and merchant vessels, and the local British countryside took a dent to its image: with the discoveries of distant new lands it seemed a little tamer, a little less strange. Meanwhile, exotic flora and fauna began arriving from far-off lands and populating noble parks and gardens.

Besides providing such exotic new attractions, exploration also affected the layout of noble parks. The need for more reliable charts and tables for navigation spurred developments in mathematics and astronomy, including the writings and theories of Copernicus and, later, Johannes Kepler, which were to spin the whole cosmology of the galaxy around, placing the sun rather than the earth at the centre of the known universe. This fascination with geometry seeped into all areas of late Tudor life. The upper classes wore it on their bodies. On the doublets and hoses, jerkins, padded-shouldered jackets and narrow-waisted outfits of the wealthiest were John Dee's beloved Euclidean proofs in satin, velvet, fur and silk. And, perhaps most of all, it was written into the landscape of royal gardens, parks and country estates – gardens which were now framed by the window-pane glass of ever more stately homes, the same glass whose manufacture was simultaneously being refined to produce the lenses for spyglasses to observe the constellations of the heavens and the shorelines of foreign lands.

At Quarrendon in Buckinghamshire – the seat of Sir Henry Lee, who'd entered service at the court of Henry VIII at the age of fourteen and weathered the reigns of Edward and Mary to become 'Champion' to Elizabeth I – a noble house stood in grounds that were composed of a park, a rabbit warren and a quadrilateral water garden, with channels, terraced promenades and platforms, all neatly subdivided into geometric patterns. More orderly still was Sir Francis Willoughby's estate at Wollaton in Nottinghamshire. Aside from accommodating early coal mines – the source of much of his wealth – and a deer park, it had eight square gardens. These were arranged around a new hall, designed and built by the architect Robert Smythson in the 1580s.

Each of these contained further smaller 'knot' gardens in an almost Matryoshka doll regress of algebraic greenery. In an era when few flowering plants outlasted the summer months, patterning or 'knotting' was used to create interest. Hedges of evergreens, trellises of flowers, dwarf shrubs and raised beds of herbs such as lavender, hyssop, marjoram and thyme were planted in geometrical maze-like arbours, around a central feature, such as a fountain or statue. The patterned knot garden was to become ubiquitous in the sixteenth and seventeenth century, with 'the quartered garden' of four knots among the most popular iteration of the form.*

Willoughby's house and gardens had largely been remade to accommodate a visit by Queen Elizabeth and her court. Sir William Cecil – Lord Treasurer and Elizabethan spymaster extraordinaire, who 'fetched his gentry from Oxford not from heraldry' – added Cheshunt Park to his manor Theobalds in Hertfordshire in 1570, and embarked on a similarly extravagant redecorating programme there in preparation for the same royal visitor. He would spend nearly as much on the park and gardens as on his new mansion, completed in around 1585. There was an intimate walled privy garden, with fountains, gravel paths, shaped topiary and cherry trees, with borders of lilies, tulips and peonies giving off heady scents. Beyond that was a seven-acre grand garden, itself composed of nine individual square knot gardens – and all of it tended by John Gerard, author of *The Herball*, one of Elizabethan gardening's most sacred texts.

Such tidiness, though, was to be criticised by Cecil's own nephew, Francis Bacon, in *Of Gardens*, a celebrated essay from 1597. If accepting that gardens were 'best to be square', Bacon mocked 'knot

---

* It strikes me that the popularity of mazes in this era is partially a response to deforestation. Where formerly there had been great wild acres of trees to lose yourself in, the Tudorbethans were increasingly compelled to rely on mazes to recapture that primal thrill of being bewildered by apparently unending green stuff at every turn.

gardens' as 'but toys' and called for a spot of 'natural wildness', advocating: 'Thickets made only of sweet-briar and honeysuckle, and some wild vine amongst; and the ground set with violets, strawberries, and primroses. For these are sweet, and prosper in the shade. And these to be in the heath, here and there, not in any order ... wild thyme; some with pinks; some with germander, that gives a good flower to the eye.'

Among the more novel elements of Theobalds was a majestic avenue of trees that ran through the park and up to the main gate. An example of trigonometry in action, it evidently impressed the Queen herself, as it was appropriated for her own Hyde Park, where an avenue of walnut trees was planted not long afterwards. Such avenues were to become prevalent features of all parks in the coming century and a half. Their growth was both an acknowledgement in England of the arrival of the *novus homo* who transcended the old constraints of feudal society, but also – and vitally – a graphic assertion of the right of the privileged to bend nature, and therefore society, to their will.

It was for this very reason that parks would be deliberately targeted by Parliamentarian-types during the English Civil War. The petty blocking off of local footpaths and the removing of acres of parish grazing ground by Charles I when he walled up Richmond Park in the 1630s was a move which echoed the persistent enclosing carried out by all his royal predecessors. Still, it was reason enough for those of a Republican mindset to subsequently trash pales and kill deer at Royalist estates such as Fawley Court in Buckinghamshire. But the English monarchs' authoritarianism was as nothing when compared to what several regal exiles were to encounter on the Continent.

CHAPTER 2

Playing in the Park

On a warm August day in 1901, two genteel English ladies on vacation in France paid a visit to the Palace of Versailles and its gardens. Charlotte Anne Moberly and Eleanor Jourdain were academic spinsters – or blue-stockings, in the language of the day – who knew each other only slightly. Moberly was the principal of St Hugh's, a women's college at Oxford. Jourdain, an Oxford graduate and the headmistress of a girls' school in Watford, was being considered for the post of vice-principal of St Hugh's. The trip had been arranged as a chance for the two women, both daughters of clergymen, to get acquainted and see if they would be compatible as colleagues. Evidently it was a success, as they would live and work together for thirteen years, until Jourdain's death in 1924. A far less predictable outcome to their French sojourn was an encounter with the ghosts of Marie Antoinette and her entourage.

The pair had begun their trip cautiously, circling each other with all the stilted delicacy of characters from a Henry James novel. Soon, though, the practical task of consulting Baedeker and accumulating sights, sounds, buildings, museums and galleries eased them into affable companionability. Neither of them had thought much of the Palace of Versailles itself, the grandiose centrepiece of Louis XIV's court – their mutual dislike a pleasing confirmation of shared sensibilities and maybe a certain English prejudice against the baroque and rococo. With this item on their itinerary ticked off, actually and figuratively, they decided to venture out into the palace grounds and went in search of Le Petit

Trianon, the garden chateau favoured as a residence by Marie Antoinette before the French Revolution. According to their map, it lay half a mile away to the north, but the weather was fine, the landscaped surroundings inviting, and the women were in the mood for a walk.

As they strolled beyond the bottom of the Long Water and deeper into a park landscape of delicate mazy paths and meandering streams, dark glades and little knolls, they became disorientated and soon realised they were lost. Passing an empty farmhouse and an old wooden plough, they saw a peasant woman hanging sheets from an outhouse window. From here on in, the day went out of joint. Jourdain recalled being gripped by 'a heavy dreaminess' and walking as if asleep. Moberly noted that everything looked 'unnatural ... flat and lifeless ... no life stirred in the trees' and everything was 'intensely still'. A succession of figures dressed in eighteenth-century costume now appeared at every path, lawn, bower and ornamental bridge, some proffering directions and others warnings. There were footmen in 'long greyish-green coats with small three-cornered hats'; a woman and a child in white bodices; a sinister-looking man with a dark complexion and a smallpox-pitted face in a black cloak and slouch hat; and a solicitous fellow with curly hair, raffish in a large sombrero hat and silver-buckled shoes, who showed them the way to Le Petit Trianon. Finally there, Moberly alone spied a fair-haired noble-looking woman in a shady white hat, her shoulders covered by a pale green shawl, sitting on a stool sketching. At that instant, they were ushered inside the Trianon chateau, where – to their relief – a wedding party of a thoroughly contemporary kind was in full swing.

Neither woman, apparently, said anything about what they'd experienced until after their return to England. It was 1901. Queen Victoria had only just died. Electric trams were a new thing. Skirts continued to touch the floor. Any indelicate topic had to be broached privately, and then only nudged toward, once several willow-patterned china plates of cucumber sandwiches and cups of tea had been exhausted. Still, after finally comparing notes and undertaking lengthy investigations and further field studies at Versailles, the answer became completely and unquestionably obvious to them: they'd fallen through a time slip and telepathically 'entered a daydream' of Marie Antoinette. Le Petit Trianon, enjoyed so happily by that doomed queen, had manifested itself before them, replete with loyal servants and treacherous chateau conspirators. Nothing else could possibly explain what had happened.

Their earliest accounts of that afternoon's events were rejected out of hand by the Society for Psychical Research – a body often forgiving enough of no less batty reports of visitations by royals and others who had met with a grisly end. But a decade later a book entitled *An Adventure*, embellished by further researches in France and published under pseudonyms to protect the authors' university positions, became a sensational bestseller, and would go through some five reprints.

It, too, was denounced as preposterous. Critics pointed to gaping inconsistencies, the languor of its construction, the gender of its twin authors and their inability to read maps or negotiate the simplest of garden paths. Several theories were advanced to explain what they might or might not have seen. 'Cinematograph' shoots, fancy-dress parties, full-on theatrical re-enactments, or just a basic miscomprehension about what still passed for 'ordinary' uniforms for French grounds people, were mooted as alternative explanations of their spectral apparitions.

For the rest of their lives, the book's authors clung to their story, supplementing new editions with responses to their detractors. But with the death of Moberly in 1937, their true identities as a couple of female Oxford dons became known. Far from ending interest, it excited it further. To those incredulous already, it seemed genuinely astonishing that these supposedly intelligent people had remained wedded to such palpable nonsense. Others wondered if there might not be some truth in it after all. Barely veiled accusations of lesbianism and, conversely, their own spinsterish disgust at stumbling upon a gay orgy were offered as possible solutions in the latter half of the twentieth century.

Their odd tale reaffirmed Versailles as a region of strange, often transcendent, spectacle. Parks, of course, had always been about performance – in British hunting parks, for instance, the number of kills and prowess in the field was coupled with pageantry – but Versailles raised this to stage-set proportions.

* * *

The palace started life as a relatively modest hunting lodge for King Louis XIII before being rebuilt along far grander lines by his son Louis XIV, the so-called Sun King. In 1661, having decided to shift his court and the seat of French government to Versailles from the Tuileries Palace in Paris, Louis XIV commissioned the gardener and architect André Le Nôtre to remodel the grounds into a lavish 117-acre park. The park took over twenty years to complete, with 36,000 workers toiling on it. An immense project, its construction involved transplanting hundreds of tons of earth and thousands of trees – full-grown oaks, beech, elm and limes – from across France in wheelbarrows and carts, and diverting the River Eure by some fifty miles to form its main water feature, a Grand Canal populated by Venetian-style gondoliers who serenaded visiting dignitaries.

Such guests were at the mercy of byzantine rules of etiquette that pervaded all aspects of court life. A control freak in modern parlance, Louis succeeded in reducing most powerful nobles to gibbering syco-phants by rigorously ordering their every action at Versailles from sunrise to sunrise. It was a testament to his superego's grip on the psyche of his courtiers that even in his absence hats would be removed at royal dining tables. Portraits of the monarch were afforded almost as much respect as the ruler himself, with no one daring to turn their back on a picture of the King, and a good many choosing to reverse from state rooms, bowing to a likeness in oils, just to be on the safe side.

They were, however, unlikely to be surprised by Louis, whose daily life ran like clockwork. Louis de Rouvroy, duc de Saint-Simon, the great chronicler of life at Versailles in Louis's time, once observed that 'with a watch and an almanac, at three hundred leagues from court, one knows what the King is doing'.

Nothing at Versailles was spared this regimentation. The symmetry of the parterres, the level gardens likened to Turkish carpets with their neatly clipped box hedges and gravel paths, drummed that message home. And the gardens were arguably the greatest gesture of the Sun King's love of order and mastery of all he surveyed: if even rivers could be forced to flow in any direction Louis chose, what hope had French peasants of ignoring his will?

In the remodelled gardens, acting the part never ended. Three times a week courtiers were 'entertained' at '*appartements*', where the King and Queen and whole royal family descended 'from their heights to play with members of the assembly', as *Mercure Galant*, the official gazette, described their manoeuvres in 1682. Play here was cards, billiards and dancing, and also the exchange of witty repartee and gossip, everything in effect an elaborate display of courtly manners to equal the masquerades staged there. Huge painted canvases dotted about the grounds served as the scenery for outdoor musical and theatrical performances.

Even the gardens themselves – arranged around a central axis whose focal point was Louis's bedroom, from which everything radiated in the sun symbolism adhered to throughout – had to perform on tap for the King. The fountains were magnificent features. But there was only enough water to keep the ones closest to the palace at a constant spurt. The others were switched off and on as the King approached and departed, his movements closely monitored and signalled to staff, with flags waved and whistles blown in a complex system of field telegraph.

Stagings of Louis's military triumphs – his crossing of the Rhine in 1672 and the Peace of Nijmegen of 1678 – were rendered as permanent fixtures in the form of statues by Antoine Coysevox. The Grotto of Tethys – its theme the Sun God Apollo descending from the heavens – placed the monarch on par with the ancients of classical myth.

The King also penned a guidebook, *The Way to Present the Gardens of Versailles*, of which there were six versions, some handwritten. This offered his personally authorised tour of its groves and basins. 'We'll stop to see the Southern parterre, where from there, while moving towards the balustrade of the Orangerie, we can see the Orange Tree parterre, and the Latone of the Swiss', runs a typical entry, though some dispute remains as to whether it was intended to be published or was merely drawn up for minions to use while leading the most esteemed visitors around. And esteemed visitors were always thick on the ground.

Indeed, every two-bit monarch, elector, prince or duke who clapped eyes on Versailles returned home fired with the idea of replicating its harmonious avenues, axes, parterres, beds, boxed hedges and *tapis vert*. Mini Versailles popped up in aristocratic country estates all over Europe. In 1688 the Holy Roman Emperor, Leopold I, commissioned his court architect, Johann Bernhard Fischer von Erlach, to build Schloss Schönbrunn in Vienna, a palace and garden 'to outshine Versailles'. Here too a former student of Le Nôtre, Dominque Girard, created the Belvedere Palace and grounds for Prince Eugene of Savoy in around 1712. And in the 1720s, another pupil of Le Nôtre, Martin

Charbonnier, was responsible for Duke Friedrich's Herrenhausen Garden at Hanover.

Charles II of England, assuming the throne in 1660 after years of exile on the Continent, yearned for a Versailles of his own and set about recruiting French gardening experts to his court almost from the moment he landed back on English soil. First, he poached Robert Morison from Gaston d'Orléans's botanic garden at Blois. Luring him to England with a professorship of botany at Oxford University and the appointment as both king's botanist and physician, Charles also made Morison master of St James's Park and Hampton Court in the first months of the Restoration. But Charles had his eye on a bigger fish, and wished for Le Nôtre himself to design a royal garden at Greenwich with the scale and formality of Versailles. He wanted him to take a crack at St James's Park, too. Le Nôtre dutifully supplied plans for Greenwich in 1662, knocking out suitably grand proposals for basins, flower beds and fountains. But the English king either lacked the resources or could no longer be bothered to fork out for the whole scheme, so only the lower section of a Grand Axis and flanking avenues was ever realised – and this by the hands of lesser-known horticulturalists.

And while Le Nôtre was certainly consulted on St James's Park, it is another Frenchman, André Mollet, who is credited with its revamp. Le Nôtre supposedly argued that the area's 'native beauty, Country Air … had something greater in them than anything he could contrive'.

The park, nevertheless, was to be the beneficiary of a new Versailles-style central canal and a lengthy avenue of trees. Another Gallic addition was a long fenced court for playing the mallet and hoop game Pelle Melle, which the King had gained a taste for during exile in France. The game lives on in the names of the area, The Mall and Pall Mall (as well as a brand of fags).

But Charles's park was to have one fundamental difference from Louis's, for the King chose to open the new St James's to the public. That said, its hours, keepers, a perimeter wall and locked gates – with keys licensed only to courtiers, officials and the illustrious residents of the new town houses and mansions that sprang up north of St James's Palace – meant the park retained its upper-bracket exclusivity. Still, the sight of the Merry Monarch and his entourage of society fops, hangers-on and high-class harlots promenading about the greenery became an entertainment to be gawped at by these slightly lowlier visitors. That, as much as the scenery. Thirsty visitors of all ranks could usually avail themselves of milk sold by a comely young farm maid with a cow tethered to a tree.

'The company' played to the gallery in St James's Park – to see and be seen being the very essence of aristocratic Restoration society. Theatres themselves were back in vogue with the return of the monarch. Closed by Puritan parliamentary ordinance in 1642, with any actors and ballad singers caught defying the edict imprisoned as common 'rogues and vagabonds', they now provided another arena in which members of high society showed themselves off to one another. Parks, too, began to make an appearance here. The Bridges Street theatre, for instance, rebuilt on nearby Drury Lane after a fire and renamed the Royal, would stage a revival of *Hyde Park*, a 'sentimental comedy' by James Shirley first performed 'on the occasion of the opening of Hyde Park to the public by the Earl of Holland' in 1632. When it was restaged in July 1668, Samuel Pepys attended its first night. Charmed by the use of real live horses in a racing scene which was set, like the rest of the action, in the eponymous park, and 'an excellent epilogue' by Rebecca Marshall, an actress admired for her 'portrayal of tempestuous, passionate women', Pepys ultimately concluded that it was 'a very moderate play'.

By the end of the century, its fashionability had also secured St James's Park its place as the setting for witty comedies of manners, among them John Vanbrugh's *The Provok'd Wife*, William Wycherley's *Love in a Wood; or, St James's Park* and George Etherege's *The Man of Mode*. All, as often as not, were lapped up by the sort of fops and floozies whose amorous and sartorial antics in said park provided material for the action on stage. In his poem *A Ramble in St James's Park*, the court rake John Wilmot, second Earl of Rochester, was less circumspect about the bawdier activities going on in the park, writing: 'And nightly now beneath their shade / Are buggeries, rapes, and incests made.' Dead at thirty-three, most likely from a combination of syphilis, gonorrhoea and alcoholism, he, if anyone, would know.

In 1672, another poet, John Dryden, would coin the phrase 'park-time' in his worldly (Sicilian-based) comedy of love and marital relations, *Marriage à-la-Mode*. The term describes the hours in which the wealthy, the respectably marriageable, flakes and the wanton might be abroad savouring topiary, a parterre and a tree-lined avenue. But by the end of the reign of Queen Anne in 1714, a distinctly English challenger to such French-style gardening had arrived on the scene. It was overtly patriotic and driven as much by politics as aesthetics, its appearance coinciding with the end of the War of the Spanish Succession and the emergence of Great Britain as a force to be reckoned with on the world stage. Broadly speaking, the idea put forward by British writers, thinkers and horticulturalists was that looser, less formal – and, importantly, less French – gardens were the mark of a more liberal society. Only countries ruled by tyrants – i.e. France – would enforce such regularity and rectilinear garden design.

For instance, in his 1711 book *The Characteristicks of Men, Manners, Opinions, Times*, the Earl of Shaftesbury denounced parterres as 'a corruption of taste' and a sign of an excessive 'Love of Grandure and Magnificence'. Such edifices and formal gardens, unknown to this country's ancestors, he stated, were 'unnatural to such climates as Great Britain!'

But the most comprehensive assault on parterres and the artificiality of French gardens as a whole was made by Joseph Addison in an influential essay published in the *Spectator* magazine on 25 June 1712. Instead of 'humouring nature', he claimed, gardeners

> love to deviate from it as much as possible. Our trees rise in cones, lobes, and pyramids. We see the marks of the scissors upon every plant and bush. I do not know whether I am singular in my opinion, but, for my own part, I would rather look upon a tree in all its luxuriancy and diffusion of boughs and branches, than when it is

thus cut and trimmed into a mathematical figure; and cannot but fancy that an orchard in flower looks infinitely more delightful than all the little labyrinths of the most finished parterre.

Promoting here a new aesthetic principle that hymned nature over artful contrivance, he wrote:

There is something more bold and masterly in the rough careless strokes of nature than in the nice touches and embellishments of art. The beauties of the most stately garden or palace lie in a narrow compass, the imagination immediately runs them over, and requires something else to gratify her; but in the wide fields of nature the sight wanders up and down without confinement, and is fed with an infinite variety of images without any certain stint or number.

Elsewhere in the piece, he enthused about reports of Chinese gardeners, who apparently didn't see anything especially clever about placing 'trees in equal rows and uniform figures', and quoted the Roman poet Virgil praising lives that knew 'no falsehood' and were instead spent by 'Grottoes and living lakes' and in 'sylvan slumbers soft'. In conclusion, he offered, as an aside, what amounted to a manifesto for this new English school of garden- and park-making. If 'the natural embroidery of the meadows were helped and improved by some small additions of art, and the several rows of hedges set off by trees and flowers that the soil was capable of receiving, a man', he wrote, 'might make a pretty landscape of his own possessions.'

Addison's references to Chinese gardens and Virgil, and his use of the word 'landscape', an import from Dutch painting of scenery, are telling details. In 1711, the British East India Company had established a trading post in Guangzhou – this new arrangement piquing interest in all things Chinese, from tea to porcelain, at home. The eventual appropriation by British gardeners of facets of Chinese horticulture – especially the winding paths, bubbling brooks, spindly crooked wooden bridges and pagodas to be seen on the willow-pattern plates popularised by Turner in Shropshire and later mass-produced by Wedgwood in Stoke – was therefore tinged with national pride and a symbol of the country's increasingly global reach. The East, either China or India, was often also the source of a park-owner's fortune.

In any event, the concept of responding to the lie of the land, even exaggerating a certain crookedness, became as quintessentially English as – according to Americans, at least – the country's dentistry today. This idea, along with informality, was given further philosophical heft by the poet and satirist Alexander Pope, who in *Epistles to Several Persons* of 1731 counselled: 'In all, let *Nature* never be forgot' and 'Consult the *Genius* of the *Place* in all.' Again another nod to Virgil. Beauties 'instanced in architecture and gardening' and 'even in works of mere luxury and elegance', he reiterated, had 'to follow Nature' and 'must be adapted to the genius and use of place … resulting from it' rather than being 'forced into it'.

Variety and irregularity were what Pope expounded as the replacement to Gallic geometry and contrivance – and he put his ideas into practice at his own garden in Twickenham. And after him, Edmund Burke, the foremost exponent of the theory of the 'sublime', would raise the untamed to an even higher spiritual and moral plane. For Burke 'terror' was 'in all cases whatsoever … the ruling principle of the sublime'. But by then the leading English gardeners and park landscape artists to the gentry, William Kent and Lancelot 'Capability'

Brown, had already absorbed a type of contrived naturalism as a commercially viable creed.

Another leading figure in the move towards the artfully natural was Charles Bridgeman. He was schooled in – and, indeed, an able exponent of – the formal style, as the neatness of the avenues of the Dutch-inflected Kensington Gardens he helped Henry Wise devise in 1691 affirms. Getting on for forty years later, Bridgeman would oversee their removal and the 're-naturalising' of the Gardens. As his own name perhaps suggests, he was a transitional figure in gardening. At Houghton Hall, the Norfolk country seat of Sir Robert Walpole, Britain's first Prime Minister, he 'harmonised' the 'contiguous ground of the park without the sunken fence' with 'the lawn within' and – in the opinion of Walpole's youngest son and man of letters, Horace – set the main garden 'free from its prim regularity' so that it 'might assort with the wilder country without'. More innovative still was his use of large plantations of 'plumps' of trees as opposed to straight lines, though Walpole senior complained that these irregular formations looked like the 'ten of spades'.

Bridgeman was also the propagator of the ha-ha – the concealed ditch, based on a defensive military trench, that kept livestock out of the main grounds of any country pile, but created the illusion of a seamless expanse of verdure between house and garden and the countryside beyond. Its development rather obviously implied that a certain manipulation of the raw materials was still okay – so long, of course, as it adhered to, and enhanced, the quite specific form of naturalistic reality gardeners yearned to replicate. Or, more truthfully, contrive.

At Stowe, the seat of the Temple-Grenville family in Buckinghamshire, and working in conjunction with the architect Sir John Vanbrugh to a cod-classical ideal, Bridgeman created a perimeter ha-ha, which exists to this day. This very effectively melted the visual boundary between the house's then main garden and outer parkland. But it was William Kent, with James Gibbs, Bridgeman's and Vanbrugh's respective successor at Stowe, who fully 'de-formalised' the park, melding the landscape into an undulating expanse containing an array of temples and grottos, walks and vistas.

Trained as a painter and having visited Italy between 1710 and 1719 to study its ancient ruins and its Renaissance treasures, Kent thought in pictures – though he was not, as we shall see, technically 'Picturesque'. He used 'perspective, light and shade' when it came to planting and, encouraged by his patron Lord Cobham, installed temples and sculptures as focal points at Stowe. If modelled on the ancient world, these additions were layered with allegorical details of contemporary political significance. An artificially decayed Temple of Modern Virtue came calculatingly with a headless statue of Walpole. Elsewhere, a Temple of Ancient Virtue housed Greek heroes such as the Spartan lawyer and scourge of corruption, Lycurgus. A Temple of British Worthies, on the other hand, contained representations that ranged from Alfred the Great and Elizabeth I to Shakespeare, Inigo Jones and John Milton.

Such classical touches were an increasing presence in the new British naturalism. The vogue for young English gentlemen (and women) to expand their cultural horizons by undertaking the Grand Tour of Europe had been in the ascendant for some time. These secular pilgrimages to a largely prescribed set of sights and cities, the art-and-antiquity-stuffed, if crumbly, bits of Italy – Florence, Venice, Rome a must – were becoming a rite of passage for the offspring of the aristocracy, along with those who aspired by dint of wealth to enter their orbit socially. Many of the places accorded importance were mountainous, overgrown and full of bashed-up statues and shattered buildings, having gone to rack and ruin in the fall of an empire; or during its conquering by unfeeling, philistine barbarians. Taking this look almost at face value, the English, especially, delighted in it as an aesthetic. Politically, too, the nascent British Empire was viewed as a potential Athens or Rome in the making, a growing imperial power that with the right kind of wise government could be a 'just' sponsor of life and liberty, commerce, invention and the arts. So, again, there was a patriotic strand to this incorporation of the classical into the present way of life.

Eventually, this style – combining the natural with supposed relics of the classical, a kind of decayed bucolic with a ruin or two *in situ* – became the dominant aesthetic. New private parks and gardens, with rolling hills, freshly laid serpentine paths and lakes, were created, their greenery augmented either by armless statues pilfered from the ancient world or by replicas. Here a fetish was made of follies, temples, rusticity and the sort of gone-to-seed Arcadianism advocated in Addison's *Spectator* piece. The end result, rather like spaghetti on toast, was a thoroughly English hotchpotch, one that Ancient Romans perhaps would not have had much time for.

Despite these vital touches of the classical, William Kent's 'ruling principle' remained that 'nature abhors a straight line'. This 'new wave of naturalism' was to be an unstoppable force, and by 1718 there was already a primer on how to turn country seats into suitably 'natural' parks, in the form of *The Ichnographia Rustica; or, The nobleman, gentleman, and gardener's recreation* by the gardener and garden writer Stephen Switzer. Among the next generation, such naturalism's predominant ambassador was Lancelot 'Capability'

Brown, who picked up the trowel at Stowe after Kent. Brown would have a hand in the landscaping of over 200 estates as gentlemen competitively funnelled their swelling wealth into gardens and parks in this latest style.

For the Duke of Marlborough at Blenheim, Brown pulled out the topiary of the earlier baroque garden, grassed over the parterre and great court, contoured the land, drowned a hundred acres of parkland to install a magnificent lake, and replanted cedars, limes and chestnuts in 'clumps and belts'. His alterations for the Viscount Irvine at Temple Newsam near Leeds were saluted in a poem by an anonymous versifier entitled *The Rise and progress of the Present taste in Planting, Parks, Pleasure Grounds, Gardens etc.* in 1767.

By 1783 there were calculated to be some 4,000 such private parks in Britain. A few became tourist attractions and were opened to the public at certain times for a fee, the fees keeping visitors largely to the upper middling sort, and foreshadowing, to an extent, the lives of some of these properties under the National Trust in two centuries' time. The rise of such parks, of course, for all their claims to 'naturalism', marked one of the most radical transformations of the countryside to date. After all, their formation often involved the rerouting of rivers and roads, shifting of tons of earth, and the planting of thousands of trees.

William Gilpin, an Anglican vicar, schoolmaster, watercolourist, inveterate tourer of the countryside and the author of a largely positive monograph on the gardens at Stowe, questioned the pretence of naturalism. Disparaging the rash of parks in the style of Capability Brown as 'flat and insipid' and 'unlike nature' and as exhibiting 'false taste', Gilpin advanced instead the theory of 'Picturesque' landscapes.

Unhelpfully, the term, which he coined, has come to be applied often indiscriminately to a huge variety of different landscapes, tended and wild, even including some of Brown's own parks and gardens. Its central conceit in the 1780s, though, was the celebration of nature at its most rugged and dynamic – the ravine and meadows of the Wye Gorge in Herefordshire, for example, was Gilpin's ideal. It was an ideal because it possessed 'that peculiar kind of beauty', which was 'agreeable in a picture'. The kind of pictures he had in mind were the brooding landscape paintings of Claude Lorrain and Salvator Rosa, awash with savage crags and gloomy skies.

And just as the artist – while daubing a likeness of the Wye Valley in ink and wash in a sketchbook – responded to its ruggedness and verdure, adding shade and tone to draw these out and complete the picture, so a landscape gardener should, Gilpin argued, use artistry to amp up those elements in the real world. Whatever would make for a good picture was, in essence, a good or 'Picturesque' landscape. If this could be found in the wild, that was great. But sometimes the wild wasn't up to the job and people had to give it a helping hand. Famously, Gilpin suggested that 'a mallet judiciously used' on the 'gable-ends' of the ruined Tintern Abbey would improve the scene.

In his *Three Essays: On Picturesque Beauty, On Picturesque Travel, On Sketching Landscape* of 1792, Gilpin expanded on his thinking:

Why does an elegant piece of garden-ground make no figure on canvas? The shape is pleasing; the combination of the objects, harmonious; and the widening of the walk in the very line of beauty. All this is true, but the smoothness of the whole, tho right, and as it should be in nature, offends in picture. Turn the lawn into a piece of broken ground: plant rugged oaks instead of flowering shrubs: break the edges of the walk: give it the rudeness of a road; mark it with wheel-tracks; and scatter around a few stones, and brushwood; in a word, instead of making the whole *smooth*, make it *rough*; and you make it also picturesque.

Humphry Repton, Brown's self-styled successor as landscape gardener to the gentry, was initially critical of the Picturesque school, and was in turn criticised by Gilpin and its other leading advocates. But by 1803 he too had become a convert and would later argue that the tradition of 'surrounding a house by a naked grass field ... introduced by Brown' was a 'bald and insipid custom'. In its place would come gloom and savagery aplenty as park-makers, Repton among them, strove to supply their patrons with the fashionably Romantic scenery hailed by contemporary poets and that littered phantasmagorical three-decker novels of mystery, adventure and young girls driven mad by their own bedclothes.

Tom Stoppard's 1993 play *Arcadia*, set in Sidley Park, a country estate in Derbyshire around the turn of the nineteenth century, delights in sending up the Gothic excesses of landscape gardening in this era.

After studying plans drawn up by her gardener, Lady Croom, the manor's formidable matriarch, observes:

> Here is the Park as it appears to us now, and here it might be when
> Mr Noakes has done with it. Where there is the familiar pastoral
> refinement of an Englishman's garden, here is an eruption of
> gloomy forest and towering crag, of ruins where there was never
> a house, of water dashing against rocks where there was neither
> spring nor a stone I could not throw the length of a cricket pitch.
> My hyacinth dell is become a haunt for hobgoblins.

Constable, one of the pre-eminent artists of the early nineteenth century, was no fan of parks, Gothickly sublime or otherwise. He claimed to have a complete aversion to 'Gentlemen's parks', contending that they were 'not beauty' as they were 'not nature'. This did not, however, preclude him from accepting an invitation from Major-General Rebow, a friend of his father's, to spend some weeks at his seat, Wivenhoe Park in Essex. Here he committed its glories to canvas at Rebow's expense.

The finished 1816 picture doesn't have a Gothic feature in sight. It's a scene of grazing cows, their udders pink and plump as inflated rubber gloves, and grey-white swans dipping their heads, in a somewhat ungainly way, into the muddy green water of a lake. Near these birds a robustly carpentered wooden rowing boat carries two men fishing with nets. The whole composition in fact emphasises the day-to-day labour of the estate.

But the common man undertaking such day-to-day labour was seeing his own right to enjoy the landscape around him severely curtailed by these parks. During this period four million acres of open and common land were fenced in by its neighbouring landowners. This process of enclosure was carried out with the aid of around 2,000 Acts of Parliament between 1761 and 1844. That last year saw the passing of the Marsh Improvement Act, which gave local authorities the right to acquire and build on ancient Lammas lands, those areas of common pasture freely available for grazing between Lammas Day in August and Lady Day in March.

Enclosure, emparkment and the fate of peasant farmers was examined in Oliver Goldsmith's 1770 poem, *The Deserted Village*:

> ... The man of wealth and pride
> Takes up a space that many poor supplied;
> Space for his lake, his park's extended bounds,
> Space for his horses, equipage, and hounds:
> The robe that wraps his limbs in silken sloth,
> Has robbed the neighbouring fields of half their growth;
> His seat, where solitary sports are seen,
> Indignant spurns the cottage from the green:
> Around the world each needful product flies,
> For all the luxuries the world supplies.
> While thus the land adorned for pleasure, all
> In barren splendour feebly waits the fall.

By that time, though, the tumbledown park with its classical or Gothic additions was becoming something of a major British export; stylistically at least. Prince Franz of Anhalt-Dessau exceeded almost all originals with his own Englische Garten at Wörlitz in Saxony, among whose joys were a Palladian villa, a Gothic House, an 'English seat', a grotto and a scale model of *the* 'iron bridge' at Coalbrookdale.

The English garden's triumphant march across Europe as a horti-cultural ideal was crowned when Marie Antoinette instructed her architect Richard Mique and the painter Hubert Robert to replace a botanical garden at Le Petit Trianon with a *jardin Anglais* – the one that two genuinely English academics seemed incapable of negotiating over a hundred and thirty years later.

* * *

Versailles is occasionally described as the world's first theme park. And while there was no shortage of sham in the English gentry's rustic country parks, nor, obviously, in its Picturesque peer, the gaudier excesses and spectacles of that original French confection lingered on much more visibly and well into the nineteenth century in the commercial pleasure gardens of London. Opened as hard-headed business ventures instead of horticultural indulgences, the brightest – Vauxhall, Marylebone, Ranelagh and Cremorne – set their stalls out for an urban population seeking amusing entertainment rather than verdure. At this point, the London commoner still didn't have freedom to roam the parks, but there were pockets of recreational greenery available on commons and heaths, at Moorfields, Goodman's Fields and Lincoln's Inn Fields. Along with these were various taverns with cockpits and greens, where rough blood sports and marginally more genteel bowls could be played in the open air while ale was supped. But the new pleasure gardens were different – and a sharp contrast to the aristocratic parks and the purpose-built public parks that would follow them later in the nineteenth century, while never-theless containing some elements of both.

Their clientele were always a broad mix – from the wealthy and fashionable to the lowest of the urban low. Though dress codes were enforced and intended to keep out the complete riff-raff, pleasure gardens were in principle open to all comers, as long as they could afford the entrance fee. Trading on spectacle and the social cachet of their more famous regulars, pleasure gardens were from the outset strongly associated with sex. Its actual accommodation, if managed discreetly enough, added to their appeal for the respectable, who could enjoy the frisson without compromising their own reputation; or indulge in it without being found out.

Perhaps the most famous of them all was Vauxhall Pleasure Gardens, which Addison, who looked upon it as a 'Mahometan Paradise', once visited with a friend who longed for 'more Nightingales, and fewer Strumpets'.

What were at first called the New Spring Gardens were opened just after the Restoration in 1661 on a patch of land at Lambeth, on the south bank of the Thames – land which had fallen within the manor of Falkes de Breauté during the reign of King John. As the 'New' in the title suggests, it was not the first such garden to bear that name, which, strikingly, derives from hunting (according to the *Oxford English Dictionary*, one meaning of 'spring' is a plantation of young trees, 'especially one enclosed and used for rearing or harbouring game').

Palace documents from the Elizabethan era confirm a predecessor – Spring Gardens at Whitehall – with a copse of trees and a preserve for pheasants and 'wild fowl'. By the time of James I this part of the royal grounds had, it appears, been leased out as a semi-public garden with a walk, fruit trees and a bowling green. Closed in 1635, after its patrons, most likely dissolute gentlemen of means, stood accused of 'continual bibbing and drinking Wine all Day' and engaging in 'two or three Quarrels every Week', the first 'New Spring Gardens' promptly opened round the corner, 'near the Mews' at Charing Cross. This prospered until the Civil War. Its suppression by Roundhead killjoys was noted by the gardener and diarist John Evelyn, who recorded on 10 May 1654 that 'Cromwell and his partisans' had 'shut up and seized ... Spring Garden, which till now, had been the usual rendezvous for ladies and gallants at this season'. It later resurfaced in a somewhat diminished form, but its proximity to the restored royal court and the park at St James's made the land itself desirable to developers. The bowling green was later enclosed as a garden for the Admiralty Office, but by then its south-of-the-river namesake had superseded it anyway.

Evelyn was one of its earliest visitors, judging it, in July 1661, a 'pretty contriv'd plantation'. Samuel Pepys, that era's other great chronicler, inevitably – predictably – also called upon it several times. On 28 May 1667, he observed a 'great deal of company' at New Spring Gardens and judged 'the weather and garden pleasant'. He also noted decidedly democratic pricing principles at work, observing that it was 'cheap going thither, for a man may go to spend what he will' and could 'hear a nightingale and other birds, and here fiddles, and there a harp, and here a jews trump, and here laughing, and there fine people walking, is mighty divertising'.

However, a facet of the garden that did not evade his gaze was its salaciousness. Though hardly averse to flirtation or full-on extramarital dalliance – the following April Pepys would himself enjoy an assignation with an actress in New Spring Gardens – on this occasion he was distressed to see 'two pretty women alone, that walked a great while' having to flee to avoid the unwelcome sexual advances of 'some idle gentlemen'.

Its avenues and roofed arbours became notorious as haunts of both the amorous and those who offered amours for a fee. A little too notorious, perhaps, as the gardens soon gained a reputation for being plagued by prostitutes, peeping toms and 'rogues'. An Anglo-Irish lady of society, Mrs Percival, maintained in 1713 that the New Spring Gardens was where 'wanton venus' kept her court. 'I could not,' she wrote, 'help thinking ... the delights that abound there are all sensial ... 'tis pitty it should be made the Sconce of Ludeness and debauchery.'

But in 1728 the lease of New Spring Gardens was taken over by Jonathan Tyers, a Bermondsey leather merchant turned impresario and patron of the arts. Crowned 'the master builder of delight', Tyers, at considerable expense, set about 'improving' the 12-acre site (in both senses of the word, since he barred known whores) with paved paths, tree-lined avenues, a piazza, grottos, lawns, Chinese pavilions and supper boxes decorated with paintings by Francis Hayman and William Hogarth. In time it would gain spectacular colonnades, an Italian ruin and rows of triumphal arches, a pond graced by a gigantic model of Neptune and eight white seahorses, and the Rotunda – an exuberantly rococo concert hall that could hold 2,000 people.

Beginning as Tyers hoped they would go on, the revitalised Vauxhall Pleasure Gardens were launched in 1732 with a lavishly staged *ridotto al fresco*. This masked ball was attended by 400 guests in domino costumes, among them Frederick, Prince of Wales, and Handel. The German composer would go on to debut his Music for the Royal Fireworks in Vauxhall and later be honoured with a statue by François Roubiliac, valued at a thousand guineas (though, unusually, depicting the composer wig-less and déshabillé in a dressing gown).

With a fee of a shilling and the only other requirement of entry decent dress – one that Handel's statue would have failed – Tyers aimed to supply edifying entertainment, not vulgar diversions, in tasteful surroundings. This was in a period when bears were still commonly 'torn to bits by mastiffs simply for the amusement of the mob', as one history of Vauxhall Pleasure Gardens puts it. The gentry would be attracted, but those of lesser means would not be excluded from sampling some finer things in performance, art, music and architecture.

As in later public parks, there was a distinct pedagogical element in this. There were to be open-air concerts, firework extravaganzas, ballooning and high-wire trapeze artist displays, and visits by Cherokee chieftains and Iroquois tribesmen. For its day, this was quite astonishingly egalitarian stuff. Some of Vauxhall's subsequent reputation as an unfettered bacchanalia can partially be put down to the snobbishness of those who objected to the mingling of different classes in the gardens.

Given the boisterous nature of London society, the sheer numbers of people (an average of 2,000 a night and up to 18,000 for gala events) and the quantity of ale, brandy and water and punch sunk until the small hours of the morning, it was almost inevitable that Vauxhall had its fair share of louche and disorderly behaviour. Recalling the gardens of the 1770s some fifty years later, Henry Angelo, one-time fencing master to Lord Byron, claimed that they were 'more like a bear garden than a rational place of resort'. Fisticuffs between inebriated punters, and even punters and the serving staff, were almost nightly occurrences.

In fact, the low quality and high cost of the food at Vauxhall Gardens was as recurrent a joke in the Georgian era as British Rail catering was in the 1970s. Though visitors were welcome to bring their own food – picnicking was popular across all classes and fruit could be picked from the trees for free – a plate of beef or ham sliced so thin it 'might answer the purpose of a skylight' cost a shilling. A slap-up dinner in a tavern or chop-house, with beefsteak, bread and ale, could be had for the same price at that time. Since pickpockets were a constant menace, holding on to your money was hard enough anyway.

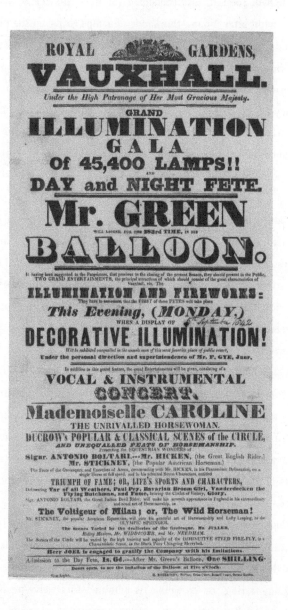

Vauxhall, though, was acclaimed for the brilliance of its night lights, with, after 9 p.m., thousands of lamps firing up the pleasure grounds and twinkling, suspended between the rows of trees. But their beams did not penetrate the deeper recesses of the gardens, where dark walks could hide any criminal element. These also offered privacy for couples out strolling, and out-and-out coupling. Despite his early efforts, Tyers wasn't able to stamp out prostitution. He probably didn't want to, anyway; a practical man, he more than understood that the chance of romance and even sex was reason enough for some to visit the gardens. If coming down hard on obvious pox-ridden harlots, high-class courtesans who could pass as society ladies added to the glamour and excitement of the place. And there always remained as much secluded space as could be deemed seemly for those who wished to pursue their private passions after dark. Less provision was made for other bodily functions; as one piece of doggerel about 'Sweet Vauxhall' quipped: 'In splendid scenes we eat and drink/In sordid huts evacuate.'

In May 1742, a challenger to Vauxhall appeared across the Thames. The Ranelagh Gardens at Chelsea were opened with the Prince of Wales and the Duke of Cumberland and 'much nobility' present. The rank of those first guests and the location, which could be reached by coach rather than boat, was indicative of the type of customer Ranelagh set itself the task of poaching from Vauxhall. Horace Walpole, the writer, politician and catty front-seat observer of his times, visited Ranelagh in its first week and recorded his impressions in a letter to Horace Mann. 'There is,' he wrote, 'a vast amphitheatre, finely gilt, painted and illuminated, into which everybody who loves eating, drinking, staring, or crowding, is admitted for twelve-pence. The building and disposition of the gardens cost sixteen thousand pounds.

Twice a-week there are to be Ridottos, at guinea tickets, for which you are to have a supper and music.'

Walpole, however, confessed he 'did not find the joy of it'; he judged the garden at Vauxhall 'pleasanter' and preferred the journey to it by water, too. But Walpole's response proved rather atypical of his class, and Ranelagh soon eclipsed its predecessor in fashionability, becoming the preferred pleasure ground of 'the quality'. Its admission fee, at 2s. 6d, even if it did include tea and coffee, was over twice that of Vauxhall, and intentionally pegged at a rate to discourage the true hoi-polloi. But not high enough to prevent the likes of Miss Ledger from being 'a constant frequenter' of Ranelagh – her favours, according to *Harris's List of Covent Garden Ladies*, being 'difficult to gain without a handsome present'. The gardens were promoted by James Lacy, joint patentee with the actor David Garrick of the Drury Lane Theatre, and boasted a canal with gondolas and a Chinese house. But its *pièce de résistance* was what Walpole rightly called its amphitheatre, the Rotunda: a rococo structure some 150 feet in diameter. With a bandstand at the centre and an organ, it was an upgrade on its equivalent in Vauxhall. A painting by Canaletto from 1754 captures the wedding-cake-like interior, with its incredibly high circular ceiling, creamy columns, glittery gilt, and two tiers of galleries of boxes for spectators. Samuel Johnson, another frequenter of Ranelagh, judged its *trompe l'oeil* 'the finest thing he'd ever seen'.

The gardens' season ran from April to July, with music performed in the Rotunda most evenings between seven and ten-thirty, the Italian composer Felice Giardini a regular and popular attraction. The young Mozart even performed at Ranelagh in 1764. The 'chief amusement' was promenading around the Rotunda itself while the orchestra or organ played; the vast floor was coated with matting to muffle footsteps.

Like Vauxhall, it possessed discreet walkways with their attendant charms, and no less brilliant lamps, its own foliage-embedded illuminations advertised as 'firetrees'. But having scaled the heights of high-society popularity, it would seemingly prove less capable of weathering shifts in taste than its forerunner. In 1803, 'the unending promenade, with its sentimental songs and elegant regale of tea and coffee had ceased to attract' and Ranelagh closed. The Rotunda was demolished two years after that, and the gardens sold off piecemeal to housing developers. Most of the land was purchased by the Chelsea Hospital, originally for allotments. By 1871, only a single avenue of trees remained to remind anyone that Ranelagh had ever stood there.

Vauxhall was gone by then too, but it had hung on, with stops and starts, until 1859. It survived by upping its prices and by adding an ever-growing roster of attractions and mounting increasingly opulent extravaganzas, its playbills in the opening decades of the nineteenth century swelling in corpulence in tandem with the Prince Regent. Indian jugglers, puppet shows, equestrian demonstrations, Siamese twins, ventriloquists, chin melodists, lion tamers and living sculptures: it seemed the shows would never end.

In 1822, Vauxhall was home to 'The Heptaplasiesoptron', a 'splendid exhibition', according to the volume *Real Life in London*, 'fitted up with ornamental draperies ... [it] presents a fountain of real water illuminated, revolving pillars, palm trees, serpents, foliage, and variegated lamps; and mirrors are so placed to excite universal admiration, inspiring the company with the ideas of refreshing coolness', its whole 'an appearance of enchantment, which sets all description at defiance'.

The following season, there was 'an 80-foot high panorama of the Bay of Naples' in which Mount Vesuvius erupted nightly, spewing fake lava all over the place. In 1827, more than 1,000 soldiers and horses mounted a spectacular re-enactment of the Battle of Waterloo, with the Duke of Wellington himself watching as the guest of honour and laughing 'loudly' whenever 'he' appeared in the drama.

Like Wellington, though, Vauxhall was getting on. They'd both live to see gas lighting and the locomotive steam railways. But however affectionately they were regarded posthumously, both were fundamentally associated with earlier, more intemperate, less industrious and less industrial times. Rising prudishness – which also finished off the unabashedly vulgar and boozy St Bartholomew's Fair in 1855 – and the pollution from the new railway at Nine Elms did for Vauxhall in the end.

The same two things, to a certain extent, would lie behind the creation now of a whole new type of park.

CHAPTER 3

Park Land of Hope and Gloria

A cursory flick through a modern thesaurus for synonyms of 'Victorian' brings up 'prudish, conventional, priggish, straight-laced, smug, prim and narrow' – all of which are of course entirely pejorative. The author and magazine editor E. P. Hood is credited with being the first person to use Victorian as an adjective, in 1851 – the year of the Great Exhibition in Hyde Park. As a self-educated orphan who overcame considerable disadvantage to become not only a successful writer but a Congregationalist minister, temperance campaigner, supporter of philanthropic ventures and the composer of lyrics for hymns with such rousing titles as 'Unless the Lord the City Keep' and 'There's a Beautiful Land Where the Rains Never Beat', Hood himself is an almost comically stereotypical 'Victorian'. Right down to the mutton-chop sideburns he sports in a sepia portrait: his face attempts to convey dignity, serenity even, but actually looks rather drained of expression, his jaw stiff and eyes glassy, no doubt due to the primitive exposure rates. And his middle name – Paxton – could scarcely have been more apt for his times, as we will see.

For Hood, 'Englishmen' lived to 'move and to struggle, to conquer and to build' and the nation's watchwords were 'industry, Protestantism and liberty', and commitment to 'the civilisation and progress of the world'. To be Victorian, then, was to be self-confidently modern, to be better than those who had gone before. The notion of 'improving' things, whether machines, places, people or the self, can be seen as a leitmotif of the whole era, from the 1830s to the dawn of the following

century. It was to be square and centre of Darwin's theory of evolution, where species were said to adapt and improve to withstand
competition from other, also improving, species.

If pressed to come up with another adjective to describe nineteenth-
century England, many would plump for 'Dickensian', which the nearest
dictionary to hand defines as 'resembling or suggestive of conditions
described in Dickens' novels, esp. squalid and poverty-stricken'.* Indeed,
Victorian progress came at a price. Urbanisation and industrialisation
went hand in hand with poor harvests, enclosures and mechanisation,
forcing thousands off the land and into mills and factories. Between 1801
and 1831, the population of London increased from 900,000 to 1.5 million,
while Manchester had swollen from a modest 40,000 to over 187,000
people. At the time of Wordsworth's death in 1850 – just thirteen years
into Victoria's reign – more people in Britain would be living in towns
and cities than in the countryside. The poor, meanwhile, had seen traditional rights eroded and for twelve hours a day were forced to toil,
alongside their children, as compliant and interchangeable cogs in a
machine. The peaks and troughs of profit and loss, like the output of
each factory worker, were all to be measured against clockwork, stand-
ardised Greenwich Mean Time. Time, in this newly industrialised society,
was money, after all, and so the hotchpotch of differing local and regional
zones and the flickering shadows of the sundial were soon cast aside in
favour of the wrought-iron rigour of the railway timetable.

The railways themselves are among the most significant achieve-
ment of the Victorians, many of their major termini and hotels

---

* It should be noted that Dickens, of course, was as much a historical novelist as
chronicler of his age, with many of his books – *The Pickwick Papers*, *Great
Expectations*, *David Copperfield*, *Little Dorritt* and *A Tale of Two Cities* among
them – set either partially or completely in pre-Victorian or late-Regency times.

considered the supreme architectural achievements of the nineteenth century, just as the cathedrals were to the thirteenth. In 1830, the Duke of Wellington, then Tory Prime Minister, had boarded a train from Liverpool to Manchester on the first scheduled steam-powered railway line in the world. But even this inaugural run had to contend with protests, largely against Wellington's intransigence on political reform, and then there was the gruesome fatal wounding of the Liverpool MP William Huskisson by Stephenson's *Rocket*. But more significant, perhaps, were the group of demonstrators who gathered to meet the train at its destination that day – some of whom had erected a loom tended by a 'tattered, starved-looking weaver' – to express their disgust at 'this triumph of machinery, and the gain and glory which the wealthy Liverpool and Manchester men were likely to derive from it'. Even here, progress could not avoid an encounter with its victims.

Just a few weeks after that maiden journey, the first park to bear the heir presumptive's name was opened. The honour went to the Royal Victoria Park in Bath. 'Very opportunely', as one of the park's committee was later to write, 'her present Majesty, then the youthful Princess Victoria … arrived in Bath in October 1830 with HRH Duchess of Kent and they agreed to open the park and name it.' As with many future municipal parks, the project was backed locally to add lustre to the resort and as an attraction in its own right. The scheme had been drummed up by two prominent Bath businessmen, J. Davies and T. B. Coward, who were concerned about 'the general welfare of the city' and assembled a committee of twenty 'public spirited' members to back the idea. Commerce was foremost in their mind. The park, it was hoped, would make Bath 'a place of summer residence as well as of winter resort' – sojourns in spa towns, like bathing places, then being undertaken predominantly in winter months and supposedly for the improvement of health. With Napoleon nine years dead and peace reigning on the continent for the moment, the city was especially keen to court such visitors, since the gouty and affluent malingerers who formerly patronised its pump rooms had again begun journeying further afield for their seasonal restoratives.

Their choice of the name Victoria for the new park suggests that the city may have been especially desperate to court future monarchical patronage. Amusingly Victoria's uncle, King William IV, was insistent that she change her name to Elizabeth or Charlotte. Writing to the Prime Minister, Earl Grey, the following June, the monarch complained that Victoria was 'a name which is not English, had never been known heretofore as a Christian name in this country, not even German but of French origin'.

Like Victoria's name – a last-minute concoction apparently supplied at the christening font by an inebriated George IV – this park in Bath was something of a novel hybrid. It was laid out by the city's architect Edward Davis, a pupil of John Soane, mostly on common land held by the freemen of Bath, and it was open to the public – although those on horseback or using a carriage were expected to pay a subscription to use it.

Beyond those restrictions, 'a decent appearance and good behaviour' were the 'only passports for admission and free enjoyment of its beauties'. What might be considered 'decent' is, of course, rather loaded, but the park was clearly intended to be a civic amenity. It was not, however, a fully municipal park. Though initially supported by the municipality financially, the land was in fact leased, and for the first ninety-odd years of its life the bulk of the cost of upkeep and management was met by private donations from subscribers. Such largesse was not always to be relied upon, and in 1837 the *Bath Journal* complained about the poor maintenance of the park, calling its neglect a 'reproach both to our morality and decency'. It was, then, a park open to the public, but not the first truly public park. Still, it was an important forerunner.

Even to build the park and grant the public such relatively open access was a very progressive move, and one most likely influenced by the writings of John Claudius Loudon. Publisher and editor of the *Gardener's Magazine*, the first organ of green-fingery, Loudon had been using its widely read pages to call for the creation of public parks, and the previous year had published 'Hints for Breathing Spaces' – an essay in which he'd set out an astonishingly prescient plan for a series of 'green belts' for London. Formulated in the context of a Britain where there was nothing even approaching a welfare state and municipal government was only being mooted, and with free trade and charity the binary forces of the age, Loudon's arguments for public parks were radical and far-sighted.

But then Loudon – who had lost an arm following a botched operation and a fortune thanks to a banking fraud, and a further fortune when his definitive catalogue of trees and shrubs, *Arboretum et fruticetum Britannicum*, failed to sell enough copies to cover its hefty production costs – always had one eye on the future. Arguably even beyond that – to the afterlife, since he campaigned for, designed and built money-making 'sanitary burial grounds' and in the process helped promulgate the Victorian cult of the cemetery. He was first drawn to his wife and amanuensis, Jane Webb, after reading her novel *The Mummy*, a tale of Gothic science fiction set in a twenty-second century where the fields were tilled by steam-powered ploughs and houses could be moved from place to place on rails.

Ever a man with an eye for technological innovation, Loudon (along with Joseph Paxton) was also a pioneering advocate of new-fangled lawnmowers. The earliest of such devices, which called time on the skilled handyman's scythe but vastly extended the potential for well-tended lawns and much tidier-surfaced playing fields for sports, was

only patented by Edwin Budding of Norwich as 'a Machine for cropping or shearing the vegetable Surface of Lawns, Grass-plots, &c.' in 1830 — the same year that agricultural workers across Hampshire, Kent and East Anglia rioted against threshing machines.

The eldest son of a respectable Lanarkshire farmer, he designed his first garden as a boy on a plot of land donated by his father from the family holdings in Kerse Hall outside Edinburgh. After receiving schooling at a 'good Scottish liberal' institution, he was apprenticed to

Dickson and Shade's nursery in Edinburgh. Loudon, though, continued his education, studying botany, chemistry and agriculture at the University of Edinburgh, poring over his books through the night, and night after night. This habit continued throughout his working life, and he later claimed to need 'no more than four hours' sleep', which goes some way to explaining how he kept up a publishing output so extensive that *Country Life* magazine judged it 'exhausting merely to browse'.

Aged twenty, Loudon set out for London, where he wasted little time in becoming acquainted with Sir Joseph Banks, President of the Royal Society and the botanist and plant collector who'd sailed with James Cook to Australia. He also befriended the Utilitarian philosopher Jeremy Bentham. Bentham's doctrine of cost-benefit, bean-counter ethics, where emphasising the 'greatest good of the greatest number' was what mattered most of all, would inform Loudon's subsequent promotion of public parks. Loudon's first published article, 'Observations on Laying out the Public Squares of London', in which he advocated the planting of plane trees over ferns and conifers, appeared in 1803 and was to have a lasting effect on the capital's arboriculture, despite fears – some justified and others exaggerated – that they would shed 'irritant spicules' that aggravated bronchial conditions such as asthma.

For the next ten years, Loudon enjoyed considerable acclaim as a writer, farmer and landscape gardener, though he was dogged by ill health. He had first supposedly come down with a persistent rheumatic condition somewhere near Pinner, after travelling on the outside of a coach one rainy night. Nevertheless, he formed an agricultural college in Oxfordshire and exhibited three of his landscape paintings at the Royal Academy during this period. Having accrued a tidy fortune of £15,000 and moved to Pall Mall, he took advantage of a lull in hostilities during the Napoleonic wars to undertake a grand tour of Europe, visiting gardens and parks in Sweden, Russia and Germany. He later returned to inspect France, Switzerland, Italy and take another look at Germany. These European field studies were to supply Loudon with the essential data for his first major publishing success in 1822. His *Encyclopaedia of Gardening* went through five editions and he followed it up with an *Encyclopaedia of Cottage, Farm, and Villa Architecture and Furniture*. But it was further trips to the Continent that expanded his horizons, and his next – and, for a while, immensely lucrative – venture, the *Gardener's Magazine*, which was subsequently to carry his clarion call for public parks in Britain.

'Every part of the Continent', Loudon maintained, was pervaded by a 'spirit of general improvement', something he felt was sorely lacking in Britain. One of its most visible manifestations, he believed, was in the number of gardens and parks that were freely open to the people and often supported by local taxes. While he was in Paris in 1828, the then verdant Champs-Élysées became municipal property, and was soon followed by the Jardin des Plantes. Yet it was in Germany – and partly in response to the events of the French Revolution – that he found the notion of the public park was most advanced.

Ironically, perhaps, the majority of the public gardens Loudon visited in Germany were laid out in 'the English style' – which flourished there in both municipal and private forms. As a boy, Prince Albert enjoyed gambolling around the English Garden at Rosenau, the neo-Gothic family schloss outside Coburg. But if he admired their social utility, Loudon thought them poor acts of horticultural homage, complaining that 'the defects of the English style' were 'more frequently copied than the beauties'.* Its style aside, in Munich Loudon found an almost perfect representation of the kind of public park he was proposing for England.

---

* The authentically French artificiality of Versailles wasn't to Loudon's taste either. He claimed to find it 'dreary beyond what could be imagined'.

The Englischer Garten at Munich, cherished, incidentally, as a nudist hang-out since the 1960s, was the brainchild of the American-born English diplomat, army officer and inventor Sir Benjamin Thompson – a man who, although working in the eighteenth century, was the kind of improver the Victorians would have approved of. Tasked in the 1780s by the Elector Karl Theodor with reforming a Bavarian army whose ranks were significantly composed of convicted criminals, Thompson used his office to enact sweeping changes to the whole economy. He created military workhouses and gardens to feed and clothe the army and provide employment for the poor. Vagrants and brigands were also arrested and put to work in a war against idleness that saw troops, somewhat notoriously, being deployed to clear the streets of Munich of beggars on one New Year's Day – by ancient tradition a date when alms were dispensed to the pox-ridden, scrofulous and needy across Bavaria.

These changes ruffled more than a few feathers, especially among the lower classes, and with a revolution brewing in France it was with some guile that in 1789 Thompson persuaded the Elector, a monarch of absolutist inclinations, to turn over the land of his private hunting estate – the Hirschanger, or 'Red Deer Grassy Plains' – for a public park. The Elector was known to dislike almost everything about Munich apart from this estate, which served as his retreat from the hustle and dirt of the city. It had been a place where he and his court-iers went to cavort, at no little expense, dressed as shepherds and milkmaids. So its transformation into the public Englischer Garten by the court gardener Friedrich Ludwig von Sckell was seen as a great gesture of the supreme ruler's benevolence. In truth, it was – perhaps inevitably – something of a sop to the common man, still as likely to be hanged for a spot of poaching or slung into one of Thompson's workhouses for sloth.

Back in Britain almost a half-century later, more practical measures were being taken to aid the lower classes. Though fiercely resisted by several leading industrialists, 1833 saw the passing of the first Factory Act, which banned the employment of children under the age of nine and restricted nine- to twelve-year-olds to a nine-hour working day. The legislation was drafted in response to growing unease, and moral outrage, about the often abysmal conditions in Britain's mills and factories. Its appearance on the statute book was part of a broader acknowledgement that progress wasn't always that progressive, and that doing business more efficiently often led to inefficient outcomes. Bad, if cheap, conditions, could, for instance, help spread diseases far beyond poor neighbourhoods, or maim and kill off the very workforce needed to increase productivity.

Far from reducing profits, concern for the welfare of the workforce might, in fact, prove as forceful a means of improving performance and profit as installing a chunk of new machinery. Such thinking was to underscore the British government's first official investigation into 'Public walks' and the 'problem' of working-class recreation, launched in the same year as the Factory Act.

Couched in terms of productivity that might just appease Dickens's Bounderby or Gradgrind with his 'what I want is, Facts' and 'deadly statistical clock', a parliamentary committee was assembled to consider 'the best means of securing Open Spaces in the Vicinity of populous Towns, as Public Walks', having seemingly accepted the premise that 'the spring to industry which occasional relaxation gives' was 'quite as necessary to the poor as to the rich'. This was, however, a far from widely accepted opinion in the 1830s. During this period, the Scottish academic Andrew Ure published an account of his own investigations around Manchester, entitled *The Philosophy of Manufactures*, in which he wrote trenchantly in favour of mill and factory work, even praising child labour. He maintained that, far from being exploitative or dangerous, 'the work of these lively elves seemed to resemble a sport'. He also argued that since the ventilation systems of many mills was far better than that of the Houses of Parliament, it was ludicrous for the government to legislate on factory conditions. Among the even madder claims Ure put forward was his notion that cotton workers were less susceptible to 'Asiatic' or 'blue' cholera, a disease which had arrived in Britain from Bengal at the Sunderland docks in 1831, and, stranger still, that most common sickness among such workers was caused by 'their inordinate taste for bacon'.

Even the greatest champion of parks, John Claudius Loudon, was not immune to doubting the British working class. In his articles for *Gardener's Magazine* and the responses to them published in its letters pages, the English public, and especially the English lower classes, were frequently found wanting when held up for comparison with their continental cousins, as encountered by Loudon on his travels. One typical letter begins, 'Perhaps you will allow me to occupy one or two ... pages, in stating that all my observations, in my various tours in the south of Germany, fully confirm your opinion, expressed in recent Numbers of the *Gardener's Magazine* and *Magazine of Natural History*, as to the decided superiority of the German peasantry over the same class in England, in civility, information, morality, and, I may add, independence of character.' The supposed defects of the English peasantry were matters of grave concern, the correspondent went on, as they threatened to prevent the British Empire from becoming 'a perfect paradise'. The answer was 'better education and more humanising amusements', so that they would 'no more make beasts of themselves by drinking fermented liquors' and would learn 'that moderation' was 'the condition of real enjoyments'. Looking at the German models, where a compact between the public and authorities appeared to have been reached, Loudon, along with such letter writers, would later suggest that public parks were exactly the kind of 'humanising amusements' that Britain now needed.

Fortunately for the future of parks in Britain, the parliamentary committee, if perhaps no less likely than Ure to condemn the over-consumption of bacon, felt that, 'for their health's sake', those who spent their lives 'shut up in heated factories' (another of Ure's gems was that working in temperatures of 150°F was 'not harmful') should 'on their day of rest' be able to 'enjoy the fresh air ... and (exempt from the dust and dirt of public thoroughfare) to walk out in decent comfort with their families'.

The committee was chaired by R. A. Slaney, the Liberal MP for Shrewsbury. As a member of the landed gentry who enjoyed riding, hunting and shooting, and as a representative of a largely rural constitu-ency in Shropshire, albeit one whose local mines and ironworks had some claim to be called 'the cradle of the Industrial revolution', Slaney might seem an unusual figure to lead an inquiry into a problem afflicting 'populous towns'. But Slaney, in lots of respects, can almost be seen as a coming man of Victorian Christian philanthropy. Well versed in the new-ish socio-political and economic theories of Adam Smith and Thomas Robert Malthus, Slaney was a statistician and pamphleteer wedded to free trade and industrial capitalism, and a member of the Society for the Diffusion of Useful Knowledge, which published penny encyclopaedias and almanacs for autodidacts. He was also touched by evangelism and, by all accounts, 'imbued with a sense of social respon-sibility' that set him far apart 'from most landed gentlemen'. Though opposed to wider electoral changes after the Reform Act of 1832 and holding some dubious opinions on migrant Irish labour, as a parliamentarian he concerned himself with the Poor Laws and pressed tirelessly for legislation on better housing, education and sanitation.* In the year of the Reform Act, he pronounced the condition of the working classes in industrial towns 'a dark stain' on the country and argued that they had to be given 'the opportunities to improve' but that this could only be achieved with the support of the government and their elders and betters.

Parks and public walks, as a 'means of rational enjoyment', presented for Slaney an ideal 'opportunity' for working-class improvement. He argued that 'the prosperity of the country depended' on them. An over-riding hope of the committee, expressed by various witnesses and again in its conclusions, was that a provision of parks might help wean the labouring classes from such 'low and debasing pleasures' as 'drinking-houses, dog-fights and boxing matches', pursuits, it was suggested, to which 'they were driven for want of opportunity of other recreation'. That the working classes may well have been perfectly happy, and even thoroughly enjoyed drinking-houses, dog-fights and boxing matches, was not something the committee could seriously contemplate.

In a letter to the committee, the Manchester-based physician Dr James Kay expressed a similar faith in the redeeming qualities of parks. Kay – author of *The Moral and Physical Condition of the Working Class Employed in the Cotton Manufacture in Manchester* (which was later consulted by Engels), and founder of the Manchester Statistical Society; a man judged 'nine points out of ten ... utilitarian' by Charlotte Brontë – stated that if parks were provided, one of the first results would be 'a

---

* Slaney would bemoan, in particular, the 'pernicious' influence of Irish immigrants, who, as Catholics, he deemed incapable of restraining their bestial impulses, breeding, drinking and gambling with abandon and generally leading their indigenous English peers astray.

better use of the Sunday, and a substitution of innocent amusement at all other times, for the debasing pleasure now in vogue'. Having treated cholera victims in Manchester during the appalling epidemic of 1832, Kay went on to note that the health of the lower classes was 'much depressed by the combined influence of municipal evils'. 'Healthful exercise in the open air', he noted, was 'seldom or never taken by the artisans' of Manchester, whose health suffered 'considerable depression from this deprivation'. And those who fell sick were an added burden, since they or their dependants would call on poor relief.

Such 'want of recreation', the committee would conclude, not only generated disease; it also brewed discontent, 'which, in its turn, led to attacks upon the Government'. As so many of the long-standing wakes and fairs – those social occasions where steam in a pre-steam age was let off – had been closed down amid claims of immorality or the regimented shift-patterns of industrialisation, the modern-day mechanic, Slaney pointed out, had few options but to go 'sotting in alehouses' on holidays. And alehouses were places where working men's tongues, loosed by intoxicating liquids, wagged unchecked by better-informed minds, and political dissent might ferment as easily as the hops and barley.

There were further economic benefits, too. Making the point directly to the Vice President of the Board of Trade, Slaney urged the government to consider that public walks could actually prove a huge stimulus to industry by increasing the consumption of manufactured goods. The logic of this was somewhat convoluted, but it rested on the idea that in a decently set-out park people would feel positively compelled by their own vanity to dress up decently. It would be a space where – like the Restoration aristos before them – the workers could 'display their neatness or their finery' to the world. Was it not a fact, after all, that 'the maidservant and the mechanic's daughter took as much pride in displaying their rich ribbons, as a lady her fine equipage, or a duchess her diamonds?' And while he was not in the habit of encouraging vanity or pride – sins both, as he didn't have to remind the honourable members of His Majesty's government – the boon to the nation's ribbon-makers could be considerable; if public walks 'promoted cleanliness, decency, and self-respect' among 'both sexes of the lower orders' then that was all to the good, as far as he was concerned.

Not everyone in the Houses of Parliament was sold on public walks. Dr Herbert Baldwin, MP for Cork, for example, maintained that the 'cleanliness and the ventilation of houses which were too much neglected in large towns, were more essential'. But the committee's findings, which flagged up a particular dearth of decent green space in London, recording that on the south bank of the Thames from Vauxhall to Rotherhithe there was 'no single spot reserved as a Park or public walk', helped kindle what quickly became an almost quasi-evangelical movement for public parks, with approximately twelve laid out between 1840 and 1852.

The Church itself would prove an enthusiastic force in the call for public parks. During their work, Slaney and the committee had drawn parallels between parks and religious institutions, arguing that they should be financed by public subscription matched by government funds, in the same way that 'money had been advanced for the building of new Churches'. As the new industrial working population had begun to rocket in the first decades of the century, city churches had increased in parallel: some sixty new churches being built in London between 1815 and 1835, the Church feeling its work was especially necessary in the newly packed conurbations. This work took the classic do-gooding form – orphanages for abandoned children, reform homes for 'fallen women', temperance 'pubs' and lemonade-dispensing working men's clubs, city missions, Mechanics' Institutes, soup kitchens, and much bible-in-hand door-knocking and hymn-singing on street corners.

The needy in some respects had never been more obviously needier. Or, perhaps more accurately, their needs were much more evident now that more of them thronged into metropolitan districts. But part of the impetus for all the church-building, do-gooding and door-knocking was an underlying fear that the urban poor – unlike their rural predecessors, who were locked into the hierarchal panopticon of village life – were slipping into ungodliness.

As the historian Asa Briggs notes in *Victorian Cities*, there had always been an 'anti-urban bias' in English society. 'Towns were places where men made their livelihood: country houses were places where people lived. Man made the town: God made the country.' This was not unique to the UK. Briggs also quotes J. H. Ingraham, a popular nineteenth-century American religious novelist, who wrote, 'Adam and Eve were created and placed in a garden. Cities are the result of the fall.' But it remains deeply ingrained in the English national psyche and is evidenced in everything from suburban architecture to the viewing figures for *Countryfile* today.

Parks, then, were potentially one means of making cities more godly. And it was not infrequently thanks to the efforts of dog-collar-wearing second sons in city parishes and similarly Christian-minded greats-and-goods that parks were laid out. For instance the Reverend Charlton Lane of the nearby St Mark's Church was to chair a committee campaigning to preserve Kennington Common as 'an open and uncovered space' – but, more significantly, he would eventually lead the charge to make it 'a place of resort for respectable persons' which would see the Common converted into a park in the 1850s. Similarly Battersea, a few miles to the west, was to 'benefit' from a spiritually minded individual's intervention.

The site of what would become Battersea Park was formerly occupied by Battersea Fields, a marshy common of market gardens on the southern bank of the Thames opposite Chelsea. The then 'lonely character of the neighbourhood' made it a popular spot for duellists, with the Duke of Wellington defending his honour there against a slur by the Earl of Winchilsea in 1829. Recalling the fields in 1873, the antiquarian George Walter Thornbury described the area as

> one of the darkest and dreariest spots in the suburbs of London. A flat and unbroken wilderness of some 300 acres, it was the resort of costermongers and 'roughs,' and those prowling vagabonds who call themselves 'gipsies.' The week-day scenes here were bad enough; but on Sundays they were positively disgraceful, and to a great extent the police were powerless, for the place was a sort of 'no man's land,' on which ruffianism claimed to riot uncontrolled by any other authority than its own will. Pugilistic encounters, dog-fights, and the rabble coarseness of a country fair in its worst aspect were 'as common as blackberries in the autumn'.

If Thornbury's retrospective verdict was not damning enough, a more contemporary observer, writing for the *London City Mission Magazine*, maintained that 'if there was a place out of hell that surpassed Sodom and Gomorrah in ungodliness and abomination this was it'. That said, the London City Mission, founded in Hoxton in 1835 by David Nasmith, a young and enterprising evangelical from Glasgow, was rather wont to see Sodom and Gomorrah where others might see just a pub, a bit of pigeon-shooting, some bathing in the river and a couple of fiddle players.

Nevertheless, to have Sodom and Gomorrah on your doorstep, if possibly welcomed by some churchmen as just the sort of Daniel-in-the-lions'-den challenge they were looking for, was evidently not something that the local vicar, the Hon. and Rev. Robert Eden, could tolerate indefinitely.

As Vicar of Battersea, a peer, and former chaplain to William IV and a young Queen Victoria, Eden had the advantage of an influential ear or three to bend. So he wrote to the Prime Minister, Sir Robert Peel, urging the immediate purchase of the fields to serve as 'a lung that is almost necessary to the health of the Neighbourhood'. Stressing the unsavoury conduct of the people cavorting in the fields, Eden argued that many 'of these persons would become orderly if pains were taken to provide for them healthful recreation ... By encouraging healthful recreations ... social and domestic happiness' would ensue, since 'feelings that are now deadened by dirt, by drink and by discomfort' could be implanted. He would eventually get his way, but not until the 1850s, when James Pennethorne, one of the great tidy-uppers of early Victorian London, who we will meet again soon, was set to work.

Before then, though, the first public parks had begun to pop up around the country – Southampton's East and West Parks begun in 1846, West Park (now Kelvingrove Park) in Glasgow in 1852, Reading's Forbury Gardens in 1856. By 1860 there were over twenty in England and Scotland. But many contend that the very first of these truly public parks was the Derby Arboretum, which opened its gates in 1840. Unsurprisingly, that champion of the park John Loudon had a significant part to play in its creation.

* * *

Since publishing his call to public-parking arms, Loudon had not been idle; but then, he rarely was. In 1835 he was engaged to build his first park in Gravesend, Kent. This he purposefully turned into a demonstration of what could be achieved for a 'Corporate Town' on a site 'not much exceeding three acres and with very unfavourable circumstance, at the least expense'. In essence, it was a 'Come Hire Me Other Corporations' advert for his own park-making skills, and it would pay off.

Though a port, and scarcely twenty miles east along the Thames from Limehouse, Gravesend at that time was a bathing resort, served by steamers bringing Londoners eager to take the supposedly health-giving air and waters. Hardly surprisingly – given his help in bringing plane trees to the streets of London, and having just lost a small fortune with the ill-fated publication of *Arboretum et fruticetum Britannicum* – Loudon was to make trees the centrepiece of his park. Then as now, Loudon was far from alone in considering them especially virtuous. Rising towards the heavens and reaching for the sun, trees are lofty things, and for a nautical nation they were the stuff its ocean-spanning, empire-building ships were made of – until the introduction of iron, at least. A mighty oak had sheltered young Charles II from his Puritan enemies, etc.

Loudon's Victorian near-contemporary the Reverend Charles Kingsley (the 'muscular Christian' author of *The Water-Babies*) went so far as to suggest in *True Words for Brave Men*, his volume of sermons and religious musings for the soldiers' and sailors' libraries, that if 'real trees' were not to hand, then the townsman might still get his fill of nature and 'the paradise of refreshment' by visiting a picture gallery. There 'the toil-worn worker' could enjoy a garden that flowered as 'gaily in winter as in summer' and so step 'beyond the grim city-world of stone and iron, smoky chimneys and roaring wheels into the world of beautiful things – *the world which shall be hereafter*'.

Loudon went a little further at Milton-on-Sea, a 'new town' at Gravesend whose master plan by Amory Henry Wilds was unfortunately never to be realised. Here Loudon would create an outdoor picture gallery, a kind of living museum. This was to be the main feature of his Terrace Garden: a fine collection of different varieties of trees and shrubs, selected and planted as much for their educational merit as their aesthetic beauty, with each species, from Virginian junipers and rhododendrons to *Cercis canadensis* and Spanish daggers, clearly labelled.

In fact, trees were enjoying something of a boom in Britain in this period. Thanks to improved glasshouses, global exploration and steamship-borne imperial trade, many once-exotic specimens were finding homes in English country gardens. All of this was of course aided by the pioneering work of the Royal Horticultural Society with its army of overseas collectors and its gardens and glasshouse at Chiswick, as well as commercial nurseries like Loddiges' in Hackney. The latter's tree collection – open free to the public on Sundays – Loudon had singled out for imitation in his 1833 salvo on public parks in the *Gardener's Magazine*. The elaborate wooden-framed conservatory of the RHS, on the other hand, he grumbled, was too 'gloomy'; he preferred (and promoted) his own unique design for wrought-iron-framed greenhouses – the rights for which he foolishly signed away, in what his biographer John Gloag dubbed 'a misguided sense of public service and total lack of business acumen'.

It was while putting together his financially disastrous *Arboretum et fruticetum Britannicum* in 1838 that Loudon calculated that in the first thirty years of the nineteenth century alone some 700 new plant species had been brought to England. Most were imported as seeds or cuttings by explorers-cum-plant-hunters such as William Lobb, Robert Fortune and David Douglas. Of Douglas fir fame, this particular Scottish botanist and mountaineer almost single-handedly altered the whole hue of the English landscape by introducing evergreen conifers like the Monterey pine and the Sitka spruce (as well as lupins) from North America.

These trees, together with the monkey puzzle – a South American import which, with its branches like writhing snakes, especially delighted the Victorians – would comprehensively transform the all-round greenery of England. Until then, and aside from other overseas arrivals like the cedar of Lebanon, the country had been dominated by deciduous local species, with their seasonal leaf droppings and work-shy refusal to do anything to leaven the cold, dark months with so much as a cheering bud or bloom.*

---

* It is worth considering that the wider planting of conifers on these shores closely coincides with the spread of the tradition of having decorated fir trees in the home at Christmas. The 1898 edition of *Brewer's Dictionary of Phrase and Fable* states that 'the custom of having a Christmas tree decorated with candles and hung with presents came to England with the craze for German things that followed Queen Victoria's marriage to Prince Albert of Saxe-Coburg-Gotha in 1840.' As a matter of fact, Queen Victoria was already familiar with the tradition as her mother was German, and even before that, Queen Charlotte, the German wife of George III, is recorded as bringing a tree for Christmas to the royal household at Windsor in 1800. But it remained a decidedly rare and royal habit in England until the 1840s, when advances in greenhouse gardening also encouraged the Victorians to invite alien plants, not unlike the era's fictional vampires, into their homes in the form of aspidistras, ferns and potted palms. In 1833, Dr Nathaniel Ward, an amateur botanist and doctor with a medical practice near St Katharine Docks, perfected his Wardian case, a hermetically sealed glass jar capable of supporting ferns and other exotics over long distances. Afterwards, not only did the range of indoor plants expand but few middle-class drawing rooms or high-class ladies' boudoirs were without these portable Lilliputian greenhouses bursting with orchids and similar other-worldly foliage.

In any event, Loudon's living museum of varied and exotic species clearly caught important eyes, and four years later he was hired to create the Arboretum at Derby by Joseph Strutt, a Benthamite Utilitarian industrialist with an enlarged social conscience.

Strutt was the youngest of the three sons (and five children) of Jedediah Strutt. A Nonconformist former wheelwright who'd prospered in hosiery – patenting the 'Derby rib machine' for manufacturing stockings – Strutt Sr went on to make the bulk of his money in mills for cotton and calico. One of the more socially minded employers of his day, he built 'model' factory communities at Belper and Milford in Derbyshire, with decent housing for his mill hands – who, admittedly, did include children. But he usually drew the line at hiring anyone aged under ten.

Joseph, along with his brothers, William and George, was to inherit the business and his father's liberal instincts. At the presentation of the Arboretum to the town in September 1840, a three-day affair with trumpeters, cannons, fireworks, a ball, tea, balloonist displays and a

procession with portraits of Queen Victoria and Prince Albert conveyed to eye-worthy positions in the shrubbery, Joseph stated that: 'It would be ungrateful in me not to employ a portion of the fortune which I possess, in promoting the welfare of those amongst whom I live, and by whose industry I have been aided in its acquisition.'

But the Strutts were rather more than just slightly kindlier-than-usual mill owners. The family – not unlike their near neighbours in Staffordshire, the Wedgwoods – formed the hub of intellectual life in their corner of the Midlands. William, the most technically minded of the brothers, was a close friend of Erasmus Darwin, with whom he founded the Derby Philosophical Society – a local version of Darwin's earlier Lunar Society which was famously attended by James Watt, Matthew Boulton, Joseph Priestley and other industrialists and dissenting bigwigs. His circle of literary and scientific acquaintances and correspondents ran from Jeremy Bentham and architect Charles Bage to the poets Robert Southey and Samuel Taylor Coleridge, who both visited the Strutts in Derby. Coleridge, who was very nearly employed as a tutor by the family, found Derby 'full of curiosities' and wrote that William Strutt was 'a man of stern aspect, but strong, very strong abilities'; while Joseph, whom he would meet again in Humphry Davy's lecture room in London, he described as in 'every way amiable' and a man who deserved his wife, 'a sweet-minded Woman ... lovely, handsome, beautiful &c'.

Whatever impressions the Strutts (or their wives) left on the author of *The Rime of the Ancient Mariner*, the brothers' mark on Derby would be pronounced, for they equipped the town with schools, an infirmary, a Friendly Society, a Mechanics' Institute, at least one bridge (designed by William), paving, gas street lighting and, of course, an arboretum.

Situated on the southern outskirts of the town, the 11 acres allotted for the Arboretum had previously served as Joseph's summer garden retreat, a kind of dacha by the Derwent. In 1839, when he hired Loudon to convert the land into a park, Strutt was seventy-three years of age and nearing the end of his life.* But while in increasingly poor health, he remained active in local affairs. As his later remarks to the town council about the Arboretum show, he'd evidently been following all the debates about public walks with some interest. From the beginning, Strutt was 'desirous', as he put it, 'of uniting, as much as possible, information with amusement'. For this reason, he had first proposed putting a botanic garden on the site – Loudon had form in this field, having laid out a botanical garden for the Birmingham Horticultural Society in Edgbaston a decade earlier – but it was concluded that the maintenance costs would be too high for it to be run as a civic amenity. Edgbaston, by contrast, was really a private place of horticultural study, sustained by subscriptions and fees.

On the other hand, a simple park would not cut it for Strutt: the idea of a 'mere composition of trees and shrubs with turf' he dismissed on the grounds that such a garden 'would become insipid after being seen two or three times', which perhaps reveals his own attention span and rather ignores how pleasingly different the most basic gardens can look from hour to hour and day to day, let alone season to season. And so it was that Strutt and Loudon – a landscape gardener laden with debt from the debacle of his *Arboretum et fruticetum Britannicum*, an arboretum in book form published, in part, to promote the creation of arboretums – agreed that 'the most suitable kind of public garden' for

---

* He would, however, outlive Loudon, who was over twenty years his junior, by a month.

their needs was 'an arboretum or collection of trees and shrubs, foreign and indigenous, which would endure the open air in the climate of Derby, with the names placed to each'.

Such a collection, they maintained, would: 'have all the ordinary beauties of a pleasure-ground viewed as a whole; and yet, from no tree or shrub occurring twice in the collection, and from the name of every tree and shrub being placed against it, an inducement' was 'held out to walk in the garden to take an interest in the name and history of each species, its uses in this country or in other countries, its appearance at different seasons of the year, and the various associations connected with it'.

The Arboretum was, if you like, a great leafy game of Top Trumps. One where parkgoers, desperate to acquaint themselves with the full set – and Loudon sourced and planted over 1,000 species and varieties in Derby – would be 'induced', in their phrasing, to tramp from tree to tree, reading and absorbing the information on each sign in turn, thereby improving themselves in body and mind simultaneously.

However, Derby's status – or, possibly more accurately, renown – as 'the first truly public park' is problematic. Under the conditions of the bequest, Strutt stipulated that the park should be open to all and free of charge two days a week, and that one of those days should be Sunday 'during proper hours' (i.e. after morning church services had finished). On other days, the rules went on, a small sum should be required from persons entering the gardens; or yearly admissions should be granted for certain modest sums.*

---

* A rather touching, compassionate detail of Strutt's demands was that the two lodges, built in the olden-times Tudorbethan style, should each have a public room 'into which strangers might go and sit down, taking their own refreshments with them without any charge being made by the occupant of the lodge, unless some

These admission fees and yearly subs were required for its upkeep, as the town council, although it had gifted the park, was unable, legally, to allocate money from local rates to pay for its maintenance at this time. And while it was also open to all comers 'from dawn to dusk' on Wednesdays throughout the year, the Derby Arboretum was, in the judgement of the park historian Hazel Conway, only 'a semi-public park, not a freely accessible public one'.

Preston in Lancashire probably has some rights to claim it promoted the first fully public park, having by 1833 already enclosed a nearby moor and turned it into a public recreation ground, named Moor Park. But until formally landscaped by Edward Milner in 1862, it remained not much more than common, and was in the main still used for grazing cattle by the freemen of the city. Peel Park in Salford is another contender. Named after the former Prime Minister, Sir Robert Peel, it was funded by subscriptions from the local residents and opened to all in 1846.

Even as an arboretum, Derby's thunder was slightly stolen as the firm of Loddiges in Hackney, so admired by Loudon, who had published the plans of their gardens in his *Encyclopaedia of Gardening* in 1830, were involved in planting an arboretum in a new non-denominational cemetery in Stoke Newington – one of the so-called Magnificent Seven built in outer London during this period. Completed in May 1840, a few months before Derby's Arboretum, the Abney Park Cemetery boasted a stock of nearly 2,500 trees, over twice that of Strutt and Loudon's, arranged A–Z around the outer perimeter of a 32-acre site landscaped and open to visitors.

---

assistance, such as hot water, plates, knives, and forks, &c, were required, in which case a small voluntary gratuity might be given'. And 'that there should be a proper yard and conveniences at each lodge for the use of the public'.

Built by a joint-stock company, all of whose trustees were Congregationalists, Abney Park quickly established itself as the preferred final resting place of many prominent Dissenters, and became among the 'Nonconformist portion of the religious world ... scarcely less sacred than ... Bunhill Fields', in the view of the writer George Walter Thornbury, who also considered the Arboretum 'formed with great taste'. As an attraction, it would, sadly, soon lose out to those buried luminaries, with the cemetery doing a brisk trade in guidebooks for those who wished to pay their respects to the dearly departed worthies. (Even in death, that most stereotypical of Victorians, E. P. Hood, kept to type, finding his final resting place among the distinguished at Abney Park.)

But while the Derby Arboretum may not have been the first truly public park – or even the first great arboretum – it exerted a powerful influence on the first generation of public parks. Since the man who designed it had spent nearly twenty years banging on about public parks and helping to frame a national debate about what they could and should be like, that shouldn't really come as too much of a surprise. But, Strutt's gift of a park for Derby would inspire similar donations by Lord Vernon (Stockport's Vernon Park in 1858) and Henry Bolckow (Albert Park in Middlesbrough in 1868) – though neither of these bequests were quite so purely philanthropic, with both men looking to develop 'villa residences' on nearby land they had retained for 'building purposes'.

Yet the Derby-style public and public-run Arboretum was to be replicated almost exactly in Ipswich, Norwich, Nottingham and Worcester in the following decade. During the same period the Royal Victoria Park at Bath was transformed into an arboretum, largely thanks to a crusade by the local registrar and surgeon Frederick Hanham, who felt they were invaluable in 'combining science with recreation and pleasure'. But if arboretums were not, per se, part of the main fittings, a look-and-learn element still permeated most of the earliest public parks with their often stated commitment to 'rational recreation'.*

This was notably the case at the first great public park in East London. Its planner and architect, James Pennethorne, had hoped to give Victoria Park its own in-grounds museum. It became a matter of lasting regret for him that lack of budget eventually prevented the realisation of his plan to build a structure like the one he built on Jermyn Street, Piccadilly for the Museum of Practical Geology – an imposing palazzo-facaded neoclassical building with a vast glass- and iron-roofed central gallery stuffed floor to ceiling with cases of ores, minerals and fossils.†

Pennethorne is often referred to as the 'favourite pupil' or 'adopted son' of John Nash, the Prince Regent's architect and planner. Diligent and largely self-effacing, he was certainly groomed as his successor, working closely on most of Nash's grand projects, and he inherited his mentor's role as architect and surveyor to the Commissioners of Woods, Forests and Land Revenues. This position, despite its Herne the Hunter-esque name, was fundamentally all about 'metropolitan

---

* Not all varieties of trees were suitable for city parks. At Phillips Park in Manchester, which opened in 1846, the trees and flowers had to contend with belching smoke from 'Mr Johnson's copper wireworks' nearby. By the 1870s 'the trees in the higher part of the park' and much of the other vegetation was suffering badly from the ill-effects of pollution. On certain days, the air in the park itself was said to be 'perfectly clouded' with factory smoke, and its smell, reportedly, 'stifling'.

† Apparently devoid of staff and other visitors by the 1920s, James Lees-Milne and John Betjeman would haunt its deserted rooms, taking great pleasure in pushing pebbles bearing labels of made-up Latin names into its dusty cabinets, amused to return weeks later and still find them there among the genuine exhibits. It was demolished in the 1930s and replaced by Simpson's department store, now occupied by Waterstones bookshop.

improvements' – something later acknowledged when the 'Woods and Forests' part of the title was axed and replaced by the far less botanic 'Works'. Here the aim of the game was really slum clearance, and Pennethorne would be tasked, on the basis of two reports in 1836 and 1838 by the government's Select Committee on Metropolitan Improvements, with carrying out three major road 'works' in the capital.

Their direct precursor was Nash's own Regent Street, which in neatening up an unruly rabble of lanes and common wastelands had also acted like a prophylactic in brick and stucco, protecting the grander districts of Mayfair and Belgravia from the squalor of Soho next door. (Regent's Park still remained closed to the public – 'contrary to explicit understanding of the Government', as the Committee on Public Walks had pointed out in 1834. Earlier attempts to open the park had been batted away with the excuse that the newly planted trees might be damaged by visitors – a ruse that meant it remained the exclusive preserve of residents of Nash's new villas for close to twenty years.)

In the 1830s there had been a fearsome cholera epidemic, believed to be carried in the miasma of bad air, and ever more festering political dissent in the squalid back alleys of the capital. What was hoped for was a wider redrawing of London's map, not only physically but socially and morally. In the words of the Committee's report:

> There are some districts in this vast city through which no great thoroughfares pass, and which being wholly occupied by a dense population, composed of the lower class of labourers, entirely secluded from the observation and influence of wealthier and better educated neighbours, exhibit a state of moral and physical degradation deeply to be deplored ... The moral condition of

these poorer occupants must necessarily be improved by immediate communication with a more respectable inhabitancy; and
the introduction at the same time of improved habits and a freer
circulation of air will tend materially to extirpate those prevalent
diseases which are now not only so destructive among themselves,
but so dangerous to the neighbourhood around them.

The 'Rookery' of St Giles and Holborn, Whitechapel and Spitalfields,
and the catchily named Devil's Acre stretching from behind
Westminster Abbey and into Pimlico – areas notorious for their rabbit
warren of streets running with filth and a surfeit of threepenny-a-
night, eight-to-a-room lodging houses catering to 'cadgers, thieves
and prostitutes' – were upgraded with 'great thoroughfares' for a 'freer
circulation' of air and traffic. These took the form, respectively, of
Pennethorne's New Oxford, Commercial and Victoria Streets, and
involved the mass displacement of hundreds of former residents – most
of whom were faced with either homelessness or cramming themselves
into already overcrowded tenements in nearby streets and districts.

Pennethorne's engagement at the Commission of Woods, Forests
and Land Revenues virtually coincided with calls led by Joseph Hume
for a park in East London along the lines suggested by Slaney's Public
Walks Committee. A Scottish-born ex-Tory radical Whig MP for
Middlesex who'd made his fortune in India, Hume was posthumously
described by Hansard as 'a burly man with a massive head and virtually
no neck' and 'rather dim in many respects'; and one who 'established
himself as an irritating and almost permanent fixture in the Commons'.
A man of many causes, who perhaps irked his parliamentary peers by
avidly promoting bills that ranged from calling for the abolition of
flogging in the army to Catholic Emancipation.

By 1840 Hume had solicited the support of George Frederick Young, the first MP for Tynemouth and North Shields – and, according to Charles Dickens, 'a prodigious bore in Parliament'. Despite this assessment, Dickens thought Young a model philanthropist. Born off the Ratcliffe Highway and the son of a vice-admiral, Young was a prominent figure in London shipping and had a profitable line in passenger steamers. A committee member of Lloyd's Register, he nevertheless chose to live near his yard and was a paternalistic employer rather in the Fezziwig mould, who supported the building of public wash houses and, as chair of the Stepney Board of Guardians, was instrumental in the creation of the Limehouse Children's Establishment and, with Hume, of Victoria Park.

On 10 June 1840, the pair convened a meeting at Young's Limehouse home of some 'gentlemen of Tower Hamlets' and drew up a petition for a 'royal' park – i.e. a public park, but one with the financial support of the state. The petition eventually attracted over 30,000 signatures and was presented to Queen Victoria, then only recently married and in the third year of her reign.

The document drew the young Queen's attention to the contribution of the district's docks, sugar refineries and silk weavers in making her metropolis 'the Common Emporium of the World', swelling the 'resources of the Empire' and adding 'strength and dignity' to her Crown. But if the 400,000 or more 'Artisans, Manufacturers, Labourers and others' of Tower Hamlets were by their 'ceaseless toil' adding 'wealth to the community, and stability to the throne', they laboured in 'closely crowded ... confined districts', with 'no open spaces in the vicinity of their humble dwellings for air, exercise, or healthful recreation: circumstances which produce the most painful effects on their physical and moral condition'.

This medical-cum-moral case for an East End park had, in fact, already been put forward in the first report by William Farr, statistician for the newly formed Registrar General of Births, Deaths and Marriages, the previous year. Pointing to figures which showed that the mortality rate in East London far exceeded that of the rest of the capital, Farr wrote that a

> good general system of Sewers, the intersection of the dense crowded districts of the Metropolis by a few spacious streets, and a park in the East End of London would probably diminish the annual deaths by several thousands ... and add several years to the lives of the entire population. The poorer classes would benefit by these measures, and the poor taxes reduced. But all classes of the community are directly interested ... for the epidemics, whether influenza or typhus, cholera, small pox, scarlatina or measles, which arise in the East End of the town, do not stay there, they travel to the West End and prove fatal in the wide streets and squares.

In any event, Hume & Co.'s scheme for a park in Tower Hamlets met with the approval of the monarch: an official wrote that they had the great pleasure of announcing that Her Majesty had 'expressed her entire approval of the steps which have been taken for complying with the memorial of the inhabitants of the Tower Hamlets for making a Royal Park in that populous district'. The proposal received vigorous backing in the Commons from Slaney when it was brought before the government. He recommended that Lord Duncannon, the Commissioner of Woods, Forests and Land Revenues, support the plan. It was partially to be funded by a royal grant from the sale of York House, Westminster,

and partially by speculative developments of grand residential properties around the park grounds. This, though, proved far less successful
than was originally hoped and much of the land set aside for housing
was eventually absorbed into the park.

Pennethorne was now charged with drawing up a plan and finding
a suitable site. Reporting back in April 1841, he suggested two potential
locations: one beside Bonner's Fields (near the Regent's Canal between
Bethnal Green and Bow) and another much closer to the Thames. The
latter, which was larger and is long since lost to bricks and mortar, was
Pennethorne's preferred option. But it was immediately rejected by a
cost-conscious Treasury, since it was already partly occupied by houses
and factories whose compulsory purchase and demolition would have
added to the initial outlay.

The Bow location was of course some distance from the dockland
communities it was supposed to serve, and this would come in for some
criticism, *The Builder* magazine in 1847, for instance, castigating it for
'not being near enough to the poor'. Indeed, part of the proposed site
next to Bonner's Fields was known colloquially as Botany Bay because
it was a popular hideout of wrong'uns avoiding transportation to
Australia, a hint that it was rather out of the way as far as the docks
were concerned.

The Tudor-era Bishop Edmund Bonner was the Bonner of Bonner's
Fields. The last episcopal lord of the manor of Stepney, Bonner, if
Foxe's *Book of Martyrs* is to be believed, was an unstinting and rather
hands-on burner of heretics during Queen Mary's reign. His former
manor house – though converted into an inn, where the Methodist
preacher John Wesley stayed in 1754 – still stood on the Bethnal Green
side of the land (an early nineteenth-century watercolour by T. H.
Shepherd shows the house bearing a sign that reads 'GINUNE ALES').

Beverages of a less intoxicating nature could also be had at the Three Colts Tea Garden nearby. And while the ground was now unkempt, in parts downright unsavoury, and home to thirteen decrepit cottages, in fact it had a long history as a place of recreation: prior to Bonner, aldermen of the City of London (see Chapter 1) hunted hares, coneys, foxes and other beasts there.

The largest landholders, now, were two charities, St Thomas' Hospital and the estate of Sir John Cass, a wealthy eighteenth-century city merchant and Hackney resident who'd left a sizeable portion of his fortune for the establishment of schools for the poor. But there were numerous other freeholders and tenants, and a small parcel of the land had only recently been sold to a group of Sephardic Jews to serve as a burial ground for their community.

If the plan he first submitted to the commissioners is anything to go on, Pennethorne's own ambitions for the park, housing around it aside, were somewhat sketchy. A case of here be green stuff for you to enjoy, and little else – but then, as Fanny Price puts it in Jane Austen's *Mansfield Park,* 'to sit in the shade on a fine day, and look upon verdure' was 'the most perfect refreshment'. The basic design would go through several drafts, and even then many of Victoria Park's major features would only arrive over time.

The park never officially opened, but came into use from 1845, with the work to finish it, and all manner of embellishments, continuing for several years after that. For instance, Pennethorne was an architect first and landscape architect second, and not, as he happily conceded, much of 'a plantsman'. This meant the initial plantings were not up to much. Indeed, his one-time collaborator Joseph Paxton would later be quoted in Parliament denouncing the forestry of Victoria Park, maintaining that the husbandry had been done by 'men who didn't know the names of half-a-dozen kinds of trees they were planting'. But the planting did come on in leaps and bounds after 1849, following the recruitment of a new park supervisor, John Gibson, an ex-Chatsworth employee once dispatched to South Africa to collect orchids for the Duke of Devonshire. As grazing was a source of much-needed revenue for the park in its infancy, keeping animals away from the new trees and the more ornamental flora presented its own challenges. As did preventing the light-fingered from picking a posy or two, with keepers needing to be vigilant about Artful Dodgers around some of the pricier plantings.

Water features were perhaps the most glaring omission in Pennethorne's original plan and the decision to add a lake to the design appears to have stemmed from a sense that the park would not be thought aristocratic enough without a scenic pool or two. Or certainly that was how Pennethorne sold it to the commissioners when he presented his revised version to them – though local people, now banned from bathing in the River Lea and with only the oily canal to fall back on, seemingly expressed more of an interest in acquiring decent washing facilities than an aquatic exercise in the Picturesque. Nevertheless, Pennethorne reminded the commissioners of 'the good effect which rational amusements produce on the lower orders', arguing that 'the ornamental water in St James' Park, Hyde Park and the Regent's Park' had 'been the source of such enjoyment to the Public as to induce a general feeling that ornamental water' was 'almost an integral and indispensable part of a Royal Park'.

In 1847, Pennethorne got his lake, which also served the purpose of obliterating some unsightly brick pits within the grounds. A second lake, approved by the commissioners in that same year and laid out in the east of the park, would, however, be devoted to bathing, a use that Pennethorne himself heartily disapproved of, arguing that it would 'quite destroy the value of the Park as a place of residence'. If thwarted in this and in his museum, Pennethorne did manage to persuade the park's board to fork out for a genuine curio: a Chinese pavilion for one of the islands on the western lake, known to all as 'the Pagoda', though it wasn't technically a pagoda at all. Or truly Chinese.

This building, a single-storey oriental-style pavilion with turned-up red eaves and 'taken after a correct model', had stood at the entrance to a Chinese exhibition staged at Hyde Park Corner. Surplus to requirements at the exhibition's end, it was advertised for sale in 1847. Claiming that it 'cost £800 to build', the advert described it as 'well worthy of the attention of Noblemen and Gentlemen for country seats'. For Pennethorne, anxious to ensure that his new royal park was sufficiently regal, there could scarcely have been a better pitch. The Pagoda was purchased for 100 guineas (plus £25 for transportation) and was installed in the park before the first lake was even finished, making a folly one of the earliest components of London's first purpose-built public park.

George Lansbury, the MP for Poplar and leader of the Labour Party, who visited the park as a small child, recalled in his memoirs believing that the Pagoda was inhabited by a Chinese family who came out at night to tend to the plants and feed the ducks. Lansbury, who cut his political teeth attending trade union rallies in the park, also remembered that the area of Bonner's Fields had been notorious for political meetings and speeches by radical theologians and atheists. Certainly John Wesley had preached there during his sojourn at Bonner's Hall. But the park had been considered a means of realising what the frock-coated and mutton-chopped 'gentlemen' of Tower Hamlets most probably called 'the reconciliation of classes': i.e. quietening or calming seditious political agitation – or suppressing it entirely, if you were feeling harsh. William Gaspey, the author of a contemporary guidebook, *Tallis's Illustrated London*, saw the park in exactly those terms. He took it as living proof 'that the rich and powerful no longer deem the poor beneath their contempt'. Writing that: 'No nobler monument exists of the kindly disposition which now generally prevails for ameliorating the condition of the operative classes; no surer antidote is found to the incendiary harangue, which would make the humble discontented with their governors, than Victoria Park.'

But incendiary harangues were never to be silenced quite so easily around Victoria Park, and the Bonner's Fields area, in particular, attracted regular gatherings of Chartist campaigners in 1848. Pennethorne's immediate response then was to recommend they enclose the Fields and let some of the land for building to prevent those of 'irreligious or democratic principles' from holding any further meetings there. Most of it in the end was simply incorporated into the park, but his reaction demonstrated the disquiet created by Chartism among the political establishment at that time.

Beginning a decade earlier as a draft parliamentary bill, and in response to the limited expansion of the franchise under the Reform Act and the draconian Poor Law Amendment Act of 1834, the opening People's Charter called for six major reforms to the electoral system. These included manhood suffrage (but not womanhood), pay for MPs, secret ballots and still-to-be-realised annual elections. The belief that a more representative and less corrupt government would alleviate economic injustice and suffering led to 'Chartism' becoming a kind of catch-all banner to rally under. Especially strong in the mill towns of the North and the Potteries in the Midlands, where it was more closely aligned with strikes for higher wages, direct industrial action and the odd riot, its supporters ranged from chapel-going moderates to blood-up would-be revolutionaries. This latter group, come spring 1848, could only gaze

Chinese Pagoda.   Cascade.   Rustic Seat.

Hot House.   The Lake.

Refreshment Saloon.   Swings and Roundabouts.

rather enviously across the Channel to where Louis Philippe of France had been forced from the throne in the February Revolution* and anti-establishment rebels in Austria, Germany, Italy, Poland and Hungary looked close to bringing the Habsburg Empire down. They failed, but it seemed to many Chartists that at last their moment had come. And so in the spirit of 'if not now, then when?' they decided to again press the British government, which had rejected two earlier petitions, on the small matter of voting reform.

In London in early March 1848, Chartist sympathisers assembled on Kennington Common, at Spa Green, Clerkenwell, Blackheath, Stepney Green, Bethnal Green and Bonner's Fields to hear speeches, shake fists, throw hats into the air, break the occasional petit-bourgeois window and loot a shop on the way home. A more formal rally on 6 March, in the as yet unfinished Trafalgar Square, had been banned by the authorities but went ahead anyway and resulted in skirmishes between the police and what the *Annual Register* referred to as 'artisans, labourers out of work, idle speculators, and thieves' and 'the refuse of a crowded city'. The stage was, in effect, being set for what would inaccurately become famous as the final act of Chartism – a demonstration to amass on Kennington Common on 10 April and then march across Westminster Bridge to deliver a fresh petition to Parliament.

Kennington Common, not unlike its north-eastern London cousin Bonner's Fields, had a long history as a gathering place for political meetings, if also serving as the former site of more authoritarian, though often no less festive, public executions. For instance, the hustings for candidates for the first elections after the passing of the Reform Act in 1832 had been held there. At that time, over 400 tenants could claim the right to graze

---

* and into exile in Britain as Mr Smith.

their animals on the common. A herd of cows owned by one local milkman was an almost permanent fixture and was judged by one observer to be the cause of the common's down-at-heel appearance since they chewed through, or trampled on, its 'stunted herbage' and shat all over the place. An encircling ditch, meanwhile, received waste from a vitriol factory on the eastern side of the common. Its excretions were enhanced by 'constant contributions' from what, in an era notorious for apocryphal stories about the covering of table legs, were described in compellingly veiled terms as 'numerous unmentionable conveniences attached to a low line of cottage erections'. If this were not enough, there was also a cemetery 'of all the dead puppies and kittens of the vicinity'. Their decaying carcasses were supposedly to be 'seen floating on the surface of ... watery graves, in all the green and purple tints of putrefaction'.

Despite all this, the common, 'for want of anything better', was where the local population repaired to relax, take exercise and get some fresh(ish) air. 'Idle youths' were noted for indulging in 'low gambling' and for playing games of cricket that obstructed 'the path in all directions' and threatened to break the noses and knock out the eyes of any unwary passer-by. These innocent pursuits, along with putrefied dogs, were perhaps the reason why Slaney & Co. in 1833 had recommended that Kennington be 'properly laid out' and 'planted round the edge' and transformed into a 'handsome Public Walk'. The committee's suggestions had, however, been kicked into the cow-shit and vitriol-soaked long grass. As had a plan a decade later to build a park on the back of a villa housing scheme à la Regent's and, in part, Victoria, and named Albert in honour of the Queen's consort.* Kennington and

* Villas and crescents serving here as obvious code words for 'improving' an area, just as 'luxury flats and loft-style living' stand in our own time for gentrification and absentee overseas owners.

Prince Albert would become more acquainted in due course, but it was to the decidedly common common that the 'refuse of a crowded city' trekked on 10 April 1848.

Like James Bond turning up at Blofeld's shark-primed underwater lair, their arrival had been rather more than expected. Over 170,000 citizens were sworn in as special constables to help police the march. William Makepeace Thackeray, whose rollicking satirical novel *Vanity Fair* was being serialised at the time, was among them, and went out armed with a purple staff with a lion and unicorn painted on it. Pennethorne's Geological Museum in Piccadilly, then still under construction, was one of the recruiting venues. Some 5,000 policemen were on duty for the march, and over 7,000 troops were deployed around the city. A special force of over 1,000 Chelsea Pensioners 'armed to the gums' were stationed at the entrances to the bridges over the Thames. At the crack of dawn, the Duke of Wellington, who was now seventy-eight and hard of hearing, rode over to the common with an escort to personally take stock of the situation. Queen Victoria and the royal family were out of harm's way, having been packed off to Osborne House on the Isle of Wight.

Estimates of just how many people crammed themselves on to the common vary, with the Chartists on the day claiming 300,000 and the government just 15,000. But even conservative estimates now reckon that over 150,000 took part. At Kennington there were speeches and an address by Feargus O'Connor, known as 'The Lion of Freedom', the Irish-born MP for Nottingham and de facto leader of the movement. Since the planned procession was declared illegal, the petition of six million signatures (the government, days later, maintained there were 1.9 million, and most of those forgeries) eventually had to be conveyed to the House of Commons by O'Connor in three hansom cabs.

The crowd, facing the armed might of the British state and suffering after hours on a boggy common in perpetual rain, slipped gradually (and almost entirely peaceably) away. And with them, or so the story goes, went Chartism – with O'Connor now moving into the syphilis-induced mental decline that seven years later would see him die in a Chiswick insane asylum. But in actual fact, the cause carried on in Parliament by Joseph Hume and a fifty-strong group of radicals was not entirely spent in the streets and on the commons. There were further assemblies over the summer of 1848, in Bradford in May and, significantly, in June, at Bonner's Fields, where Chartist heads were cracked by gentlemen-at-arms bearing cudgels.

The blood on the Bonner's Fields grass was barely dry before Pennethorne and his gardeners had swept in and re-landscaped, and a suspiciously similar re-landscaping would occur at Kennington in 1854, when its common was remade as a park – the spot formerly used for the electoral hustings proving an early casualty of the new design.*

* * *

When the re-landscaping of Kennington was done, the most notable addition was a new building. The so-called Prince Consort's Lodge had been moved brick by brick from the grounds of the Knightsbridge Cavalry Barracks in Hyde Park, where it had first been erected in 1851 for the Great Exhibition. Sponsored by the Society for Improving the Conditions of the Labouring Classes, whose president was Prince Albert, the lodge was designed by Henry Roberts, the architect earlier responsible for the Society's houses at Bagnigge Wells, Pentonville, and Streatham Street, Bloomsbury – two of the earliest attempts in the

---

* It was with a tip of the hat to the Chartists, that on 31 March 1990 around 70,000 demonstrators against the Conservative government's 'Community Charge', or 'poll tax', set out from Kennington Park to match on Trafalgar Square.

capital to provide decent, purpose-built modern housing for the poor. Built with new hollow bricks that were lighter to use and cheaper to manufacture, Roberts's 'model dwelling' comprised four generously sized, three-bedroom flats, each with its own scullery, closet, water supply, fireplace and dust shaft. Re-erected in Kennington, it was intended to house two park employees, and a 'Museum for Articles relating to Cottage Economy'. The museum part of the plan seemingly never materialised, leaving South Londoners to fend for themselves over the economics of cottaging, but the Great Exhibition's main themes, industry and education, were still very much the animating force behind the laying out of Kennington – and countless other public parks. Indeed, the significance of the 1851 Great Exhibition to the parks formed in Victorian Britain in subsequent decades cannot be overestimated.

The idea of staging the Exhibition had first been broached by Henry Cole. As an assistant in the Public Record Office at Carlton Terrace, Cole was instrumental in the founding of the 'penny' postal system, and in 1842 also published the first Christmas card in Britain. Under the pseudonym 'Felix Summerly', he wrote unofficial guides to the likes of Hampton Court, and children's books; he was also a promoter of the docks at Grimsby and the publisher of the *Journal of Design*. In 1846, he even picked up the Society of the Arts' Prize for his own design of 'a good simple nursery tea set' – one of which the Queen herself reputedly esteemed enough to use as a sole set for breakfasts at Balmoral.

It was Cole's meticulousness at the Public Record Office – his use, specifically, of a small hand press for producing on-the-spot docket tickets – rather than his tea set, that had caught the attention of the no-less i-dotting consort Albert when they first met in 1842. Though initially sceptical of Cole's suggestion, the Prince, having been personally troubled by the political upheavals of 1848, came to see an exhibition as a means of cementing peace in Europe and promoting wider international co-operation through trade.

Later Albert was to assert that he believed the Great Exhibition to be 'a new starting point from which all nations' would 'be able to direct their future exertions'. And certainly Joseph Paxton's exhibition hall – christened 'a palace of very crystal' by Douglas Jerrold of the humorous magazine *Punch* – established a compellingly futuristic tone for the whole. The structure was, after all, as one historian put it, an 'unprecedented building using unprecedented fabrication and assembly methods'.

Starting out as 'a common gardener's boy', as Queen Victoria described him in her diary, Paxton was in many respects the ideal person to supply the centrepiece for an exhibition supposedly dedicated to 'the Industry of All Nations'. Dickens, hardly a slacker himself, reckoned that Paxton's 'very leisure would kill a man of fashion with its hard work'. A horticulturalist and landscape architect by profession and by appointment to the Duke of Devonshire at Chatsworth, Paxton in fact bagged his fortune in railway shares.* Publishing, at that time a rapidly expanding 'communication', was another of his major business interests; his *Horticultural Register* had lured many readers away from Loudon's *Gardener's Magazine*. And a young Dickens had, as it happens, edited the opening seventeen issues of the *Daily News*, a Paxton bank-rolled paper whose stated first principles were to fight for the 'improvement; of education, civil and religious liberty, and equal legislation'.

It was Paxton's canniness with 'the media', to use the current phrase, that ultimately helped secure the last-minute adoption of his design for the Exhibition. Paxton had already furnished an Exhibition building

---

* Later in life, he claimed to have passed Kennington Common on the morning of the Chartist rally in April 1848; surmising that a revolution was not imminent, he hotfooted it to his broker and made a £200 killing buying stock while the market seesawed in panic.

committee – that counted Isambard Kingdom Brunel, Charles Barry and William Cubitt as members – with a design: a low brick number topped off with an iron dome twice the size of that sported by St Paul's. This had been tentatively accepted. But the design, whose construction was estimated to require some twenty million bricks, was in the end judged ugly and widely condemned as inappropriately bulky for the proposed temporary exhibition site in Hyde Park. There was also a feeling that such a structure would not go down well with the local residents. The Hyde Park site remained contentious with affluent locals; the upper-crust equestrians of Rotten Row and *The Times* doing their damnedest to persuade the committee that other, earlier contenders, including Leicester Square, Victoria or Regent's Park and (a then still prison-free) Wormwood Scrubs, would be more appropriate.

Paxton alighted on his successful design quite fortuitously. Ensconced in Chatsworth, he was hard at work on the glasshouse cultivation of giant Amazonian water lilies. For several years, Paxton, on behalf of the Duke, had been engaged in a polite race to see which gentleman gardener (or gentleman's gardener) could first bring a giant Amazonian water lily to flower in Britain. This 'titanic water plant', whose leaves could reach over six feet in diameter, had been discovered by the Bohemian explorer and botanist Thaddäus Haenke in Peru at the beginning of the century. Attempts to bring living samples back to England from Guyana had failed, forcing Paxton and Sir William Hooker, the Director of the Royal Botanic Gardens at Kew, to attempt to raise lilies from a handful of prized imported seeds. Paxton emerged victorious in November 1849, coaxing one plant to bloom in a tank rigged up to emulate the warm tropical conditions of its natural habitat inside the Great Stove – a vast iron-framed glass conservatory he'd designed and built at Chatsworth and whose overall dimensions exceeded those of the Euston Station railway terminus.

Paxton named the plant *Victoria regia* in honour of the Queen and travelled to Windsor to deliver in person to Her Majesty what was, in the event, a somewhat wilted blossom. But in a cultural epoch when the unusually large (Jumbo the Elephant) and the unusually small (General Tom Thumb)* exerted a powerful, if peculiar, fascination over the general public, it was a picture of Paxton's young daughter Annie standing on one of its enormous leaves and published in the *Illustrated London News* that led to the lily becoming a full-blown phenomenon. And, perhaps unsurprisingly, it was to the *Illustrated London News*, with a readership of over 200,000, that Paxton turned, in due course, with an engraving of his plan for a glasshouse for the Great Exhibition.

The plant's load-bearing abilities, however, were ultimately as important as the publicity it generated. Richard Bruce, another horticultural collector, had already observed that the red-ribbing of the lily's firm leaves suggested 'some strange fabric of cast iron just taken from the furnace'. And Paxton, inspired by the organic 'cross girders' of the leaf, applied the same principle of construction to a 'ridge and furrow' iron-and-glass roof, at first for a new lily house, and then as one of the guiding structural motifs of his 'Crystal Palace'.

The railways, too, would prove a sometimes unwitting handmaid to the final Exhibition Hall. It was at an appointment in Westminster with the chairman of the Midland Railway Company that Paxton first mooted the idea of designing such a building for the Exhibition. John Ellis, MP and chair of the Midland, was instantly convinced – and there and then dragged Paxton off to meet Henry Cole. A week later, while chairing an evidently boring Midland Railway Company board meeting,

---

* Or, in *Alice's Adventures in Wonderland*, a magical combination of the two.

Paxton knocked out a rough sketch of the 'palace' on a piece of blotting paper between the various matters of business. On top of this, a chance encounter with Robert Stephenson on a train to London garnered the backing from the father of the *Rocket* for the soundness, in engineering terms, of his design.

From the moment its image appeared in the *Illustrated London News* on 6 July 1850, Paxton's Exhibition Hall was an object of fascination, attracting gasps of admiration for the audacity of its engineering, grumbles about its viability and prophecies of catastrophe in tea shops, tap rooms and club lounges. A Cinderella's slipper of a building, over 1,800 feet in length and close to 500 feet wide, it dispensed with bricks and mortar: instead it was to be assembled from prefabricated modular glass panes, cast- and wrought-iron columns and crossbars, and wooden beams and bars. The whole building was eventually put up in under twenty-two weeks and was an attraction before it was finished, with Londoners paying a small fee to gawp at its construction *in situ*. And what a truly remarkable impression it must have made. Here, in the year of the abolition of the window tax, was a piece of engineering that suggested the possibility of a brighter and better world to come.* After the soot and smoke of the preceding decades, what else could anyone wish for?

The gaiety of Paxton's palace was not solely down to the glass. Owen Jones was employed as a superintendent of works for the Exhibition and devised the Hall's festive colour scheme. Architect, antiquarian, designer, Jones was the author of the lavishly illustrated *Plans, Elevations, Sections and Details of the Alhambra*, one of the first books produced using chromolithographic printing. He was among a

---

* This tax had been condemned by medical campaigners in the wake of another typhoid outbreak in 1849 for forcing the nation's poorest tenants to live and work in dark, dank, miasma-fermenting rooms.

generation of Victorian artists (particularly the Pre-Raphaelites), architects, designers, scholars and gardeners whose work was informed by
Goethe's *Theory of Colour*, which had appeared in English translation
in 1840. For the Exhibition Hall, Jones employed a warm white for
upper glazing bars and light blue for the girders, whose undersides were
in striped red. A light yellow was used on some of the moulded details
and elsewhere, brightening the overall effect even further.

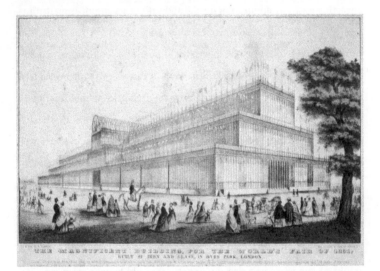

THE MAGNIFICENT BUILDING, FOR THE WORLD'S FAIR OF 1851,
BUILT OF IRON AND GLASS, IN HYDE PARK, LONDON

In the interior, translucent streamers of 'turkey red' garnished the
15,000 exhibits from more than forty countries. These included the first
gas stove, the Koh-i-Noor diamond, a steam loom, the Jacquard lace
machine, a pneumatic railway, a steam brewery and stuffed frogs from
Württemberg. From his crown lands, Prince Albert himself exhibited
grain, wool, and, most revealingly of all, a garden seat assembled
from coal designed by his artistic advisor, Ludwig Grüner. Even rest,
this artefact surely implied, could only come after often grubby and
dangerous industry.

The availability of group excursion train tickets, pioneered just a decade earlier by the former temperance campaigner turned travel agent Thomas Cook, would give many thousands of ordinary people a chance to visit the Exhibition on special cheap 'shilling days'.* However, although the Exhibition was funded by private subscription with backers receiving season tickets which entitled them to attend the opening and mingle within sight of the Queen, all classes would be welcome. This was not a prospect to gladden all hearts; the Duke of Wellington, ever the Cassandra, gloomily foresaw looting and mob riots. He was far from a lone voice in predicting doom for what from its inception was viewed as the Consort's pet scheme. Paxton had, for instance, argued in favour of free admission for the labouring classes, or what he called 'the sinews of the land', suggesting in a piece for *The Times* that the Exhibition should be 'as free as the light it pervades'. But this was rejected by the committee, who, like Wellington, feared the prospect of hordes of the unwashed (and, worse, the unwaged) invading the site.

The pessimistic predictions of Wellington and others that the 'common' sorts would arrive drunk and disorderly, 'destroy the things' and 'cut their initials or scratch their names on the panes of the glass lighthouses' proved unfounded. Remarkably, throughout the Exhibition there were just twelve arrests for pickpocketing, another eleven for petty offences and only three recorded assaults on women. According to the social researcher Henry Mayhew, on the shilling days the working people 'surpassed in decorum the hopes of their well-wishers'. He argued that to them the Great Exhibition was 'more of a school than a show' and 'what was a matter of tedium ... and a mere lounge, for gentle-folks' the less well off 'used as a place of instruction'.

---

* From now on, special excursion trains would be laid on for the opening of new public parks, like Halifax's People's Park in 1857.

At the Great Exhibition, the public had, in a sense, shown that they could behave themselves when let loose in a gigantic, potentially lethal and eminently breakable glasshouse and exposed to the highest examples of mechanical and horticultural craft.

Paxton had hoped that his palace would become a permanent fixture of Hyde Park after the Exhibition closed, and suggested it be re-purposed as a 'winter garden' so that people could amble in greenery in all weathers. While its stock was still high that summer, he also proposed the creation of a crystal sanatorium as part of City of London Hospital for Diseases of the Chest, which stood beside Victoria Park. This idea came to nothing and to his frustration proved the first of several other thwarted 'crystal' structures he proposed. Paxton now became almost as monomaniacal about glasswork as Chubby Checker with the Twist. Each project failed to get off the ground.

Under the official terms hammered out between the Queen, the government and the committee for staging the event in the first place, the Exhibition Hall had to be removed and the ground restored to the park by June 1852. A new home, however, presented itself in the comparative wilds of Sydenham – but this move was as much a result of private as of civic enterprise. The Crystal Palace Company, of which Paxton was a director, bought the 'People's Palace', moved it, piece by piece, to South London (Surrey, as it then was), enlarged it by a further half again and turned it into a jewel of Koh-i-Noor proportions at the centre of a whole new park.

Perhaps taking its cue from Mayhew's educationally minded Great Exhibitioners, Crystal Palace Park deliberately set out to be a superior type of private pleasure ground. Chief among its refined attractions was an extensive array of concerts of classical music – a particular passion of the company's secretary, George Grove, later the founding editor of *Grove's Dictionary of Music and Musicians*. Promising to be an 'illustrated encyclopaedia', it contained classical Graeco-Roman sculptures and inside the rebuilt palace a full-scale mock Ancient Egyptian court was created. Like the set of an early Hollywood sword-and-sandals epic, this was rammed floor to ceiling with sarcophagi, mammoth columns decorated with hieroglyphs, and giant ornamental cat after giant ornamental cat. All of the room's contents were copies, but most were cast from genuine artefacts held in the British Museum's collection by Joseph Bonomi, a sculptor and artist who'd undertaken two sketching expeditions to Egypt.

This kind of historical tableau, antiquity as awe-inspiring spectacle, extended to one of the park's most endearing and still extant features: its collection of life-sized replica dinosaurs, a few of which, like the palace, were refugees from the Great Exhibition. This 'family of monsters ... destined to roam, as in their native state, through the deep Penge morasses', as one contemporary observer rather fruitily put it, were sculpted by Waterhouse Hawkins, a one-time illustrator for Charles Darwin, under the direction of Richard Owen, the palaeontologist who coined the term 'dinosaur'. Hawkins described his role as a God-given chance 'to call up from the abyss of time and from the depths of the earth, those vast forms and gigantic beasts which the Almighty Creator designed with fitness to inhabit and precede us in possession of this part of the earth called Great Britain'.

That both he and Owen rejected Darwin's theories of evolution, and styled their creatures accordingly, undermined their eventual peda-gogical value. But as monuments to the curiosities (and controversies) of mid-nineteenth-century science, they remain fascinating. Though their rather mammalian features could be seen as the first step on a long and dangerous anthropomorphic road to Barney the Dinosaur.

However, in an increasingly desperate hunt for entrance-fee-paying punters, Crystal Palace Park was quickly forced to lower its highbrow tone and was soon hosting cat-and-dog shows and displays of tightrope acrobatics by that French wonder of the wires, the Great Blondin. In an interesting twist, Paxton now complained that when it came to one of Crystal Palace's most noted horticultural features, its floral displays, it faced unfair competition from public parks.

Back at Chatsworth in the 1840s, Paxton had been an enthusiastic early promoter of ornamental or 'carpet' bedding – the practice of greenhouse-rearing a mixture of brightly coloured flowering plants, like the yellow or crimson Tom Thumb nasturtiums, and then replanting them in beds, in mass formation, to create a botanical mosaic or tapestry. Not unlike arboretums, carpet bedding, in providing a fresh way to display a wide variety of often non-native or specially cultivated flowers, had first won plaudits for being as educational as it was showy. Which partially explains their widespread planting by Paxton at the Crystal Palace Park, that 'illustrated encyclopaedia', etc. But as with Hawkins's dinosaurs and the Egyptian court, the massed rows of gaudy multicoloured flower beds at Crystal Palace were a captivating (and crowd-pleasing) visual extravaganza first and foremost, and one that any dunderhead could admire.

And that dunderheads clearly did admire the flowers at Crystal Palace was one reason why carpet bedding was promptly adopted by public parks and, in time, formal flower beds would become virtually synonymous with municipal gardens. The Scottish-born horticulturalist Donald Beaton was among those who helped nudge this trend along. Beaton argued that such displays were an important tool in the public park's reforming arsenal. Flower beds, he reasoned, were a means to wean the less fortunate from ignorance and depravity by giving them a stunning experience beyond their grubby humdrum lives. 'In these public gardens, where the bulk of visitors know little or nothing,' he wrote, 'get the multitude first into a frame of eye, so to speak, to *see* flowers by presenting them in brilliant masses of the strongest colours – a blaze, in fact.'

The dearth of natural beauty was reiterated in the *Gardeners' Chronicle*, which maintained that: 'Flowers are wanted in the people's parks just because the people's houses have no gardens, and nine-tenths of those who frequent the parks have no opportunity of seeing growing flowers anywhere else.' The issue was also picked up by Lord John Manners, Commissioner of the Board of Works, who proposed increasing the 'public benefit' of the royal parks in London by laying out flower beds. His plans met with stiff opposition from Paxton, now the MP for Coventry and far from flattered by this obvious imitation of the floriculture of Crystal Palace, in which he retained a financial interest and which people of course had to pay to see. He spoke out against Manners's scheme in the House of Commons, but his objections were ignored and by the summer of 1859 close to 40,000 bedding plants had been installed in Hyde Park. Their arrival was saluted by Samuel Broome, the 'floral oracle' of Temple Gardens and author of *The Culture of the Chrysanthemum*, because now 'the working classes could see a display of summer flowers' at no additional expense. Elsewhere, Hyde and Regent's Parks were praised for their transformation into 'feasts of colour'. While 'even' Kennington Common, 'which now aspires to the name of Park', as the *Gardeners' Chronicle* noted, had a 'bordering of flowers, as bright as the smog and vapour from an adjoining factory' would 'let them be'.

Such blooms did not appeal to the American landscape architect Frederick Law Olmsted when he visited England in 1851. But he did like at least one of Paxton's public parks enough to use it as the basis for another of the world's greatest civic creations.

CHAPTER 4

Central Parking

At this point in the twenty-first century, no vehicle is quite as orange as the Staten Island Ferry. This tubby little boat is a deeply 1970s sunburst orange; it's a Super 8 film-stock orange; the orange of fizzy drinks before tartrazine was banned. Against the sludgy greeny-grey of the Hudson River and the shiny towers of Manhattan, its colour is even more pronounced, and rather charmingly dated. And if the Farmers' Market near the entrance to the ferry on the Manhattan bankside, with its array of expensive home-grown produce and a certain business-like briskness, exemplifies a contemporary New York of bankers and loft apartments, boarding the boat still feels like stepping back in time. It's free, for a start. Then there is the view: as the island of Manhattan recedes, its sheer island-ness becomes genuinely astonishing. The whole place seems perched on a mere sliver of water, like a pond skater on a meniscus, as its underlying, and ancient, topography is brought into clear view. The city, despite, or possibly even because of, its monumentalism, appears surprisingly vulnerable – an Atlantis that could slip suddenly and sink deep into the river below.

Thoughts of such a calamity are almost unavoidable when you glance at a skyline dominated by the absent presence of the twin towers. It was to Staten Island that many Manhattanites were evacuated after the 9/11 attack, and where a good deal of the rubble from the towers was sifted before burial in the Fresh Kills landfill. The island in earlier times had served both as a garden nursery and a beach retreat for the growing metropolis – a kind of short-hop Long Island. Albeit one that in the early nineteenth century was home to a quarantine station, was plagued by outbreaks of malaria, and that remained rather more precariously linked to Manhattan by a supposedly 'dismal' sail-ferry service.

Most of Staten Island back then was rural. Today, a half-hour bus ride from Staten Island's St George's ferry station brings you to 'Historic' Richmond Town, a living heritage village. Here actors in starched white bonnets and heavy petticoats diligently stage scenes from the agrarian past, kneading chunky dough by open hearths and churning butter with heavy implements beside suitably spartan furniture inside restored period houses. Their passing knowledge of Dutch colonial settlements and George III's taxation policies are no less impressive. But surprising fragments of old Staten Island endure beyond such a well-tended preservationist reservation. Due south from Richmond Town, in an area once known as the Woods of Arden, lies an old stone and clapboard house with a red-tiled roof. It's tucked away up a narrow lane and almost completely obscured by a dense cat's cradle of trees. A slightly mildewed picket-fence white, it's a property you can well imagine being menaced by evil spirits in a story first published in *Weird Tales* or in a film widely circulated on Betamax back in the day. Any ghosts it may hold, however, are more likely to be friendly than fiendish. For this building was once the central hub of Tomosock Farm, a rather ill-fated (certainly unprofitable) venture in 'scientific' agriculture advanced in the late 1840s by Frederick Law Olmsted, a youthful New Englander inflamed by the writings of Emerson and Ruskin. The farm's failure, or perhaps more accurately its founder's inability to fully commit to farming, has to be cause for celebration, though. Had the farm succeeded, or its founder succeeded in knuckling down to farming, he might never have strayed into landscape architecture – and New York would never have had its Central Park. The debt is arguably even deeper than that: before Central Park America had virtually no public parks. Afterwards, parks would become an issue of municipal prestige, with cities across the states vying to out-park one another.

Few meeting Olmsted in bucolic Staten Island could have guessed at such a future turn of events. The figure he cut then was of a perhaps rather earnest, slightly fussy, gentleman farmer. Tools, former hands later recalled, were expected to be returned to their set places after each day's labours and a recurring obsession with the need for spartan tidiness and order can be discerned in almost everything he did. He was a wan-faced young man with a droopy moustache, brimming with ideas and pet enthusiasms: for plank roads, a wooden forerunner of paving; English drainage systems; cabbages; trees; and, especially, the cultivation of French pear trees on American soil. Yet a scan of his CV would have nailed Olmsted as a dilettante, an indulged abandoner of Ivy League college courses and schools, an occasional clerk with an

Ishmael-like propensity to take to the sea when nothing much else interested him on shore. In fact, as office workers, sailors, farmers and writers, Olmsted and Herman Melville had much in common. One of Olmsted's earliest articles, 'A Voice from the Sea', was 'a spirited account of the sad lot of the working seaman', and he was even briefly a partner in the firm that first published Melville's *Piazza Tales*.

But as the scion of a wealthy Hartford, Connecticut family, Olmsted, despite numerous financial scrapes and living far beyond his means for years, never quite suffered the same penury as the author of *Moby-Dick* – though from middle age on, he did sport a similarly heavy Assyrian-king-style beard. And whilst Melville made his first sea voyage as a cabin boy sailing from New York to Liverpool in 1839, Olmsted's tenure as a 'green hand' (an untested sailor) on the *Ronaldson* had taken him to China, and Europe remained uncharted territory. He did eventually head there, but not until the spring of 1850, when he boarded the Merseyside-bound *Henry Clay* as a paying passenger, having abandoned the Staten Island farm to embark on a ten-week walking tour of England, Scotland and Ireland with his brother, John, and their friend, Charles Loring Brace – a future founder of the American fostering movement.

Ostensibly the trip was undertaken (or explained away) by Olmsted as an agricultural fact-finding mission. But for his brother, it was intended as a health tonic. The Olmsted clan appear to have been afflicted with a hereditary eye condition – one that certainly disrupted Frederick's own early education. Late in life, Olmsted went so far as to attribute his career in landscape architecture to being left to roam wild and daydream under trees as a child when he was frequently too ill to attend school. In actual fact, it would be this very trip that led him directly to landscape architecture.

The trip also led to the publication of Olmsted's first book: his account of the journey, *Walks and Talks of an American Farmer in England*. This move into the literary field, like almost all of the other turns in Olmsted's life, was as much a matter of luck and elite connections as anything else. For instance, his travelling companion Loring Brace, himself a published writer who had funded his own excursions around Europe by placing travel letters in New York and Philadelphia papers, would later secure Olmsted a commission to tour and write about the southern states for the *New York Times Daily*. And it was a chance encounter with America's leading gardener (and publisher of the widely read *Horticulturalist*), Andrew Downing, that encouraged Olmsted to try his hand at journalism. The book deal for *Walks and Talks*, in another happy instance of knowing the right people, came courtesy of the great publisher George Palmer Putnam, a one-time neighbour.

At this time, travel books were among the most widely read forms of literature, bested only by novels and romances. With imperialist exploration in full swing, descriptions of other places – familiar or foreign – were a way of examining new ideas of national identity and self and of scientific knowledge. As a boy, and presumably during a respite from his eye troubles, Olmsted had read and enjoyed Benjamin Silliman's *Journal of Travels in England, Holland and Scotland*. Having attended Silliman's lectures on geology at Yale, Olmsted found in this Yank-in-Europe's travelogue the basis and inspiration for his own efforts.

Olmsted was almost genetically programmed to be an Anglophile, being a direct descendant of Essex Nonconformists who had left Braintree for the New World in 1632. After separating from the main colony at Newton (now Cambridge), Massachusetts, his great-great-great-grandfather James Olmsted was among the founders of Hartford in the Connecticut Valley, receiving a hefty 70 acres of land in the carve-up that followed. The family were proud of their roots, and not averse to referring to Olmsteds in Essex in the Domesday Book if the topic arose; modestly, of course, and quickly following up with some statement or other about their forebears' foresight in moving to egalitarian America, happily free from the yoke of such a tax-gathering Norman aristocracy.

But Olmsted responded warmly to Britain during this first visit, even writing in his account of a stay at a suitably ancient inn in Chester of 'Dear old Mother England'. Like many an overseas tourist since, Olmsted had a penchant for the storybook England of ruined castles, winding lanes, thatched cottages and smoky oak-panelled taverns. When not seeking out farms and/or drainage systems to study – and *Walks and Talks* is genuinely invaluable to the agricultural scholar as a survey of early nineteenth-century English drainage systems and the diet, housing and wages of farm labourers – Olmsted was mostly drawn to the quaint, the quirky and the arcane.

However, his New World egalitarianism wasn't easily quelled. Throughout *Walks and Talks*, the New Englander frequently slips into the rhetorical mode when faced with what he perceives to be the inequities of the old country. Following a tour of a plush stately pile, which at first inspired dreamy admiration, he wrote, moral outrage bubbling:

Is it right and best that this should be for the few, the very few of us, when for many of the rest of us there must be but bare walls, tile floors and every thing besides [a] harshly screaming, scrabble for life.

Liverpool had been the Americans' first port of call; Olmsted, his brother and Loring Brace landing there on 27 May 1850. Slightly perturbed to find other guests at their temperance hotel smoking and drinking beer in the coffee lounge, they'd pressed on the following morning, catching a ferryboat, which Olmsted, as a Staten Islander, judged 'very small and dingy', to Birkenhead. By all accounts, Olmsted was completely unaware that Birkenhead had a park, let alone a public one maintained by the municipality and open to all.

But then, Olmsted had never visited a public park, as such, before. With the exception of the odd common, private formal gardens and dime-a-go Vauxhall Garden-style pleasure grounds and cemeteries, parks in any meaningful sense were effectively unknown in America. Indeed, the word would not appear in any American encyclopaedia until 1861; and when it did, the entry for Appleton's *New American Cyclopaedia* was written by Olmsted himself. But more than that, with their aristocratic hunting lineage, the form and landscapes of parks were deemed suspect by Americans. In 1797, founding father and second President of the US, John Adams, dismissed parks as fundamentally anti-democratic and predicted that it would be 'long before Ridings, Parks, Pleasure Grounds, Gardens ... grow so much in fashion in America'. But with increasing swathes of urban America disappearing under brickwork, the likes of Olmsted's literary mentor Andrew Downing were beginning to argue that the country needed to make proper provision for open spaces.

What led Olmsted to Birkenhead Park was hunger. The visitors, peckish and with few thoughts on their minds other than the open road ahead, had popped into a local bakery for buns. There, in addition to buns, they received a lecture from the baker on the merits of French and the deficits of American flour, and were told in no uncertain terms that they could not leave Birkenhead without first seeing the new park. The baker was quite insistent about this, and succeeded in persuading the Americans to leave their bulky hiking knapsacks with him while they went to have a look.*

A new town, laid out barely twenty years earlier to plans prepared by J. Gillespie Graham – the man responsible for Edinburgh's New Town district – Birkenhead in 1850 remained a genteel if rapidly expanding industrial suburb, with a thriving shipyard and, shortly, the Britannia Engine Works, a major producer of steam-powered cranes for the nation's docks in the coming decades. As Olmsted & Co. approached the park, though, they were greeted by something far more arcadian: a band of milkmaids selling fresh milk by the cup.† Stationed at the entrance gate – dismissed by Olmsted as a 'great massive block of Ionic architecture, standing alone' – were also herds of donkeys, some with milk cans strapped to them and others saddled and bridled to hire for rides.‡ This scene, a vision of enterprising ordinary folk and the quasi-pastoral, could almost have been laid on specifically to appeal to Olmsted. It was practically a dumb show for the commercial underpinning of the park itself, which, though public, was partly financed by the selling of residential lots – a fact that did not escape the American's attention or approval for long. (Like most spendthrifts cushioned by family money, Olmsted was a great advocate of prudence and financial self-sufficiency in others.)

---

* The contemporary visitor wishing to replicate Olmsted's visit is advised to visit the local bakery chain of Hurst's for buns, which has branches on Grange Road West to the south and Duke Street to the north of the park.

† The Ableworld Mobility Superstore, a vendor of wheelchairs and the like, makes for a somewhat less agrarian offering today.

‡ Olmsted had little time for neoclassical monuments and would fight hard to prevent his paymasters saddling Central Park with pretentious Graeco-Roman gimcracks.

Birkenhead Park had been built on the site of a low-lying and waterlogged expanse called, since at least the seventeenth century, 'the Lowerfields'. Mostly a gorse-infested common favoured by foxes for its cover, criss-crossed by rough lanes and prone to 'unhealthy mists', its chief attraction in that prior incarnation had been a farm-cum-beerhouse whose premises were acclaimed for their ales and for their badger-baiting, rat-killing and dog-fighting contests. These gamy entertainments, if perhaps more authentically rustic, were naturally not to survive the Victorians. Their vanquisher, in this instance, was the railway promoter, Birkenhead resident and town-improvements commissioner Sir William Jackson, Bt, who fixed on the idea to create a country-style public park on the land.

Hailing from Warrington and 'a large family of but small means', Jackson had married the daughter of a leading member of the Corporation of Liverpool and grown astonishingly wealthy importing (no doubt dubiously bartered) West African palm oil, gold and ivory. Chairman, for a time, of the Chester and Birkenhead Railway Company, he not only had a hand in bringing the railway to Birkenhead but helped establish the local docks and the first gas- and waterworks – and the park was to be on a par with these latter municipal amenities. It was inspired, most likely, by the Princes Park, which had opened just across the Mersey at Toxteth in 1841. Funded by the well-to-do Liverpudlian grandee Richard Vaughan Yates, this was a much more hard-nosed commercial proposition, with the bulk of the park reserved for the private residents of three new terraces and a selection of villas built and sold to recoup the cost of its development. It had been designed by Joseph Paxton, with some input from James Pennethorne. It was the head gardener to the Duke of Devonshire's first essay in park-making, and he almost immediately followed it with Birkenhead.

Persuaded to sketch out a rough plan for the park, Jackson offered Paxton £800 for the job but it is the potential for glory that seems to have appealed most to the gardener. In a letter to his wife shortly after surveying the planned, if evidently unprepossessing, site, he wrote:

> I walked at least 30 miles to make myself master of the locality etc. This is not a very good situation for a park as the land is generally poor but of course it will redound more to my credit and honour to make something handsome and good out of these materials, indeed I am not altogether sorry that it is as it is, for it will suit my ingenuity to work to overcome the difficulty.

Paxton, as even his detractors might concede, was never short of ingenuity. Here working with 226 acres (101 acres sold for perimeter housing plots, 125 acres for the park itself), much of it marshland that needed extensive draining, he had a more modest 8 acres of lakes dug

out from scratch, with the tons of spare sod heaped up to form surrounding mounds, promontories and undulating hillocks. The lake in the upper part of the park was fashioned to resemble a river, as silvery and meandering as anything in nature – if nature had ever been quite so capable of precision landscaping.

Over 1,000 men worked for three years on the park under the supervision of Paxton's assistant, Edward Kemp. Kemp was to stay on as its head keeper, a post he held for the next forty years, and became the first tenant of the Italianate Lodge – one of nine lodges, purposely of differing styles and ranging from neo-Elizabethan to Gothic, erected about the park. Among the other architectural components were a stone boathouse, a pagoda and a large covered bandstand, styled after an ancient Roman temple. The lakes in the lower park were crossed by three decorative bridges: a Swiss bridge with a sort of cowshed roof and steep steps; a Chinese or rustic bridge, in latticed woodwork and in the mode of those seen on willow-pattern china; and, lastly, a cast-iron one, hinting at the encroaching industrialisation beyond the park, and perhaps at Jackson's substantial holdings in the Clay Cross Coal and Iron Works.

In all, the cost of laying out the park and the gardens, including levelling the ground, excavating the lakes and planting, came to over £70,000. It was officially and fully opened to the public on 5 April 1847 by Lord Morpeth, the verse-writing statesman and a regular correspondent of William Wordsworth's. Despite persistent showers, Morpeth planted a tree, examined the rockery, cricket pitch and swans, and judged an afternoon of 'Rural Sports', in which beefy lads raced to wolf down 'three basins of hot stir-up', and donkey riders, skilled in ambling, battled – 'no carrots allowed' – to come last and carry off a 10-shilling prize. Morpeth left for London at around 5 p.m., having managed to squeeze in another bout of ribbon-cutting that Easter Monday – opening the nearby Morpeth Docks. Here again, in this dual opening, we see Victorian industry and leisure in spades, along with order, duty and efficiency.

Some 56,000 people are estimated to have attended the opening of the park, substantially more than the population of Birkenhead itself at the time, which only reached 60,000 inhabitants by the 1870s. The park's popularity with those beyond Birkenhead was picked up by

Olmsted, who on his arrival just three years later saw 'a number of strangers, and some ... with note books and portfolios, that seemed to have come from a distance'. He himself had, of course, probably travelled further than anyone else to get there and proved to be among its greatest admirers, visiting Birkenhead Park on at least three separate occasions in the decades to follow. Pointedly, he returned in 1859 and obtained from its gardeners the 'full particulars of its construction, maintenance, and management' while midway through work on Central Park.

In aesthetic terms, Birkenhead was an exercise in the pastoral. Its meadows were rolling, trees came in clumps, and its lakes and transverse roads, especially the three-mile-long driveway snaking around its perimeter, were all studiously winding. Even today, the word 'serpentine' is never far from the mind when you tread its paths, which also have a curiously tractor-beam ability to keep the ambler on them rather than on the grass at either side. In period maps, the park's original layout with its various features tends to look not unlike an etching of Galenian anatomy or the electro-magnification of a bacillus. And yet, with its sports fields, there are flashes of the more exacting Victorian parks to come – and which Paxton, especially with his propagation of formal flower beds, later helped define.

On subsequent tours of the country, Olmsted would grow weary of what he regarded as English gardening's increasing obsession with 'botanic beauty', preferring the earlier landscape models of Capability Brown & Co. to newer and more floral British efforts. In this, his tastes were perhaps forever queered by Birkenhead Park itself. Like the cherished memory of a teenage first love, it continued to loom large in his imagination long after he had gone on to design gardens that equalled, and even excelled, it. In 1850, he was after all still technically a farmer: he came with few preconceptions and no prior experience of parks, and was bowled over by its essential scenic nature. And as a tiller of the land, he was impressed by the sheer graft that had gone into its landscaping and the quality of its horticulture. 'Gardening here,' he was to state, had 'reached a perfection ... never before dreamed of'.

What he responded to most of all, however, was the fact that it was free and open to anyone and everyone. That, for Olmsted, was close to a revelation. In *Walks and Talks*, he writes, 'I was glad to observe that all the privileges of the garden were enjoyed equally by all classes. There were some who were attended by servants, and sent at once for their carriages, but a large proportion were of the common ranks and a few women with children or suffering from ill-health were evidently the wives of very humble labourers.' After praising the park's amenities, he adds, in a tone close to stunned wonder, that 'all this magnificent pleasure ground' was 'entirely, unreservedly and forever the people's own'. There was nothing, he was slightly affronted to concede, similar or equal to it in supposedly democratic America.

Some six years earlier, the issue of a park – or the lack of park – in New York had, in fact, been raised by the poet, author and social campaigner William Cullen Bryant. In an editorial on 3 July 1844 for the *New York Evening Post*, which he then edited, Bryant pointed out that, unlike the Big Apple, 'all large cities' had 'their extensive public grounds and gardens, Madrid and Mexico their Alamedas, London its Regent's Park, Paris its Champs Elysées, and Vienna its Prater'. The answer for New York, he argued, providing 'the owners of the soil' could be persuaded 'to part with it', lay close to hand. 'On the road to

Harlem, between Sixty-eighth street on the south, and Seventy-seventh on the north, and extending from the Third Avenue to the East River', there was an as yet undeveloped 'tract of beautiful woodland, comprising sixty or seventy acres, thickly covered with old trees, intermingled with a variety of shrubs'. And here, he maintained, 'never was a finer situation for the public garden of a great city'. The matter could not be ignored for long, though. 'Commerce,' he warned, 'was devouring inch by inch the coast of the island' and if any part of it was to be rescued 'for health and recreation it must be done now'.

Bryant's call may have gone unheeded to begin with, and his preferred site was lost to brownstone but, further galvanised by a visit to London the following year, he raised the question of a park for New York again and again. Largely as a result of Bryant's editorials, both candidates in the New York mayoral election of 1850, Ambrose C. Kingsland and Fernando Wood, were forced to express their support for a park; subject to the usual budgetary vicissitudes, of course. But it was the pace of change in New York that ultimately nudged the issue on to the political agenda.

'Are the green fields gone?' asks Ishmael of Manhattan in the opening pages of *Moby-Dick*, published in 1851. Indeed, between 1840 and 1850 the number of residents in the city jumped from 400,000 to 700,000 people, and Herman Melville, who himself resettled in his native New York in the fall of 1847, dubbed it 'a babylonish brick-kiln', enthralled and appalled as he was by the 'elbowing, heartless looking' crowds who filled its streets. These were streets, it should be said, packed with horse-drawn traffic and menaced by free-living pigs, and running with human and animal excrement where the sewerage system was pitiful, as on Sixth Avenue. With immigrants, domestic and international, particularly from Germany and famine-ravished Ireland, flocking to what was rapidly becoming the American city, the pressure on available accommodation grew intense. In the rat-infested lodging houses of squalid districts like 'Five Points', new arrivals were often billeted six or more to a room.

These growing pains of the city in the 1840s, '50s and beyond were dictated by the underlying grid system of its streets that had been adopted by town commissioners in 1807, when Manhattan was a village untroubled by running water or gas. The grid plan was supposedly inspired, or so an apocryphal tale goes, by the shadow cast by a stonemason's sieve on a working map of the city. Whatever the truth of this story, a greater tendency towards tidiness – a New World Order for streets, shall we say, after the spindly thoroughfares of much of old Europe – seems a common enough feature of American cities of this era. Charles Dickens, for example, wrote of his yearning for the sight of a crooked street after visiting Philadelphia in 1842.

New York's plan dictated the building of uniform blocks 200 feet deep. With that uniformity – or so the thinking went – came equality, since all sites were the same and any variants in topography, superior views or situations were 'obliterated under the grid'. As a result, New York real estate rose tall and narrow – and monotonous – with impressive but unremitting walls of buildings springing up. A sense of the oppressiveness of that streetscape is captured in the diaries of Philip Hone, the fifty-seventh Mayor of New York City, who in 1839 wrote of his joy when the old Trinity Church near Wall Street was pulled down for rebuilding and 'an unobstructed view of the bright blue Western sky' suddenly opened up in front of him.

An unexpected consequence of the grid-and-block format was that differences in social status between buildings and areas became more, not less, pronounced. As real-estate value rose, buildings in poorer areas were carved up into tenement houses, while only the most affluent could afford to occupy a single block or several floors; accordingly, good areas got wealthier and poor areas poorer and more crowded. The response, inevitably, was to expand the grid north and east and build more blocks on previously unsullied wasteland, leaving even fewer scraps of greenery for New Yorkers of any class to enjoy.

In the face of such developments, and alongside Cullen Bryant's editorials in the *New York Evening Post*, the pages of Andrew Downing's *Horticulturalist* magazine contained equally robust calls for European-style squares and parks for New York. It was here too that the first version of Olmsted's account of Birkenhead Park appeared in 1851. As was often customary then, it was published under a pseudonym, Olmsted adopting the nom de plume 'Wayfarer', a device that served him well, since it allowed the paper to later run an unashamedly rave review of the first volume of his *Walks and Talks*. Three months after the 'Wayfarer' had sung the praises of Birkenhead Park, Downing himself supplied the magazine with its lead essay, an impassioned call for 'a green oasis for the refreshment of the city's soul and body' entitled 'The New York Park'.

Evoking a green heaven for a city already saddled with at least one Hell's Kitchen, and possibly another circle or two familiar enough to Dante, Downing was up there with the best snake-oil men in presenting the park as an earthly paradise and urban panacea. Free of entrance fees, with its acres of 'lovely, limpid lakes' and full of 'the charm of the sylvan accessories' and 'the perfume and freshness of nature', his park was sketched out in only the broadest and most romantic of strokes. But like a talented student painter's canvases, future potential and present enthusiasms were everything. As Downing envisioned it, this could be a place in the city with 'a real feeling of the breadth and beauty of green fields' that offered pedestrians 'quiet and secluded walks when they wished to be solitary' and 'broad alleys filled with thousands of happy faces when they would be gay'.

The broad alley would prove to be a key element in the eventual design of Central Park, but Downing was to play no part in its creation. Nor was he even to see a single clod of earth turned towards fulfilling his dreams of a park for New York. Less than a year after his essay was published, and aged just thirty-six, he perished along with his wife and over seventy other passengers when the *Henry Clay* steamboat caught fire and sank in the Hudson, one of the worst maritime disasters ever to occur off mainland America.*

Had Downing lived, it is almost inevitable that as the most distinguished landscape gardener in America he would have been offered the job of supplying New York with the park that he had campaigned for. But it was not to be. He did, however, play one last and pivotal role in the story of Central Park, giving a job in his Newburgh firm to Calvert Vaux, a young English architectural draughtsman he'd met in London. Vaux, short and short-tempered, with a long beard and a longer memory for perceived slights and grievances (some not entirely unjustified), would prove essential to the park's success.

But in the immediate wake of Downing's death, and for many years to come, the matter of the park was dogged by internecine battles at City Hall between Tammany Democrats and Republicans and their opposing advocates and backers. By July 1853, though, the New York State legislature had at least authorised the acquiring of the tract of land that would become Central Park. Predictably, its original owners voiced their objections. They were joined by various interested parties: financial

---

* This ship seemingly a different *Henry Clay* to the packet of the same name Olmsted took to Liverpool in 1850.

speculators, jerry-builders, brick manufacturers, hod carriers, realtors, pavement artists, and those who simply believed that America – and especially the City of New York – had no damned business building public parks on land that could be utilised for private gain. In response, the New York Supreme Court appointed a five-man team of commissioners of estimate and assessment to look into the issue. Their report, over two years in the making, found for the city, but there remained a further two years of arguments over the proposed size of the park.

In the interim, Olmsted was busy devoting himself to journalism, magazine and book publishing, embarking, among other things, on his tour of the southern states for the *New York Daily Times*. But one man, and at his own expense, had already surveyed the potential site. This was Colonel Egbert Ludovicus Viele, a graduate of the West Point Academy ('Class of '47') and a veteran of the Mexican–American War, who sported a distinguished service record and a walrus moustache that Zapata (or even Frank Zappa) might have envied. Retaining his military title, and prone to exaggerating his martial bearing on civvy street with a gruff manner and parade-ground turn of speech, Viele had set himself up as a civil engineer upon leaving the army. Uninhibited by any formal qualifications in that field, and aided by old Knickerbocker connections, some ad hoc service training, unwavering self-belief, a diligent work ethic and, as it turned out, a certain aptitude for his newly chosen profession, Viele had persuaded the New Jersey legislature to employ him as the state's topographical surveyor. And mapping would really prove to be his forte. In New York, to this day, planners, architects, civil engineers, developers, or just property owners whose basements have unexpectedly sprung a leak, still refer to Viele's 'Sanitary & Topographical Map of the City and Island of New York' – a chart which the mustachioed one drew up of Manhattan's natural springs, marshes and meadowlands in the aftermath of the insanitary horrors of the American Civil War and published in 1865.

Twelve years earlier, Viele had reasoned that somebody would inevitably have to map the Central Park site at one point. He'd undertaken the job himself, suspecting that his initiative was bound to be rewarded. It was. Not only were his map and provisional plan welcomed by the city when he presented them in June 1856, but he was appointed engineer in chief, tasked with overseeing the park's construction and awarded a salary of $2,500 a year.

Among his first duties was to issue eviction notices to the 1,600 residents of the site – practically an act of ethnic and social cleansing, since it was home to some of the poorest residents of Manhattan, and squatters who were mostly recent Irish immigrants and African Americans. When it came to dishing out itinerant jobs at the park – the less-than-a-dollar-a-day, back-breaking crumbs gained by toiling as a casual ditchdigger, stonebreaker or turf-cropper – the latter group were excluded entirely. This hiring policy was enforced largely at the insistence of – and fear of reprisals from – gangs of only marginally more empowered Irish labourers.

The voices of the poor and downtrodden, Viele could easily ignore, and few shed any tears for the evicted, who were easily demonised as feckless and unworthy wastrels standing in the way of elevating progress. But the elite world of horticulture was harder to silence, what with its nicely produced journals and lavishly illustrated books, and its access to newspaper columns and the ear of politicians. Now, some of its leading lights started to take issue with Viele's plan.

One of the most vocal, if hardly disinterested, critics was Calvert Vaux, the young Englishman hired by Andrew Downing. Upon his boss's death, he inherited Downing's business practice, and having now relocated to New York, he took it upon himself to act as his former mentor's emissary on earth when it came to the proposed park. 'Being thoroughly disgusted with the manifest defects of Viele's published plan', he later reminisced, 'I pointed out, whenever I had the chance, that it would be a disgrace to the City and to the memory of Mr Downing (who had first proposed the location of a large park in New York) to have this plan carried out.'

We can well imagine that New Yorkers, then as now, appreciated nothing more than a four-foot-ten bearded limey – a little over six years off the boat, with scarcely a year in the city under his belt – telling them their park would be a disgrace. In the opinion of Witold Rybczynski, one of Olmsted's finest biographers, 'Viele's plan was really not that bad' either, with his 'naturalistic layout' largely following 'Downing's precept'. There was to be a cricket pitch, a botanical garden and, proving that you can take the man out of the military but not the military out of the man, a 50-acre parade ground.

It's possible, though, that there was a slight feeling of insecurity among Manhattanites about what constituted a good park – such a European institution, after all. But whatever the case, Vaux, who'd by now married an American and was evidently throwing himself into the civic life of his newly adopted home, managed to secure a meeting with the park board, in which he made a convincing plea for Viele's plan to be set aside. While his was not a lone voice against Viele, it was Vaux's testimony which seemed to have swung the balance, and in August 1857 the park board announced that an open competition would be held to find a fresh design, with submissions closing the following spring.

Vaux made no bones about wanting to enter the competition himself, and was by now an experienced landscape architect with several prodigious private stateside commissions under his belt. In the end, however, he chose to seek the assistance of Olmsted. Heavily in debt and with his inky fingers badly singed by the fallout from a spell on the short-lived American literary magazine, *Putnam's*, Olmsted had let Tomostock Farm that summer and retreated to a small inn in Morris Cove, Connecticut. There he aimed to recuperate, taking in the sea air and savouring homely scenery and genteel company, while finishing a book based on what had been a bruising tour of the American South.

Whatever anxieties Olmsted may have had about his personal finances could hardly have been eased by news that the New York branch of the Ohio Life Insurance and Trust Company had failed. This firm's collapse on 24 August, amid reports of full-scale embezzlement, helped trigger a run on the nation's banks. One that was exacerbated by falling grain prices, the collapse of railway speculation, the flight of British investors, and the loss in a storm of a ship carrying gold bullion from the San Francisco Mint.

Christened 'The Panic of 1857', and felt, erroneously or otherwise, to have had less impact on the slave-owning states, it sowed the economic seeds for the American Civil War. More immediately, though, as unemployment rose steeply after the crash, the construction of Central Park was soon seized upon as a means of supplying much-needed jobs in New York. But as he sat at a corner table in the tea room of his hotel in Morris Cove, the burble of polite conversation and the chink of silver spoons against bone-china cups merging with the distant churn of surf on the Connecticut shore below, parks were not likely to have been much on Olmsted's mind. All that was to change when the familiar face of Charles Wyllys Elliot hove into view.

A forty-year-old New York ironworks magnate, man of letters and former horticultural student of Andrew Downing, Elliot was also, since April that year, a member of the Central Park board. After exchanging a few pleasantries and touching as delicately as either of them could muster on the recent difficulties at *Putnam's*, Elliot urged Olmsted to apply for an upcoming position at the park, that of superintendent.

This was classic jobs-for-the-boys stuff, and boys who both happened to be Connecticut-born, weren't-your-folks-on-the-*Mayflower*-with-mine, literary-minded Republicans. But sensing his destiny, or just desperate to secure a firm salary after the vagaries and penury of experimental farming and freelance journalism, Olmsted wasted no time, and apparently returned to New York that very evening to begin the process of canvassing supporters to back what would be his successful application.

His appointment wasn't entirely welcomed by Viele, who remained the park's chief engineer and Olmsted's superior and had every reason to believe his plan might be adopted eventually anyway. Clocking that on his first day that September the new superintendent had come dressed for the office rather than the field, the Colonel had one of his men, a Mr Hawkin, take Olmsted on a tour of the park site. Hawkin, Olmsted observed, was 'a sensible looking gentleman' whose trousers were 'tucked into the legs of a heavy and dirty pair of boots', and he led him 'through the midst of a number of vile sloughs'. On occasion, Olmsted sank 'half a leg deep' into 'black and unctuous slime'. The low grounds, he was to discover in the worst possible way, were 'steeped in the overflow and mush of pig-sties, slaughterhouses and bone-boiling works and the stench was sickening'.

Recalling this tour decades after the fact, Olmsted was to admit – with masterly, almost English, understatement – that he was 'not quite so well prepared as I could have wished for what followed'. He would not make that mistake again. Keeping one step ahead of Viele became his modus operandi and ensured, after some initial ragging from the teams of labourers, and not all of it good humoured, that he was gradually able to exert his authority over the park staff.

The worsening economic climate helped Olmsted in his bid to that end. City Hall were putting him and Viele under enormous pressure to distribute jobs more widely – 'My office,' Olmsted recorded, 'was regularly surrounded by an organised mob, carrying a banner inscribed "Blood or Bread", [and] this mob sent into me a list of 10,000 names alleged to have starving families demanding that they should immediately be put to work.' The advantage for Olmsted was that in such conditions he had no hesitation in dismissing anyone who failed to do what he asked of them, since there was a queue of willing and able replacements stretching round the block.

Olmsted had met Vaux some years earlier through Andrew Downing. When the Englishman approached him in August 1857 about joining forces on a park design, Olmsted was not immediately certain and took pains to seek Viele's permission to enter the competition, not wanting to be discourteous to his boss. Viele gave his permission – a formality, in any case – but offered a contemptuous response to the idea that Olmsted stood any chance of winning. This no doubt compelled a still erring Olmsted to throw his hat in the ring.

Under the rules of the competition, each entry had to contain certain set features. These included a parade ground 'with proper arrangements for spectators', three playing fields, a flower garden, the site for a concert or exhibition hall, an ornamental foundation, a prospect tower, and a space 'reserved for flowing with water to form a winter skating ground'. To allow for city traffic, 'four or more' east-to-west crossings were stipulated between 59th Street and 106th Street.

The site for what was already being called 'Central Park' – a two-and-a-half-mile-long, half-mile-broad parallelogram of some 770 acres of which 150 acres were reserved for the Croton Reservoirs – was hardly enticing material. Aside from a rocky ridge which passed through the centre of the site, much of the potential park was feature-less barren land, whose mediocre soil was relieved by a few stony outcroppings, knotty trees, rough bushes and the handful of squatters' shacks that were yet to be cleared by the Colonel and Olmsted's crews.

The budget for transforming these wilds into an aesthetically pleasing 'natural-looking' park was put at $1.5 million and the prize offered for the winning design was $2,000, with $1,000, $750 and $500 going to the second, third and fourth prize-winners respectively. In total, the Commission received thirty-three sets of competing drawings. These were put on display in a room above the Stanford and Delis bookstore at 637 Broadway. On 28 April 1858, and after 'long and careful consideration', the board awarded first prize to Plan No. 33 'signed Greensward' – as it happens, the last eligible entry submitted 'for the improvement of Central Park'. It was Olmsted and Vaux's submission.

Who did exactly what in their winning entry is largely a matter of conjecture. Although the two men would go on to design count-less other parks, together and separately, Vaux went to his grave feeling that he didn't get the full credit he deserved for Central Park – a suspicion rather confirmed when in 2007, following an article on the park, even the *New York Times* had to print a correction, having previously omitted his name as its co-designer. Olmsted himself, though, was always scrupulous in paying tribute to his partner. He told an early biographer, Mariana van Rensselaer, that he could have 'done nothing to good purpose' alone. And after their business relationship had ended, a photograph of Vaux remained a permanent fixture on Olmsted's office wall, alongside one of Ruskin and Édouard André, the French landscape architect and author of *L'art des jardins*.

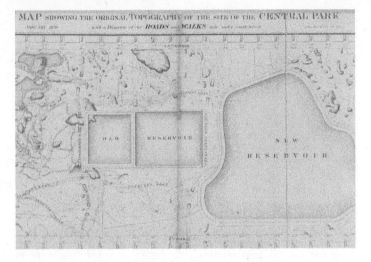

MAP SHOWING THE ORIGINAL TOPOGRAPHY OF THE SITE OF THE CENTRAL PARK
JANUARY 1859   with a Diagram of the ROADS and WALKS now under construction

On paper, Vaux was the senior partner: an architect and a fine draughtsman with a few prestigious stateside projects under his belt and Downing's good name to fling about. He almost certainly inked out much of the actual plan. His young son (named, touchingly, Downing) later remembered that since there was such 'a great deal of grass' to be put on the plan 'by the usual small dots and dashes', any callers to the house would be invited to pitch in. Olmsted, meanwhile, had a day-to-day working knowledge of the site, and was already whipping the park and its workmen into shape. Also, he could write and had many influential friends in what might today be termed 'the media'. As a result, he almost certainly penned much of the report that accompanied the design. But from what can be surmised, the division of labour was far from exact and, as with all great double acts, the magic in their 'Greensward' plan lay in the combination of their talents. From the late summer of 1857 until the deadline for submissions the following April, they met on Sundays and every available free evening at Vaux's house to work on the project, batting ideas back and forth.

The board's choice of winner was endorsed by the *New York Times*, which reported that:

> There can be little doubt that in its essential features the plan of Messrs. Olmsted and Vaux embraces all the leading requisites of a great Park ... adapted not only to the nature of the particular grounds in question, but to the prospective wants of our City.

But what had New York chosen? Well, New York certainly would not be getting a formal garden in the French style. As its name suggested, the Greensward plan looked to nature, and made as canny a use of the site's natural defects as it could, not least by burying some of them underwater for lakes. In the accompanying report, Olmsted and Vaux stated that they planned 'to create contrasting and varying passages of scenery, all tending to suggest to the imagination a great range of rural conditions'. Those 'rural conditions', varying from wooded hillsides and dinky bridges to rolling meadows and tended lawns, perhaps owed as much to the English pastoral as to indigenous American farming. Nevertheless, there was an unabashed American boldness in their aim to bring the country, log by log almost, to the city, and it was a desire underpinned by egalitarian principles. 'It is one great purpose of the Park,' their report stated, 'to supply to the hundreds of thousands of tired workers, who have no opportunity to spend their summers in the country, a specimen of God's handiwork that shall be to them, inexpensively, what a month or two in the White Mountains or the Adirondacks is, at great cost, to those in easier circumstances.'

Essential to achieving this, as far as they were concerned, was keeping Gotham and its 'discordant urban elements' out of sight and out of mind – and their plan would go to great lengths to achieve this. One of their most innovative solutions was to sink the four main transverse roads demanded in the brief deep below the ground level of the park. By then adding three additional but decidedly meandering paths at surface level, they succeeded in separating get-going business vehicles from parkgoers roaming for pleasure.

Their design was not without its detractors. Two park commissioners, Robert Dillon and August Belmont, were distinctly unhappy with what they judged to be a lack of classical showpieces, and petitioned for a grand avenue to run straight through. Such a roadway, they believed, would not only be more in keeping with the rigour of the grid plan and the line of the city – it would also add a majestic sweep to the park.

Olmsted saw off this suggestion, among a raft of others from Dillon and Belmont, by appealing to a future New York – one that to many seemed unimaginably distant, but which would arrive sooner than anyone could have realised. 'The time will come,' he pointed out,

when New York will be built up, when all the grading and filling will be done, and when the picturesquely-varied, rocky formations of the Island will have been converted into foundations for rows of monotonous straight streets, and piles of erect, angular buildings. There will be no suggestion left of its present varied surface, with the single exception of the Park. Then the priceless value of the present picturesque outline of the ground will be more distinctly perceived, and its adaptability for its purpose more fully recognized.

In short, their avenue would in time make the park identical in form to the city, robbing its inhabitants of the chance of ever going off-grid. The 'Greensward' was to be a haven from the brickwork that Olmsted rightly predicted would engulf Manhattan; its 'well-balanced irregularity', nooks, trails, bridle paths and vistas offering relief from the uniformity of the rest of the place.

FREDERICK LAW OLMSTED.

A pivotal element – 'the central feature', even – of Vaux and Olmsted's plan was a broad alley: the Promenade (later rechristened the Mall). This was not the kind of Appian Way Dillon and Belmont had dreamed of, but a quarter-mile of spacious walkway lined with American elms. Often referred to as 'a street of nature', it was quite deliberately plotted with the intention of easing the New Yorker entering at Fifth Avenue and 59th out of their city. Laid out on the diagonal, The Mall acted as effectively as a trail of breadcrumbs in a Grimms' tale, drawing the visitor deeper and deeper into the park. Walking along under its leafy canopy, parkgoers were enveloped in ever more greenery, the hubbub of Fifth Avenue and the monumental new St Patrick's Cathedral behind them gradually magicked away. Immediately ahead was a terrace built of Albert freestone, and a fountain, but beyond that further views opened up: there was the lake and, just in the middle distance, a rocky bluff laden with rhododendrons, black oak and azaleas, and ornamented by a Martello tower – and behind that, even more greenery. There appeared to be no end to the park from this vantage point, and Olmsted and Vaux were as scrupulous throughout, hiding traces of the city wherever they could. Surveying the park from a boat on the lake in 1872, James D. McCabe, author of *Lights and Shadows of New York Life,* maintained that: 'No sight or sound of the great city is at hand to disturb you, and you may lie back in your boat with half shut eyes, and think yourself in fairyland.'

It was 'hard to realise', he noted elsewhere in the book, that 'so much loveliness' had been 'preceded by such hideousness'. But this journey from hideousness to fairyland – from plan to park – would itself be quite hideous, especially for Olmsted. Now appointed 'Architect in Chief', he had to answer to City Hall for every delay and every cent spent. A music hall, a palm house and a conservatory were among the budgetary casualties – though Olmsted was never a great one for buildings anyway, preferring landscape over architecture in his landscape architecture. Nevertheless, not having the money to do a good job irked him. And long after it ceased to be his responsibility, he felt compelled to castigate New York's political leaders for their financial scrimping and corresponding neglect of Central Park's upkeep, publishing a critical pamphlet entitled *The Spoils of the Park* in 1882.

During the park's construction, an immense task that wasn't fully completed until the 1860s, its public-minded and -funded paymasters, keen to maximise use of the site as soon as possible, insisted on a quite phenomenal work rate. The skating rink, for example, was finished and opened for the winter of 1858 and the Ramble finished by the following spring. Olmsted was so exhausted that first year, he was granted six weeks' paid leave to go on the first of many busman's holidays, touring European parks, much to the chagrin of Vaux but probably to the enormous benefit of the final park.

One of the people he sought out on that first European tour was Sir Richard Mayne, whom he met in London. Mayne was joint commissioner of the still relatively new Metropolitan Police Force and had helped write the *General Instruction Book* – the first police manual. As the man responsible for the policing of the 1851 Great Exhibition in Hyde Park, there was little he didn't know about keeping order in a public place and Olmsted was to grill him on every aspect of law and lawlessness he'd experienced.

Since the concept of a public park remained an unknown quantity in America, Olmsted was especially worried about how Central Park would be treated by its first users. The American public were ignorant of parks, his thinking went, so they would have to be trained to use it properly. That job was made harder by the fact that the park was to be semi-open while construction was under way, allowing folks, or so he feared, to tramp about bits of it as they pleased, acquiring bad 'parking habits' from the beginning. To counter this, he drew up an extensive list of regulations for Central Park and had them vigilantly enforced from its infancy.

Here his fears perhaps outstripped reality. Just as with prohibition, a generation or so on – when well-meaning do-gooding tipped over into strident law-making, criminalising sherry-on-a-Sunday tipplers and grog-guzzling alkies alike – the public were not to be trusted to exercise any restraint. Olmsted unleashed the puritanical side of his nature: edicts were issued against large group picnics, walking on the grass (admittedly fairly standard at the time in nearly all parks), strenuous activities, gaming, fortune telling, riding a horse faster than 10 m.p.h., and using bad language. Schoolboys wishing to play baseball needed to provide a note signed by their principal before venturing on to the diamond. Hawking and peddling were other big no-nos from the off. On the rules went, and as each new area of the park opened, up too went the 'Keep Offs', 'Don'ts' and 'Please Refrain Froms'.

The excess of regulation in Central Park led the *Irish News* to complain that New York wanted 'a place to play leap-frog in, not a mere ornament to pass through'. Indeed, *Civilizing American Cities* is the title of a collection of Olmsted's writings – he didn't choose it, but it perfectly sums up his slightly patrician attitude to Central Park. Olmsted always saw the park's job as to educate as much as entertain, and to provide a civic space free (or freer, at least) of the capitalist impulses that raged elsewhere. And that spirit would persist, with later innovations such as productions of Shakespeare rather than vaudeville acts in the park, which kicked off in 1916 on the 300th anniversary of the playwright's death. Band concerts, begun in 1859, similarly ran to military tunes and selections from the established classical canon, studiously avoiding jigs, polkas, or any other contemporary toe-tappers that might encourage dancing or inflame unseemly passions. And, pointedly, it was to be a zoo that opened in Central Park in 1864, not a circus.

Research shows that a significant proportion of working-class New Yorkers, and especially newer Irish and German immigrants, voted with their feet, and with what few cents they had, choosing to frequent the privately run Jones Wood pleasure grounds on the Upper East Side rather than their new municipal park. The park was free, but it was also straight-laced. At Jones Wood, meanwhile, there were novelty grottos, boxing matches, magic shows and fireworks. The *New York Tribune*, under the editorship of Horace Greeley and writing on behalf of respectable Manhattan society, would take up cudgels against the pleasure ground, denouncing it as a vulgar haunt of thieves, tricksters, lewd women and rowdy men. But there, boisterous fun could be had. A lager beer could be sunk to tunes belted out by an oompah band. Hair could be let down, lederhosen donned and gay dancing done without the disapproving glances of snooty park officials or Park Avenue coachmen, for posh carriages soon commandeered the bridle paths of Central Park to the virtual exclusion of everyone else.

Geography, too, conspired against the working classes. Lying to the north of the most densely inhabited parts of the city, Central Park wasn't all that central to many. The horse-drawn omnibus fare from downtown was a nickel. When weighing up the options, why spend that getting to Central Park when a ferry could speed you to Coney Island, with its hot-dog stalls and ring-toss games? To an extent, there was, of course, room for both. And rather like the BBC in its more Reithian days, it wasn't public-funded Central Park's job to chase fairground trade. In his pitch for Prospect Park in Brooklyn (where, incidentally, he and Vaux built the first Parkway), Olmsted would write about the need to wean the public off 'debasing pursuits and brutalising pleasures' by offering 'new sources of rational enjoyment'.

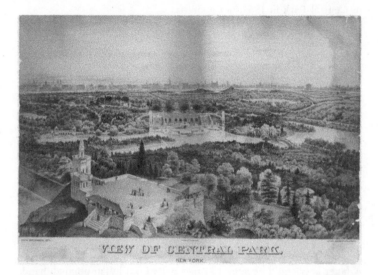

VIEW OF CENTRAL PARK,
NEW YORK

Parks, though, are man-made in every sense, and just as Wittgenstein characterised language as use, so New Yorkers, asserting at first subtle liberties, began to bend Central Park to their will. Homeless Civil War veterans camped out in its groves. Picnickers rebelled and occupied patches of grass. And in 1872, the park finally joined the rest of the island as a socially acceptable place to commit murder.

As the status of organised team games and the moral worth of fitness rose, so extra sports facilities were added, and rules regarding physical exertion relaxed. Even Olmsted himself loosened up. On one of his final jobs – overseeing the World's Columbian Exposition of 1893, in

Chicago – he pressed for the employment of troupes of strolling banjo players to serenade visitors. Shortly after this, however, his mental health went into sharp decline and his last years were lost to dementia. The fate of his ex-partner, Calvert Vaux, was no less tragic. On 19 November 1895, taking his usual morning ramble around Gravesend Bay, near his home in Bensonhurst, Brooklyn, the seventy-one-year-old Vaux evidently got caught up in a thick fog and stumbled off the river path and into the Hudson. His body was washed ashore three days later. By then, it was over twenty years since the pair had worked together, but from New York to San Francisco their legacy was in full bloom. No American city worthy of the name was without its municipal park – and arguably all of it thanks to a tip-off from a baker in Birkenhead.

CHAPTER 5

We Are Amused

There are few sights in England that can quite equal the absurd charm of the imitation Khyber Pass in Hull's East Park. This slice of South East Asia in the East Riding sits just a short stroll away from an animal house that is home to alpacas from Peru and a lake where oversized swan pedalo boats bob about. Seeing it now is to feel, not unlike Lewis Carroll's Alice, that you have fallen into a dreamland where normality has been temporarily suspended. It's a fleeting sensation: this is Yorkshire, after all, with reality quickly recalled by a couple of yapping dogs (yes, terriers, as it happens) and the inevitable arrival of rain, but the strange mock-landscape is there all the same. Though restored to something closer to a decent state in the last decade, old photographs reveal that the current stone archway and bridge once contained a grander edifice, known as the Arab door – a carved wooden doorway embellished with markings and symbols and lacking only a shaven-headed guard in pantaloons, with a flaming torch and a scimitar, to complete the oriental effect. The doorway, supposedly an exact copy of one in Zanzibar, had previously stood at the entrance to the East African Pavilion at the British Empire Exhibition, coming to Hull only after the pavilion closed in 1925.

Pictures from the 1930s capture Lowry-esque figures in flat caps and heavy woollen overcoats stepping through this strange valley as gingerly as mice emerging from a hole in a skirting board. Shot in a somewhat bleached-out monochrome and with no real establishing details to go on, the specific location of this Khyber Pass and its Arab door is obscured, leaving open the possibility that these doughty Hull folk might well be tramping to Kabul rather than the Holderness Road, their dress differing little from the tweedy get-ups worn by mountaineers and Antarctic explorers of the period.

Laid out by Joseph Fox Sharp, the Borough Engineer for Kingston upon Hull, the East Park was opened on Queen Victoria's Golden Jubilee, 21 June 1887 – a regal milestone celebrated at home and across the Empire with forelock-tugging displays of pageantry. In London, an Indian cavalry, headed up by the Maharao of Kutch in a diamond- and ruby-encrusted turban, and the no less resplendent Maharaja of Holkar, escorted Victoria to a special Service of Thanksgiving in Westminster Abbey. Up in Hull, the park-opening was preceded by a somewhat more disorganised parade. Led by the Knights of the Golden Horn and featuring the Albert Loud Lodge of the United Order of Druids and a horse-drawn float carrying basket-weaving members of the local institute for the blind, it was branded the 'Jubilee Jumble' by a local newshound in the *Hull Daily Mail*, who deemed it a disgrace to the town and the Queen.

Hull, of course, was not alone in opening a park to mark the Golden Jubilee. Both it and Victoria's Diamond Jubilee a decade later provided the stimulus for a further wave of public-park building across the country. Among them would be the likes of the St Paul's Recreation Ground in Brentford, Sheffield's Endcliffe Park, Brunswick Park, Wednesbury, the People's Park at Tiverton and Glasgow's Victoria Park. The latter was one of countless parks then christened in honour of the monarch or lumbered with similarly timely, if unimaginative monikers, such as Jubilee Gardens. More parks would ultimately be created in Britain between 1885 and 1914 than at any period before. But really, there was another factor for this fresh push for parks. It was one quite at odds with the bunting-strewn public displays of imperial self-confidence, displays that would grow shriller at the Diamond Jubilee, with the old Queen's end starkly obvious to all and a corpulent roué waiting in the wings.*

The reason for this park-building drive lay in the economy, which was near to collapse. In 1887, Britain was into the third consecutive year of the deepest slump of the century. Indeed, the word 'unemployment' was coined in that jubilee year, and the warm summer witnessed a sharp increase in homeless people camping out in London's parks.†

The Queen was booed in a rare sortie to the East End, and Trafalgar Square ran red as mounted police charged political demonstrators, among their ranks William Morris and Annie Besant, on 'Bloody Sunday'. The East Park, like so many other public works in the period,

---

* For that second jubilee, Hull's near neighbour Grimsby erected the Queen's Observatory in its People's Park – a monolithic tower that one resident later recalled as 'a brutal looking thing, black, circular but on a square base and made of what was politely described as "rough stone" but which were, in fact, chunks of slag'. It was finally pulled down in 1949.

† Over twenty years earlier, the voyeuristic civil servant Arthur Munby had already observed the ways in which public parks were acting as impromptu day centres for those with nothing to do and nowhere else to go. In a diary entry for 15 July 1864 he records:

> Walking through S. James's Park about 4 p.m., I found the open spaces of sward on either side the path thickly dotted over with strange dark objects. They were human beings; ragged men & ragged women; lying prone & motionless, not as those who lie down for rest & enjoyment, but as creatures worn out and listless. A park keeper came up: who are these? I asked. They are men out of work, said he, and unfortunate girls; servant girls, many of them, what has been out of place and took to the streets, till they've sunk so low that they can't get a living even by prostitution. It's like this every day, till winter comes; and then what they do I don't know. They come as soon as the gates opens.

was a project intended to go some way to confronting the economic issues, providing employment for idle hands, with its construction predominantly undertaken by local jobless men.

In Hull, the labourers were overseen by Edward Peak, the East Park's supervisor and the man credited in some quarters with first coming up with the idea of the Khyber Pass folly. Built of artificial stone and material foraged from the Hull Citadel, an old fort that had once defended the town's port, it was, and remains, a most curious but striking tribute to what is frequently called 'the Great Game' – the sporting metaphor applied to the battle for supremacy between Britain and Russian forces in Asia throughout the nineteenth century. In particular, it is often used to refer to the scramble for control of Afghanistan, considered a crucial strategic gateway to India and secured by Britain in 1879. Nevertheless, the Pass's presence in an English public garden is slightly ironic, since it was a horticultural feature that ultimately did for Britain in the disastrous first Afghan leg back in 1842. Retreating from Kabul, the British Army found the road to Jalalabad at Jegdalek partially blocked by two all but impenetrable six-foot-high hedges fashioned from the local holly oak. In the ultimately vain attempt to avoid annihilation at the hands of advancing Ghilzai tribesmen, hundreds of cornered and frostbitten British troops and supporting Indian sepoys impaled themselves on its prickly foliage as they tried desperately to squeeze through it and escape.

It is estimated that some 40,000 people died in that first Anglo-Afghan war, but, illustrating the strange myopia of horticulturalists, the holly- oak hedge seems to have proved a more pressing matter in gardening circles. Reviewing *Journal of an Afghanistan Prisoner* by Lieutenant Vincent Eyre in the following year, the *Gardeners' Chronicle* was happy to praise the book as 'infinitely beyond the Romance of fictions', but baffled by some of the botanical details in this soldier's illustrated account of the campaign. In particular, it implored readers to write in with any further information on the Afghan Holly Oak. Ultimately, interest in the plant faded and it failed to take hold in Britain's gardens. Similarly, mock Khyber Passes remained in the minority as far as parks went. But Victorian England's imperial skirmishes did help introduce some of the things we still most readily associate with public gardens.

The Crimean was perhaps the most influential conflict. In 1854, less than three years after the triumph of the Great Exhibition, and much to Prince Albert's chagrin, Britain along with the French had rallied to support the Ottoman Empire against a Russian incursion into present-day Romania, then under Turkish rule. The war, played out across the Danubian Principalities (modern Moldavia, Wallachia and the Ukraine) and on the Black and Azov Seas, would permeate British culture, filling the newspapers, precipitating verse, and even changing men's fashion. Most famously, in one of his many gripping reports from the field for *The Times*, the journalist William Howard Russell told of the slaughter at Balaklava of a third of the horsemen of the Light Brigade, in a heroic, if suicidal, charge against Muscovite guns, led by Lord Cardigan.

It was a story relayed across the Empire, and an account which, in turn, inspired Tennyson's most memorable verse. In due course, the wool helmets and vests worn to fend off the bitter cold of the Crimean Peninsula, and named, respectively, after the battle site and the dissolute British commander Lord Cardigan, also found themselves popularised on civvy street.

Beards were another beneficiary of the conflict. The vogue for soup-worrying, Old Testament facial hair in the Victorian era, worn by the likes of the evolutionist prophet Charles Darwin, is frequently credited to the circulation of pictures of hirsute British soldiers serving in the Crimea. Icy weather, and the appallingly insanitary conditions that would lead to as many British soldiers losing their lives to cholera as dying in the Battle of the Alma, generally militated against shaving.

The British and their French, Turkish and Sardinian allies had prevailed against the Russians. But the whole bungling mess of the British effort had been laid bare in newspaper dispatch after newspaper dispatch, filed by Russell and Thomas Chenery among others. Basic field and medical operations were shown to be inadequate and most of the nation's highest-ranking army officers revealed as grossly incompetent: madeira-sodden near-geriatrics who'd bought their commissions decades earlier when Wellington was in his prime and a gay ball still the aperitif to a good battle. This was to be a war where only a third of the total casualties were sustained in battle, the rest perishing from disease and hardship. Florence Nightingale with her lamp was all too readily seized upon as a ray of hope in a story with grim things to say about the supposed invincibility of the British Lion.

Still, a British-Franco-Turkish-Sardinian win was a British win and one not to be sniffed at, however ignominiously it might have been achieved. And whatever the contribution of the country's Colonel Blimps to the atrocious body count, the victory was saluted with patriotic monuments to the heroic dead. Streets and, in the case of the Alma, an extraordinary number of pubs continue to this day to bear the names of its major battles. Some went especially far in their efforts. The Surrey Zoological Gardens, a private pleasure ground in Kennington, and then rather on its last legs, mounted a late hurrah in 1855 in the shape of a compellingly realistic model of Sebastopol, complete with all of the topographical features, including a blockaded harbour, familiar from the news reports of the famous siege. They went so far as to hire invalided troops from the war to mime sorties 'aided by the pyrotechnical resources peculiar to the establishment' for the amusement of their paying visitors.

But it was public parks that became significant recipients of actual Russian army surplus. Large artillery guns seized after the Siege of Sebastopol quickly became choice trophies to display on plinths near park entrances, or offsetting floral beds, their bulky iron snouts raised in perpetual last salutes – perhaps, at this point, still giving off a faint whiff of gunpowder, an olfactory note somewhat at odds with the fragrance of nasturtiums and fuchsias. By the early 1860s, the Royal Victoria Park in Bath, Peel's Park in Salford and its namesake in Bradford, the Corporation Park in Blackburn, the People's Parks of Halifax and Sunderland, Glasgow's Kelvingrove Park, and even Derby's Arboretum, were all proud owners of guns hailing from the Crimean War. (Not all of the guns would survive the next century's conflicts, of course. The premium on metal in the Second World War led to Kelvingrove Park's gun, to name just one, being melted down for munitions, a case of swords being beaten back into swords rather than turned into ploughshares.)

An even more lasting relic of the Crimean War for parks domestically was perhaps the bandstand. Those now familiar circular, domed temples to music, mainly martial, share with the pavilions and minarets of seaside piers an obvious debt to Eastern architecture. With the British government assuming control of the East India Company's holdings in 1858 following the so-called Indian Mutiny, the vogue for ersatz Mughal frippery in this country grew exponentially. Much of what was built in Britain usually proved a hybrid of competing, and even conflicting, elements. The result, as often as not, was as insensitive to any single native tradition as the introduction of beef, say, to mulligatawny, or supposedly providing sepoys with tallow to grease cartridges for their Enfield rifles.

Bandstands were no exception, with secular and sacred details from India, China and Persia and God knows where else often jostling for attention on a single structure. But anyone wishing to establish a forebear for the common park bandstand could not go far wrong by taking a peek at the raised-platform kiosks seen in Turkey and across the Ottoman Empire, of which the contested Crimea formed a part. One of these certainly found its way to Paris, where it appeared among the triumphant Ottoman exhibits at the International Exhibition in May 1855 – just a few months before the Russians evacuated Sebastopol and began suing for the peace finally signed the following March, also in the French capital.

This particular kiosk was most likely seen by Captain Francis Fowke of the Royal Engineers, who was in Paris in 1855 and had a professional interest in exhibitions. As it happens, Fowke, architect of the Royal Albert Hall and the much-maligned follow-up to Paxton's 'Crystal Palace' pavilion for London's own International Exhibition seven years later, had not served in the Crimea. But by 1860, the former soldier was working on a conservatory and two band-houses for a new garden for the Royal Horticultural Society at South Kensington (now lost to the brickwork of the Science Museum and Imperial College). Described as of 'a light and tasteful design' and built in wood and iron with a sprouting dome roof topped with zinc, his band-houses look extraordinarily like jellyfish. Giant, landlocked, iron, wood and zinc jellyfish, admittedly. But that, in a sense, only adds to their odd Jules Verne-cum-H. G. Wells air. You can easily picture them giving the *Nautilus* a run for its money at 20,000 leagues, say, or suddenly springing into life and walking off and taking out parts of Woking. They were, though, nearly identical to the Ottoman kiosk shown in Paris and were soon enough widely imitated themselves. And Fowke's two bandstands had their own afterlives. When the RHS garden closed in 1883, they were moved on, edged out to parks a far cry from

South Kensington in the rather edgier South London districts of Southwark and Peckham Rye. Later, in 1890, a close copy of one of them was made and erected even further south, on Clapham Common.*

The army, of course, has always had a connection to music, and the playing of military music in public parks certainly predates the construction of such bandstands. In London, for example, there was a paucity of music in the new public parks until quite late in the century, but a military band had first started playing in Victoria Park in July 1851. The idea came from a group of local residents, who raised a petition begging Lord Seymour, the first Commissioner of Works, to use his influence to get a band from the 'Tower of London' or 'the West End' to play there occasionally. This, they stated, would 'improve the

---

* There were, as it happens, architectural precedents for these Eastern-style bandstands in parks. Inspired by the tents the Ottomans raised during their campaigns against the Habsburg Empire, Louis XIV had tents *à la Turque* erected at Versailles, and one in a similar vein was put up in Vauxhall Gardens in 1744 as a dining hall.

neighbourhood and add much to the interest and enjoyment we are already favoured with'. Whether the band from the Tower of London was held in special esteem as an elite military musical outfit is not known, but it seems that neither they nor a West End group appeared available or willing to play in Bow.

Seymour did, however, secure the services of the Royal Marine band from Woolwich Barracks. Led by Bandmaster Thomson RM, the musicians initially performed in the island pagoda, until a permanent bandstand was built in 1865, where their neighbourhood-improving tiddly-om-pom-pom could be heard on Tuesday and Friday afternoons in the summer months.

That these performances had been established by and for the local people is indicative of a growing aspirational and autodidactic strand of urban society. This same sentiment was the backbone of the Mechanics' Institutes, Co-operative shops, building societies and mutual savings clubs which flourished in this era. And it would soon have further bearing on the public parkscape.

For many, their bible in this cause, in addition to the Bible itself, was the social reformer and author Samuel Smiles's book *Self-Help*. Published in 1859, the same year as Darwin's *On the Origin of Species* and *On Liberty* by John Stuart Mill – and outselling both by the truckload in its day, shifting 20,000 copies in its first twelve months alone – Smiles's book preached a decidedly Calvinistic doctrine of strife and self-reliance. In it, he argued that hour upon hour of diligent, hard graft was the key to obtaining success and the only way of achieving personal integrity. What perhaps sounds to contemporary ears like a rather mean gruel was followed by a steady stream of books – *Character* (1871), *Thrift* (1875), *Duty* (1880) and *Life and Labour* (1887) – whose titles not only appear to encapsulate the major and grimly worthy preoccupations of his age but also proved seemingly irresistible to the Victorian book-buying public at large. It is doubtful that Smiles, if in favour of free universal education, would have advocated idling away time in a park listening to a band when there was fingers-to-the-bone work still to be done. But his self-improvement, without doubt, did capture the imagination of the era's urban population.

Smiles had some fairly radical views about the upper classes. Having never had to strive for anything, the aristocracy were, he believed, too often mollycoddled wastrels whose unearned wealth and privileges stopped more able, ambitious and industrious men (and with Smiles, it is only ever men) from getting on.

If this opinion was near to heresy, and curtseying and doffing caps to titled betters continued unabated, Smiles was not alone in worrying about decadence in the aristocracy. Many other self-made men and industrialists voiced concerns that, unchecked, the aristocracy could be a dead hand on innovation, and that they were generally storing up for the British Empire the same seeds of destruction that had done for the Romans, once the toga-wearing ones had exchanged warring for the bread and circuses of luxurious banquets, longer and longer warm baths and polyamorous sexual encounters. There was perhaps a degree of irony in the fact that these concerns were usually voiced in private, and sotto voce, by self-made industrialists in their cups, and only while eating heartily with other self-made industrialists. But, as the bungling of the old officer class in Crimea had made quite apparent, questions needed to be asked about the qualities a modern country might need in its leaders.

Eventually, a campaign for a more responsible ruling class would take shape, driven by a pincer movement: from below, by this emerging mercantile class, chippy about their supposed masters' lack of moderation and urgency, but not averse to entering their ranks by marrying in or adopting their airs and graces. And from above, by enlightened members of the gentry with an Empire to run.

Neither was entirely successful, obviously, as time has shown. But their sentiments were certainly shared by key figures in British public schools. The first of these reformers was Dr Thomas Arnold at Rugby in the 1830s – back then, the brash new educational establishment on the block. Arnold died abruptly of a heart attack in 1842, aged just forty-seven, but among the innovations attributed to him was the introduction of sports and team games as a means of instilling character. That reputation was cemented in the public imagination by the appearance in 1857 of Thomas Hughes's *Tom Brown's Schooldays*. It reads less as a novel than a didactic love letter to the school and its locker rooms and was written by an ex-pupil seized by a peculiar compulsion to pass on the good Doctor's pedagogical gospel in the form of a coming-of-age tale.

It's a book whose constituent elements (new boy at school, fiendish bully and weedy best friend) have proved remarkably enduring and can be spotted in YA novels and high-school teen movies to this day. Though Hughes's conclusion, a cricket game heavy on learning, decidedly doesn't do hugs. 'The discipline and reliance on one another which it teaches is so valuable,' runs one previously sceptical master's view of this final game. The fictional master goes on: 'I think … it ought to be such an unselfish game. It merges the individual in the eleven; he doesn't play that he may win, but that his side may.' Tom himself insists that cricket is 'more than a game. It's an institution.' Meanwhile his friend Arthur, as perhaps befits a boy with a mythical king's name, indulges in a spot of romantic nationalism by claiming cricket as 'the birthright of British boys old and young, as habeas corpus and trial by jury are of British men'.

The reality was that before Arnold's time, English public schools had taken a minimal interest in their pupils' extracurricular activities, with the result that boys largely policed games themselves. For all the wall games, boat races and cricket matches that had supposedly helped win the Battle of Waterloo, gambling and boxing were about the most popular gentlemanly pastimes – the latter always held to be a respectable way for Englishmen to settle arguments, hence young Herbert Pocket's immediate resort to his fists when faced with such a common little oik as Pip in *Great Expectations*. That Pocket leaves that encounter beaten and bloodied perhaps indicates that the upper classes now needed to up their game, which, in a way, they did.

In 1852, G. E. L. Cotton, one of Arnold's protégés, a master favourably portrayed in *Tom Brown's Schooldays*, left Rugby to become the head of Marlborough. Though the school was in only its ninth year, Cotton found it 'a hotbed of poaching, trespass and general licence' and responded by introducing organised sports there too. In the same year Edward Thring, a God-bothering Old Etonian with a fondness for football and cricket bordering on the fanatical, took over Uppingham grammar school, and immediately set about acquiring new playing fields for games. It was here, at Uppingham, in the 1860s that football matches were first limited to ninety minutes. And by then no public school worth its salt was without its regimen of cold baths, fresh air and backbone-stiffening, character-building, loyalty-inducing sports.

J. E. C. Welldon, headmaster of Harrow and himself a sportsman who played in the first FA Cup Final, summed up the now prevailing ethos best when he observed that 'the health and temper which games impart ... the pluck, the energy, the perseverance, the good temper, the self-control, the discipline, the co-operation, the esprit de corps, which merit success in cricket or football, are the very qualities which win the day in peace and war.'

Graduates of these public schools and the universities, embarking on careers in industry, the army, civil service and the Church in Britain and across the Empire, carried their games with them, often as badges of patriotism and/or emblems of muscular Christian virtue. They also now began the process of bureaucratising sports, as groups of the more fervid amateurs banded into associations and started writing rulebooks governing how each particular game or competition ought to be played. The Football Association, dominated by Old Etonians and Harrovians, was, for example, formed to establish set rules for the 'beautiful game' in the Freemason's Tavern, Lincoln's Inn, in 1863.

These organised sports would soon make their formal appearance in Britain's public parks. It's worth remembering that some parks were laid out with the intention of eradicating sports that were judged unsavoury, or at least lacking in healthfulness. 'Pugilistic encounters and dog-fights', after all, were among the gay contests lost when Battersea Fields were reborn as Battersea Park. At Preston's new Corporation Park, the traditional Whit Monday games held on the same site for generations were denounced as 'absurd' and of 'demoralizing character' and the authorities moved to prohibit all games that were not 'innocent and simple recreation'. Even cricket on Kennington Common wasn't cricket – a phrase only coined in 1867, the year the first Test Match was played. Far from being wistfully eulogised as one of the few decent sports, cricket was deemed a positive nuisance on the Common for obstructing 'the path in all directions', while stray balls worried passers-by who feared that they would lose eyes or get their noses broken.

Moreover, where there were games, there was usually gambling, or so much of the thinking went. Sinful gambling, that is; not the honest gentlemanly wagers of Phileas Fogg or the London Stock Exchange. Cricket was no exception. One of the earliest accounts of a cricket match, in Coxheath near Maidstone in Kent in 1646, includes a reference to a bet on its outcome. Before the 1840s, contests of many different stripes remained 'money-gate affairs' held in playgrounds adjoining inns or public houses. Bets being placed and beer being sunk were part and parcel of a good match – as they continue to be to this day.

Legislation that improved working conditions meant that the working class was now presented with more opportunity to indulge in such unimproving, disorganised pastimes. The 1850 Factory Act, for example, had closed all textile mills at 2 p.m. on Saturdays, and by the 1860s Saturday half-days were common among railway workers and 'superior tradesmen', with the division between work and leisure gradually becoming more sharply delineated.

The Bank Holiday Act of 1871, the brainchild of the banker, Liberal MP for Maidstone and cricket fan Sir John Lubbock, redressed the loss of traditional feast days for the ledger-keeping Bob Cratchits who, in terms of holidays, had fared as badly if not worse than the Stephen Blackpools in the mills post-industrialisation. A further Factory Act of 1874 again shortened the working day of mill workers, with Saturday labours now finishing at 1 p.m. And by the 1880s, the British labour force was privileged to be the most leisured in Europe.

Football – once the hacking, the picking up of the ball and some of the other more dangerous elements of play to survive in rugby had finally been removed in 1863 – was perhaps the greatest beneficiary of these newly free Saturday afternoons. Lasting a modest hour and a half and now a much less injurious or lethal game than it once was, it could be slotted into the industrial working week without disturbing the godly Sunday or rendering a valued employee unfit for work come Monday.*

---

* And sabbatarian societies like the Working Men's Lord's Day Rest Association and the Central Committee for Securing the Cessation of Sunday Excursion Trains, both founded in 1860, campaigned vigorously against anything other than church-going on Sundays. Many sabbatarians took the collapse of the Tay Bridge across the Firth of Forth on Sunday 28 December 1879 as a sign from God.

As ever, the extension of more free time to a wider section of society concerned Anglican ministers and moralists, who worried about idleness leading to sinfulness, or participation in the wrong kind of activity – drinking, gambling, etc. – simply equating to sinfulness. Churches and Sunday schools, therefore, campaigned to help clean up working-class team games like football, luring clubs away from pub gardens by offering changing facilities, grounds and alcohol-free refreshments. Everton Football Club, for instance, was founded as part of the Congregationalist St Domingo's Church Sunday School in Liverpool, while Wesleyans set up Aston Villa. Moreover, a decent kick-around in a park was considered good for improving the general health and fitness of a member of staff and was now welcomed by industrialists, who saw it as enhancing productivity and inculcating such virtues as loyalty and team spirit.

The expansion of elementary schools following the passing of the 1870 Education Act also increased participation in team games, and again football was the main beneficiary. And yet again, the Church played a part, as the sports curriculum set by public schools was enthusiastically adopted at Church-sponsored teacher training colleges. It was their graduates who were to provide the bulk of the staff recruited to teach the additional four million pupils now able to take up a school place. Earnest, God-fearing, lower-middle-class men, they were often as evangelical about Association Football as they were about education for the masses. It was a group of such student teachers who founded what became Sunderland FC.

As the form, character and reputation of certain games began to change, so the clamour for dedicated sporting pitches to be included in new public parks, or expanded in existing ones, grew. In Birmingham, for example, parks arrived relatively late, but coming after the first great wave of Victorian park-building, they were able to incorporate sporting pitches into their design.* This coincided with a remarkable footballing explosion. In 1874 the city had just a single football club: by 1880, it could boast 155. The sport historian Dennis Brailsford has argued that the arrival of the city's new public parks, soon filled with eager hoofers chasing after balls, was responsible.

In public parks, sports added to the gaiety of the scene. They introduced the thrill of motion and emotive action into landscapes which, as that painterly term betrays, were too often laid out only to be looked at, and were best admired at a slow walking pace. The intrusion of sports into the leafy spaces wasn't to everyone's taste. In 1867, the Reverend Charles L. Dodgson, aka Lewis Carroll – who, amusingly, had been schooled at that most sporting of academies, Rugby – was a

---

* Birmingham historian Carl Chin has written that 'too few of its leading citizens cared... to provide facilities for the education and recreation of its citizens... The dominant ideology among councillors remained one of parsimony and inaction.' In 1853 the campaigning local Quaker Joseph Sturge maintained that 'there was not a town in England so ill-provided with playgrounds as Birmingham'. And just two years later the council rejected the offer of a donation of land for a public park by Charles Bowyer Adderley on the grounds of the cost of its future maintenance.

mathematics don at Oxford. There, he campaigned against the creation of a cricket pitch in an area of the university grounds, known as the Parks. This being fruity old Oxford in the 1860s, his objection, which was successful, was conveyed in the form of a satirical poem entitled 'The Deserted Parks', in which he grumbled about 'rude pavilions' saddening the green. The tactic proved less successful twelve years later, when the proposal was revived and the pitch finally laid.*

Rude pavilions, despite Carroll's efforts, were to become a nationwide feature, as with sports pitches came clubhouses, scoreboards, manicured greens and, after 1891, even goalposts with nets. Public drinking fountains also arrived, more or less as a direct result of the greater amount of physical activity taking place within parks. Such fountains weren't always a pre-emptive measure for dehydration. At Kennington Park, for instance, an open-air gymnasium installed in 1861 was a big hit with the local children, who liked nothing better than to clamber about on the parallel bars and swing from its ropes. Having exhausted themselves and the gym's various devices, the tykes were usually left rather thirsty. To rectify this their only option was to head for the cabstands, and on most sunny days little Fannys and Alexanders were to be seen 'drinking with the horses out of their pails'. To the chagrin of the cabmen, naturally. It did not please the park's committee either, which since banishing street preachers and Chartist agitators and acquiring the Prince Consort's 'model dwelling' as a lodge, and installing constables to settle scuffles around the gymnasium, was striving for more decorous behaviour all round.

Fortunately, Felix Slade, a wealthy local landowner, antiquarian and philanthropist, whose endowments would create the London art school

---

* Carroll did come to take some interest in at least one sport, tennis, and in 1883 he penned a treatise called 'Lawn Tennis Tournaments, The True Method of Assigning Prizes with a Proof of the Fallacy of the Present Method'.

that bears his name, paid for a drinking fountain. Modelled on a classical Etruscan exhibit at the Great Exhibition and designed by Charles H. Driver, it was certainly an imposing edifice for this quarter of South London. Originally the water flowed down from a bronze fixture, cast in the shape of four lotus flowers, into a large red granite bowl inlaid with Slade's initials and coat of arms mounted on four steps.

In exactly the same year, and perhaps not to be outdone, Angela Burdett-Coutts, heir to the Coutts banking fortune and dubbed 'Queen of the Poor' for her charitable ventures, presented Tower Hamlets' Victoria Park with one of the most colossal fountains ever erected in a public park. A 'Neo-Gothic, cum Moorish' confection in pink marble, granite and stone, and decorated with chubby, sculpted cherubs, four clock faces and a grey slate roof, it was designed by the architect H. A. Darbishire and cost £6,000. At that time a domestic servant could expect to earn £12 a year. It was probably enough to make poor East Enders choke as they quenched their dusty throats with water from one

of the fountain's bronze cups, each engraved with the phrase 'Temperance is a bridle of gold' for good measure. At a ceremony to mark the presentation, William Cowper, first Commissioner of Works, described the fountain as 'the most beautiful yet built or imagined' and quoted from *The Rime of the Ancient Mariner*, Coleridge's poem inspired by James Cook's voyages into the ice-packed seas of the southern hemisphere.

Such journeys never failed to capture the public imagination. For instance, coupled with Romantic poets' promotion of sublime landscapes, they stoked among roistering English gents of an athletic or scientific bent a demand to venture into frosty realms themselves. They also contributed to mountaineering becoming a sport: while the Antarctic or the snow-capped ranges of the Sikkim were beyond the reach of most, the railways were to make Switzerland and its invigoratingly chilly Alps a far more reasonable vacationing alternative. In 1852, Londoners did not even have to go that far, as the travel writer Albert Smith brought his 'Ascent of Mont Blanc' to the Egyptian Hall in Piccadilly. A spectacular dramatic rendering of his climb, it was narrated with the aid of a moving painted panorama, native hurdy-gurdy music and Smith's own songs. The show was an instant roaraway success and was soon being staged with improvements: the hall decked out with edelweiss, packs of real St Bernard dogs, firing cannons and a pond featuring a gurgling fountain and live fish were all added to the bill. It triggered a mania for Mont Blanc merchandise, with Smith doing a brisk trade in sheet music for ditties such as 'The Mont Blanc Quadrille' and 'The Chamouni Polka', and producing a board game based on his ascent. Slightly higher-browed but no less thrilling, another contribution to the growing vogue for all things Alpine came in 1855 with Alfred Wills's *Wandering Among the High Alps*, his page-turning account of scaling the Wetterhorn, the so-called 'peak of tempests'. This was followed a year later by *Of Mountain Beauty*, the fourth volume of Ruskin's *Modern Painters*.

In keeping with the systematisation of other sports in this era, the Alpine Club was formed in 1857 by a group of dons, lawyers, clergymen and other minor worthies with the aim of furthering the cause of climbing and alpine literature, science and art. And one art that duly latched itself to the mountain-esque as firmly as Charles Barrington roping up the Eiger was horticulture.

Perhaps its most active proponent was the Irish-born gardener, journalist, publisher and vegetarian William Robinson. Rising from a nine-shilling-a-week hand at the Royal Botanic Society's garden in Regent's Park to become, at twenty-nine, the Special Horticultural Correspondent of *The Times*, and then contributing editor and owner of the *Gardener* and *Gardening* – the latter a popular, heavily illustrated weekly aimed at prosperous suburban villa owners – Robinson had a preference for herbaceous borders. This was matched with a particular horror for carpet bedding, iron railings, Latin name-labels for plants and formal French gardens. Or, indeed, formal gardens full stop.

Wildness, albeit of the artfully crafted kind, was his watchword, and his book, *The Wild Garden*, could be described as Ruskin with a hoe,

Scene in the higher Alps.

watering can and trowel. It was published in 1870, and that same year, following Robinson's first walking tour of the Alps the previous summer, he also wrote *Alpine Flowers for English Gardens*. Propitiously, its publication was virtually contiguous with that of *Scrambles amongst the Alps*, Edward Whymper's ghoulishly anticipated memoir of his 1865 conquest of the Matterhorn – a climb in which four of the party had fallen to their deaths – and the outbreak of the Franco-Prussian War. Since the war closed the Alps to tourists, booksellers stepped in to supply would-be visitors with the next-best thing. Demand was nudged along by resting mountaineers, some of whom used this period of enforced leisure to write books of their own. The end result was that there was something of an avalanche of alpine-ish literature in the early 1870s and, in the absence of the real thing, landscape architects and park gardeners consulted Robinson's sage tome and resorted to recreating mountain scenery on a more modest scale domestically.

Conveniently for them, James Pulham & Son, a family firm of cement manufacturers based in Broxbourne, were by then producing a highly convincing artificial stone for use in rockeries and other ornamental features. Known as Pulhamite, it had several advantages over proper rock. It was cheaper to make and lighter to shift about, and could be mixed in with real rock and dyed and moulded to imitate quite spectacular geo-strata from alpine lands. The Pulhams prided themselves on its verisimilitude, offering clients naturalistic copies of stratified rock, replete with 'fissures, cleavage and cracks'. Their repertoire included heatheries, caves, cavernous recesses, dropping wells, boathouses, rocky streams, cascades and waterfalls, and their clients ranged from the Prince of Wales and the Marquess of Hastings to local authorities in Buxton, Derbyshire, Stoke-on-Trent, and Her Majesty's Commissioner of Works.

In the decades to come the firm would be tasked with 'rockifying' Blackpool's seafront. But by 1877 the landscaping side of the business had already grown so successful that they ceased production of cement and published a prospectus entitled *Picturesque Ferneries and Rock-Garden Scenery* to further promote their services. Underscoring their aesthetic chops, this came garnished with lines from Wordsworth's *The Idle Shepherd-Boy*:

> It was a spot, which you may see
> If ever you to Langdale go:
> Into a chasm a mighty block
> Hath fallen, and made a bridge of rock

It would be a bridge of *artificial* rock – or more accurately, a bridge *ornamented with* artificial rock – that the Pulhams installed in the industrialist Joseph Shuttleworth's Swiss Garden, at Old Warden near Biggleswade in Bedfordshire, which has only recently been restored and re-opened as a public park, tucked behind a museum devoted to British aviation. But the public were to benefit more directly at Avenham Park, Preston, one of three local public parks the Pulhams equipped with mock-rocks, bridges and neoclassical vases. Here their Pulhamite 'Waterfall, cave etc.' was set not too far from two real Sebastopol cannons, each element lending the other an unreal kind of authenticity – the park's terrain of rocky steppes, oriental plants and cod-Graeco balustrades by the River Ribble becoming about the nearest setting Preston had to offer to that Black Sea port.

The finest Pulhamite example perhaps resides at Battersea Park, the location of what is known today as 'The Cascade'. In old postcards, it

is usually referred to as 'The Waterfall', though possibly only because postcard manufacturers and vendors feared confusing punters. Whatever its name, it endures to this day as such a splendid example of Swiss watery rock artifice that Sherlock Holmes can readily be envisaged leaping from it to stage his no less fake death.

CHAPTER 6

Urbs in Horto

Shifts in centuries tend to cause a certain amount of soul-searching, with much musing over what has gone before, or will go soon, and what might lie ahead. As the twentieth century came into view, this soul-searching took literary form, with utopian novels – along with their correspondingly less optimistic dystopian siblings – rising to popular prominence as a noteworthy genre. Thanks, in part, to increased literacy rates, mass printing and whizzy innovations such as two-stroke engines, the electric light bulb and the phonograph, over a hundred such novels are calculated to have been published in Britain during the 1880s and '90s, with more than 150 appearing in the ever-forward-thrusting United States. Of these, a surprisingly high number were to conjure up near-tomorrows where crop rotation rather than rocket ships prevailed – not that the inclusion of one necessarily excluded the other, as *Star Wars* was to later prove.

On the dystopian side, there was Richard Jefferies's 1885 effort, *After London*, which suggested that nature would have its revenge. In Jefferies's novel, with pollution killing off the British capital and the great and the good fleeing abroad, the country re-wilds. Meanwhile, human society – its culture and history lost, as books rot away and rats run free – regresses. Superstition and primitive barbarism reign again, with the railways and the telegraph soon becoming 'little more than fables of the giants and the old gods that walked upon the earth'. Alternatively, there were novels like *A Crystal Age* (1887), by the nature and travel writer W. H. Hudson. This was among those 'romances of the future' which painted an optimistic vision of an idyllic pastoral society. One, in this instance, where money has been abandoned and vegetarianism is the norm, as animals have evolved to do most of the heavy lifting, leaving people free to gambol about eating berries and singing songs.

The yearning for a future which resembled a kindlier version of the past was a hallmark of the Arts and Crafts Movement that emerged during the same period – a movement which would have a strong influence on the look of the nation's parks, and even see those parks breaking their bounds to create the first 'garden cities'. In the final decades of the nineteenth century, these kindred spirits would found such organisations as the Art Workers' Guild in 1884, the Guild and School of Handicraft in 1888 and the Central School of Arts and Crafts in 1896. These men and women were committed to preserving and revitalising the imperilled practices of pot-throwing, stained-glass work, timber-frame-building, spinning and hand weaving. The use of hands with some kind of tool rather than a steam or clockwork machine generally stands as a kind of four legs good, two legs bad of the whole Arts and Crafts scene.

The catalyst for the movement was William Morris, the wallpaper designer, poet, publisher, political activist, and proselytiser for a revival of traditional techniques of manufacturing. This was a campaign that he led through practical example, mastering, for instance, the arts of tapestry and printing. He even went so far as to cut the wood for the blocks of each new typeface he designed. Though it's doubtful he 'was ever seen with a spade in his hands', Morris was as pernickety about plants and gardens as everything else. He denounced carpet bedding, for instance, as 'an aberration of the human mind' and was especially enraged by florists' hothouse flowers and the breeding of new strains of roses. Scarlet geraniums and yellow calceolaria planted en masse he deemed so awful they showed that even flowers could be 'thoroughly ugly'.

The reason for such disgust perhaps lay in Morris's childhood. Born in 1834, he was raised in the London suburb of Walthamstow, when it was still, to his mind, blissfully unabsorbed by the capital – a rustic Essex village edged by marshland and the River Lea. Pointedly, he grew up with Epping Forest on his doorstep, in basically a meadow with a few houses in it. Morris was never to tire of recalling the succulence of the blue plums that had flourished by the kitchen-garden wall of his childhood home, the aptly named Woodland Hall. Nor the sweetness of the May blossom there.

This early environment suffused his work. In the 1860s he created wallpapers that put the fronds, buds and blooms of those native meadow flowers on to the interior walls of the smartest of houses. They were sold with appropriately floral names like 'Daisy', 'Eyebright' and 'Honeysuckle'. These patterns not only served as a recollection of their creator's childhood but evoked the indigenous varieties often uprooted from the gardens of his clients, the prevailing fashion among gardeners at that time being to diligently groom lawns to perfection and fill beds with those livelier glasshouse-reared species so reviled by Morris. And such flora's place in the British wild was no less endangered. As the cities expanded, it was perhaps an irony not lost on Morris that some of the newly erected walls his papers covered had obliterated fields of daisies and meadows decked with eyebright.

Morris's horticultural ideal is exemplified perfectly by *A Floral Fantasy in an Old English Garden* (1899), a sumptuously illustrated poetry picture book by Walter Crane. Crane – a prime mover in the Arts and Crafts scene and a long-standing friend of Morris, as well as a fellow socialist – uses the book to offer up a vision peopled by 'fayre maidens and verray parfit gentil knyghts frolicking in verdure'. Such a bricolage of mistily re-imaged neverlands was of course fantastical, but this glorification of an earlier, less mechanical, age was to create an outbreak of backward-looking gardening beyond the world of the Arts-and-Crafters.

The period of lost gardening that late-Victorian trowel-wielders most regularly alighted upon was the England of William Shakespeare – another epoch when the nation was ruled by a formidable queen and was getting the hang of helping itself to distant parts of the globe. Their enthusiasm was aided and abetted by the likes of the Reverend Henry N. Ellacombe's book, *The Plant-Lore and Garden-Craft of Shakespeare*. Published in 1884, this primer to the horticulture of the playwright's epoch fed a near mania for pseudo-Elizabethan gardens – gardens with the scented herbage, box hedges, crumbling stone walls and flagging, yew trees and the 'natural wildness' of sweet briar thickets urged by Francis Bacon back in the day.* Walter Crane himself also contributed to the genre by producing *Flowers from Shakespeare's Garden: a posy from the plays* in 1906. And this vogue for cod-codpiece-period greenswards, many incorporated into public parks, lasted until well into the 1920s. Their longevity and popularity was extended by the First World War and the tercentenary of Shakespeare's death in 1916. One such garden was laid out in Victoria Park in East London as late as 1927.

Exactly forty years earlier, Morris had ventured into the same park to speak at a demonstration for free speech organised by the Hackney Branch of the Socialist League. The left-leaning designer always cut

---

* Incidentally the author of *Of Gardens* and *New Atlantis* was himself the subject of a book by Constance Mary Pott entitled *Did Francis Bacon write 'Shakespeare'?*, published in the same year as Ellacombe's.

The Plant-Lore and Garden-Craft of Shakespeare

BY

HENRY N. ELLACOMBE, M.A.

VICAR OF BITTON

AUTHOR OF 'IN A GLOUCESTERSHIRE GARDEN'

New Edition Illustrated

EDWARD ARNOLD

LONDON AND NEW YORK

a fairly conspicuous presence. Sporting a long, flowing beard, he often wore purposely ostentatious dress and invariably sallied out with a canvas satchel full of socialist pamphlets slung over his shoulder. On this particular occasion he was wearing a great flapping grey cloak which, as he readily admitted, usually meant he was mistaken for 'a brigand or a parson'. But here in East London it induced raucous taunts of: 'Shakespeare Yah!' from a group of passing ''Arrys'.

In a letter to his daughter, Jenny, Morris judged Victoria Park 'a rather pretty place with water (though dirty)'. Given his belief that public gardens 'should be divided and made to look like so many flower-closes in a meadow, or a wood, or amidst the pavement', he would almost certainly have approved of its subsequent Old English garden. Morris duly gave full vent to this notion of flower-closes breaking out 'amidst the pavement' in his work of speculative fiction, *News from Nowhere*. A vision of an ideal socialist society, first serialised in the left-wing *Commonweal* newspaper, which Morris edited, it's arguably the fullest expression of his fetishisation of the natural world and all things medieval.

The book's protagonist, William Guest, is a Hammersmith stone-mason who awakes to find himself in 2003. Though, this being Morris, the dawn of the millennium appears closer to 1403 than to any Victorian steampunk fantasy teeming with coal-powered airships. London in the novel has been rendered virtually smokeless through de-industrialisation. Since 'the great clearing of houses' in 1955, forests of oaks and sweet chestnuts have sprung up to reclaim the sooty streets of the capital from Kensington to Clapton. There are apricot trees in what was once Trafalgar Square.

The once forbidden sexual fruit of no-strings marriages, separations and mutually fulfilling casual couplings have blossomed too. But the chaste, courtly love of Round Table fame and fable, if of a rather lance-less Lancelot variety, remains the highest ideal. Despite this, women, thanks to a lack of contraception, continue to be lumbered with child-rearing duties and the housework. Formal schooling is no more, and work is joyful folkcraft for everyone. Such nineteenth-century innovations as exploitative factories, dark satanic textile mills and iron suspension bridges have been superseded (or, more accurately, retrofitted) by collec-tive workshops, handlooms and pointy-arched stone-hewn pontoons.

Ultimately, Morris's futuristic metropolitan paradise looks more like the countryside than a metropolis. Albeit a collective countryside, with fields here 'treated as a garden made for pleasure as well as a liveli-hood for all'; the 'courtly game-keeperish trimness' of formal parks and gardens having long given way to the beauty of 'natural wildness'.

The context, as always, in which Morris's book was written is essential to its vision of a re-ruralised city and also to the increasing attention that would now be paid to the Arts and Crafts Movement's ideals. It was, put plainly, a widespread and growing unease with the pace of change. Between 1870 and 1900 the number of farm labourers, thanks in part to cheap imports and mechanisation, halved in Britain. The urban population, meanwhile, continued to rise sharply, reaching 80 per cent by 1911. To men like Morris, natural wildness appeared to be in ever shorter supply. It makes perfect sense, then, that in the 1880s areas such as the Cotswolds should have been fetishised, in direct proportion to the perceived and very real decline of rural settlements.

In his 1881, and subsequently published, lecture 'Art and the Beauty of the Earth', Morris had argued that industrial England had to be turned 'from the grimy backyard of a workshop into a garden' and wished for 'the town to be impregnated with the beauty of the country, and the country with the intelligence and vivid life of the town ... the town to be clean, orderly, and tidy; in short, a garden with beautiful houses in it'. Among the Arts-and-Crafters who carried Morris's message forth was an admirer by the name of Robert Blatchford, who upon meeting the great man himself in 1893 was pleased to report that it was 'grand to find my one hero better than his work'. Blatchford was the editor of the hugely popular socialist newspaper the *Clarion*, whose circulation would reach 90,000 by the end of the century. It had a strong Morris influence and featured illustrations by Walter Crane.

Two years after his initial encounter with Morris, Blatchford published *Merrie England*, an enormously successful and influential publication that sold over a million copies. In it, Blatchford called for the nation to be 'countrified anew', and for urban capitalism to be eschewed in favour of an agrarian life based on public ownership of the land. Subsequently, in 1901, he launched the Morris-esque Clarion Handicraft Guild, whose motto was 'Joy in work, and hope in leisure' and by 1907 he had written his own rustic science fiction novel, *The Sorcery Shop*. A *News from Nowhere* for the North West, it re-imagined Manchester as 'a garden of green lawns, and bright spring flowers and sparkling fountains, and stately trees'. As a somewhat worthy haven for vegetarian, teetotal non-smokers, it brings Morrissey to mind as much as Morris. And Blatchford, not unlike the former Smiths frontman, would disappoint many early admirers by veering sharply rightwards in later life.

But then, in England a love of the countryside has often been seen as a prerequisite of loving the nation. Canon H. D. Rawnsley, noting shortly before Queen Victoria's Golden Jubilee a rise in popularity of outdoor pursuits among what he termed 'the intelligent class of artisans', expressed the hope that the country walks and field-side rambles would nourish patriotism. Rawnsley, who'd been tutored by Ruskin, spear-headed the campaign to prevent the railways intruding on the natural beauty of the Lake District. He also set up the Keswick School of Industrial Arts to keep local crafts alive there, and was shortly to help found the National Trust, arguing that the soil and the countryside were 'not only a national need, but a racial one'.

In this battle for the soul of the nation, between progressives and patriots, even London and its parks would be asked to do their bit for Queen and country, by becoming ever more ye olden and rustified. Leading the charge, fittingly perhaps, was Lieutenant Colonel J. J. Sexby, park supervisor for the Municipal Board of Works and, with the arrival of London County Council in 1889, first Chief Officer of Parks. Born in Lambeth and qualified as a chartered surveyor, his military title was honorary and stemmed from his years as a voluntary reservist. Pale-faced and balding, with heavily lidded eyes and a substantial moustache, Sexby was a keen follower of horticultural trends, laying out voguish American gardens with rhododendrons and azaleas in Dulwich, Battersea and Peckham Rye parks in his earliest years in office.

But what has been called 'his masterstroke' was converting a former manor house kitchen garden into a walled Old English Garden at Brockwell Park. It bears all the hallmarks of the Morris-infused Arts and Crafts rustic aesthetic – though the carpet beds on the promenade else-where in the park, which spelt out 'two or three bars' of 'God Save the Queen', may not have pleased Morris.* The garden's original and

---

* In an epoch of imperial pomp and circumstance, the scope that carpet beds gave for presenting such commemorative or patriotic displays was widely celebrated. In the decades to come Cannon Hill Park in Birmingham would, for example, toast the coronation of George V by planting a bed designed to resemble a vast Tudor-style crown. With the expansion of democratically elected local government, botanical borough crests and floral civic coats of arms also became a common feature of hundreds of provincial parks. In Middlesbrough in 1898, municipal self-aggrandising extended to honouring the serving mayor, with the name of this public official rendered in blooms in Albert Park.

characterfully aged fruit trees, however, were retained. The broad flagged walks were offset with a smattering of golden yews and beds of herbaceous flowers, while an archaic well lent the entrance a fairy-tale allure.

This Old English style was, as already noted, rolled out across the capital: at Battersea Park, Peckham, in the Streatham Rookery and much later at Victoria Park.* Elsewhere, Arts and Crafts-style detailing crept into park architecture, with the bathing-pool hut at Brockwell, for example, sporting a thatched roof and wooden beams.

It's impossible to know if such new features of London's parks truly reflected Sexby's taste or were merely illustrative of the increasing general fashion for all things Arts and Crafts. Much to the chagrin of purists, the look was certainly becoming quite the thing. The department store Liberty, which had not yet acquired its Tudorbethan flagship store, constructed in part with planking from old ships, had begun stocking off-the-shelf ranges of intentionally distressed, hand-made-looking silver and pewter ware.†

Sexby may well have been prone to modishness. But his boss, George John Shaw-Lefevre, a prominent member of the LCC, was without doubt something of an apostle for 'native wildness', having battled to save Wimbledon Common from enclosure in the 1860s. Coming together with John Stuart Mill, Thomas Huxley and other like-minded worthies, he had established the Commons Preservation Society in 1865. They subsequently used the courts to defeat a plethora of attempts by unscrupulous lords of various manors – moustache-twirling villains one and all, robber barons with only bricks-and-mortar and profit-and-loss

---

* The Old English Garden in Peckham now bears his name.

† As a further example of an Arts and Craft cash-in, the Wills cigarette firm issued the first of two series of their collectable picture cards depicting fifty Old English Garden Flowers in 1911.

on their minds – from encroaching on, and even eradicating, common land at Putney, Wimbledon, Berkhamsted, Banstead, Epping, Hampstead, Parliament Hill and elsewhere.

William Morris, perhaps unsurprisingly, was a later supporter of the Society. But an early and tremendously useful recruit was Octavia Hill. A year older than Morris, she was born in Wisbech, Cambridgeshire to a wealthy Unitarian family. And, like Morris, Hill set great store by her youthful memories of being raised in a North London that remained barely urban. Often were the times when she waxed lyrical about ambling in a meadow of flowers in Finchley and romping about the heath at Hampstead, or in the woods near her grandfather's home in Highgate. Later she claimed to have dreamed, as a child, of finding a field so large that she could run in it for ever.

Humourless and sometimes quite inhumane in her moral rectitude, Hill was converted to the do-gooding strand of Anglicanism by the socialist minister F. D. Maurice and that most muscular of Christians, Charles Kingsley, who had been appointed the Queen's chaplain in 1859. She began 'working with' the less fortunate around Marylebone while in her early twenties. Obtaining some money from Ruskin, she threw herself into refurbishing slum dwellings and leasing them cheaply to poor tenants. If welcoming a decent and affordable home, Hill's tenants were nevertheless forced to accept her exacting stand-ards when it came to their personal conduct and habits as a condition of occupancy. Drink and idleness had to be forsworn, and cleanliness, godliness and industriousness embraced in their place.

Ascribing the 'deeply rooted habit of dirt' to urban dwellers' aliena-tion from nature, in 1875 Hill, with her sister, Miranda, set up the Kyrle Society, an organisation whose purpose was to distribute plants and flowers to workhouses and hospitals and generally press for the retention and extension of greenery in the capital. The conversion of deconsecrated old burial grounds into open spaces or 'public living rooms' was one of her many innovative ideas that eventually became reality, the Disused Burial Grounds Act of 1884 enabling local authorities to refashion them into pocket-sized parks.

Octavia Hill argued that Londoners needed places that would allow them to 'rise above the smoke, to feel a refreshing air for a little time and to see the sun setting in coloured glory which abounds so in the Earth God made'. She commended the existing commons and open fields on sanitary grounds as 'air holes for labourers' and, crucially, also urged those of an artistic bent to fight for whatever 'remnants of rustic beauty' were left.

Her efforts with the Commons Preservation Society were spurred on by the bitter memory of failure to save Swiss Cottage Fields from the clutches of a property developer. She'd led poor children in Marylebone out to these fields. Escorting the soot-smeared urchins away from the fetid city alleys and up into lush grass dotted with buttercups, perhaps she had felt a little like Moses proffering a promised land of milk and honey. But her pleas about the value of these fields to such huddled masses went unheeded and they were closed off and soon buried under 'a sea of house'. Their loss moved her greatly, but put iron in her soul. When it came to face subsequent bruising rounds over Hampstead Heath and Parliament Hill Fields, Blackheath and Epping Forest, Hill, Shaw-Lefevre, Morris and the rest of the Commons Preservation Society would prove victorious. Thanks to them, legislation such as the Metropolitan Commons Act 1866 and the Commons Act 1876 was passed, ensuring that no further commons were to be lost in London, though the battle continued outside the capital.

In June 1881, Octavia Hill visited William Morris's Thames riverside home, Kelmscott House, at 26 Upper Mall, Hammersmith. (In *News from*

Nowhere William Guest is also a resident of Victorian Hammersmith at the start of the novel.) She was given a tour of the garden, which stretched for 600 feet and contained arbours of almond, walnut, horse chestnut, pear and plum trees, along with a profusion of foxgloves, sweet williams, roses, sunflowers, hollyhocks, poppies and peonies. Together with the lush greenery, Hill was enchanted by Morris's 'carpet factory', a workshop in an outhouse which, she observed, was 'just in his own garden'.

This merging of horticulture and homespun manufacturing in a sense represented the Morris ideal. Gardens, both public and private, in great towns, he once argued, were 'positive necessities if the citizens' were 'to live reasonable and healthy lives in body and mind'. To that end, he was a keen backer of another Hill project that actually appears more eerily predictive of his futuristic fictional dream. This was a successful scheme to convert the grounds of a torched paper factory and warehouse on Red Cross Street in South London into a community garden. Here in 1887, in what Hill called 'darkest Southwark', nature arose from the ashes of industry, just as it had in *News from Nowhere*.

Morris himself was to die just shy of a decade later of diabetes, tuberculosis and exhaustion, but at the turn of the century, a book was published by a man infused by Arts and Crafts ideals who proved to be among the most significant civic park-makers of the late nineteenth and early twentieth century. His name was T. H. Mawson, and at the turn of the twentieth century he wrote *The Art and Craft of Garden Making*.

The scion of modest North Country Nonconformist stock, whose stock would become even more modest after the premature death of his father (fatally exhausted by a failing nursery and market-garden business), Mawson was first and foremost a practical and professional landscape architect. With a practice based in the Lake District serving an array of different and quite differently picky individuals, companies and public bodies around the world, he could never afford to be especially doctrinaire. Clients rather than Arts and Crafts dogma were always his chief concern.

That said, his extensive use of vernacular materials – he placed great, if not exclusive, importance on local stone, wood, plants and trees – put him firmly in the Arts and Crafts camp. As did his self-professed and lifelong love of the quaint.

Mawson himself put this down to spending the first six years of his existence in Scorton, a small Lancashire village. Today it promotes itself as the 'Gateway to the Trough of Bowland' and can be reached on a 'Pendle Witch Hopper' bus from Clitheroe – the said witches having been led through this moorland of peat and gritstone, a barren but undeniably arresting landscape, en route to their trial in 1612. It was not witches, but a local bridge that cast its spell on Mawson. The 'quaintness' of that bridge impressed itself so 'ineradicably' upon his memory that he could picture it exactly almost sixty years later. (He also confessed that as a youth he kept a 'vision of a tall, comely nurse in whose arms I nestled during my introduction into the world, and she always wore dress and apron of a very quaint pattern' no less frequently in his mind, which seems more suggestive of kink than quaint.)

At twelve, by which point the family had moved to Lancaster, Mawson claimed to have known 'intimately every old door-head, date-stone, sundial, quaint gateway, oriel or mullioned window, for miles around'. He took up sketching that county capital's score of ancient buildings, becoming in the process an accomplished draughtsman and steeping himself in architectural arcana, both of which, in due course, would stand him in good stead professionally. As, of course, would a spell in the family nursery, working alongside his soon-to-be-late father and his brother. (Mawson recalled that upon first acquiring the business, his father, rather ominously, had bought a book entitled *How to Earn*

£600 per Year from An Acre of Ground, a volume that he, even as a strip of a lad, found 'very unconvincing'.)

Mawson would have to complete his gardening apprenticeship in London, first at John Willis's of Onslow Gardens, Kensington and then at Hale Farm Nurseries, Tottenham. The former was close enough to the South Kensington Museum for the autodidactically inclined Mawson to spend most lunchtimes there 'improving himself'. At the latter, he was entrusted with answering correspondence about daffodils, nymphs and aquatic plants.

Finally striking out on his own with a nursery in the Lake District, his lucky break came in the form of a commission for a private garden near Windermere, on the recommendation of a relative of John Ruskin. Similar commissions would follow, but, perhaps haunted by his father's failure, Mawson was on the hunt for some more substantial projects to keep his business afloat. And among the most substantial project that any landscape gardener could really hope for at this juncture was a public park.

Picking up a paper one morning and reading about a scheme for a new park in Hanley in Staffordshire, Mawson decided then and there to 'get after' the work. Wiring an MP he knew for a letter of introduction to the local Member of Parliament, he hotfooted it to Hanley, and by 2.30 p.m. the following day was already showing examples of his work to the borough engineer, Joseph Lobley. Lobley informed Mawson that 'two men of considerable reputation' had already approached the company with an eye to the job, but he obviously liked what he'd seen. With impeccable timing, Mawson had, in fact, arrived just half an hour before the next meeting of the park committee and Lobley promised to try to induce them at least to see this young lakeside upstart, since he was there anyway.

At 3.15, he was ushered into a large wood-panelled room, municipal probity oozing from each and every plank. There he faced an assembly of aged aldermen and councillors, liver-spotted livery wearers to a man, the kind of portly, wheezy-breathed, snow-haired fingerers of waistcoats and callers-to-order whose throaty coughs interrupt proceedings and cause weighty chains of office to clank. They listened attentively while Mawson made his pitch; he offered to undertake the job for 5 per cent of the costs and expenses. At this point, one of the councillors interjected that a well-established name had put himself forward at just 3 per cent. Mawson, however, would not budge on price. Offering his youthful arrogance as a guarantee, he argued that Hanley Park would become his 'first great public work' and that he could not 'afford to do less than' his 'utmost' to give them 'satisfaction'. He was asked to step outside while they discussed the matter. Ten minutes of thumb-twiddling in a gloomy corridor, its walls decorated with sombre oils of the distinguished (and mostly dead) of Hanley, followed before Mawson was called back in and given the job.

And what a job it was. The task now to hand was, in his own estimation, to convert 'a waste of pits, mounds, and rubbish tips ... into a pleasant park'. The only redeeming feature of the 125-acre site was, apparently, 'its southern slope' – but this was nullified by 'an exceptionally utilitarian canal' which cut across the property 'at an awkward level' and carried material to and from the local potteries and ironworks. Along its eastern boundary stood a number of potteries with 'bottle-shaped kilns, belching forth smoke and fumes, poisoning the air and making vegetation very difficult to establish'. To the west lay the Cauldron irrigation works. But Mawson was 'determined to coax or bully' these unprepossessing conditions into 'a beautiful pleasance'.

As Pennethorne had found at Victoria Park in East London nearly fifty years earlier, 'a sheet of water', in this instance specifically conceived as a boating lake, would cover a multitude of topographical sins. It also served two very distinct practical purposes. Firstly, in Mawson's view, it worked to clarify 'the air of chemical fumes' and 'favoured the growth of foliage in the surrounding area'; and secondly, it provided the park with 'a source of revenue'. Similarly hard-headed considerations would govern the choice of plants and features in the park. Here in Hanley, Mawson surmised, it was 'useless for the park architect to think of quaintly clipped yew, holly or box-edged gardens where only privet would withstand such conditions'. So much for the Arts and Crafts in Stoke, then. But to compensate for its many deficiencies, enlivening lodges, seats, terraces, a bridge, a bowling green, a bandstand, boathouses and a boundary fence were introduced – some of which did boast Art-and-Crafty detailing.

Almost inevitably for any park built in this epoch, there were also rockworks and a cascade by James Pulham & Son. Another feature was a conservatory, designed by the architect Dan Gibson, which doubled up as a winter garden, and a pavilion on a terrace edged by flower beds – Mawson stating that a pavilion occupied 'the centrepiece position in a park, as a house ... in a garden'.

Most of the hard graft was undertaken by hundreds of local unemployed men, diligence being rewarded with full-time positions in the park. At the opening ceremony in 1898, a military band played Handel's 'Largo' – a short aria derived from an initially ill-received opera in which the ancient Persian king Xerxes I sang of his love of trees, and their shade, in particular – and Mawson was praised for turning 'such a desolate wilderness into a green oasis'.

He was immediately engaged by Burslem Town Council to work on their new park, where the ground was 'worse than Hanley's'. The going was little better in Wolverhampton, where he would supply both the East and West Parks. But his ability to transform these stagnant crockery-stuffed mires into verdant municipal spaces was swiftly rewarded with requests to equip Newport with its Belle Vue Park, Cleethorpes with its sports-pitch-rich Sidney Park, Rochdale with a formal sun garden at Falinge Park, Preston with its Haslam Park and Enfield in North London with Broomfield Park, a park admired for its avenue of elms, which sadly fell victim to Dutch elm disease seventy years later.

Work came in from further afield too. There were commissions from France, Germany, Denmark and Greece, and soon enough several trips to British Columbia and Calgary in Canada, as well as other parts of North America. By 1914, his firm, trading as T. H. Mawson & Sons, listed 'London, Lancaster, Vancover and New York' in its masthead. After speaking at Harvard during one American lecture tour, he met Frederick Law Olmsted's son, Frederick Law Olmsted Jr, and his stepbrother John Charles, the founders in 1899 of the American Society of Landscape Architecture, and later paid a visit to the Olmsted firm's offices in Brookline near Boston.

By then, Mawson had become not only a park- and garden-maker of note but a significant figure in the still quite nascent field of town planning – the latter discipline an offshoot, to an extent, of the former.

The move from one to the other began for him in earnest in 1903, when Mawson was invited to submit a plan for a new park at Pittencrieff, Dunfermline by the Scottish-American industrialist turned philanthropist Andrew Carnegie. Carnegie had been born in Dunfermline, emigrating to the United States with his impoverished family as a small boy in 1848, after the power looms had done for the indigenous hand-weaving industry. Prior to their departure, the Carnegie clan, like many other Dunfermline natives, had nursed a particular grievance about their exile from Pittencrieff Castle grounds and glen. These had formerly been common land until their purchase and enclosure by the Hunts, a family of wealthy local industrialists. By the turn of the twentieth century, however, the Hunts had fallen heavily into debt and had to dispose of a number of properties, among them Pittencrieff, which was eagerly snapped up by Carnegie.

In a letter to the Prime Minister, Henry Campbell-Bannerman, and clearly savouring the poetic justice of the situation, Carnegie described its acquisition as 'the sweetest event in my life in the way of material satisfaction'. Having secured the land, he intended to have it revamped as an elegant public park with a range of facilities 'to bring into the monotonous lives of the toiling masses of Dunfermline' some 'sweetness and light ... some charm, some happiness, some elevating conditions of life'. Hence his approach to Mawson.

But Mawson wasn't the only man he approached. Ever the free-market capitalist, Carnegie wanted competition, so he also solicited designs from Patrick Geddes. Geddes was not a park-maker or a landscape architect as such but a natural scientist; he held a chair of botany at Dundee College, an affiliate of St Andrews University, having studied in London under Thomas Huxley at what was then called the Royal School of Mines, today's Imperial College.

Soaking up the latest thinking on evolution, Geddes had advanced a theory of his own – a theory which was to cast towns and cities as living, organic entities. Convinced that humankind's trajectory had inevitably been affected by industrialisation and urbanisation, Geddes saw the layout and organisation of towns and cities as a matter not just of architectural or engineering concern, but of a grander moral and biological importance. Scientifically, people would get better if their cities were better. Geddes was convinced that parks and gardens were among the most potent factors in the regeneration of any city. In his report on Dunfermline, he also laid out his belief that: 'Civics as an art, a policy' was not to do 'with U-topia but with Eu-topia; not with imagining an impossible no-place where all is well, but with making the most and best of each and every place, and especially of the city in which we live.'

Mawson would shortly publish his own book, entitled *Civic Art*, but neither man would see their competing designs flourish at Pittencrieff, Carnegie instead opting to leave the site in much the same natural state as it had been in his youth. As something of a sop, he did hire Mawson to lay out a new garden at Skibo Castle, Sutherland, while Mawson's plans for Pittencrieff, which included a grand new boulevard, a lecture hall, museum, concert hall and art gallery, led to other commissions for parks in Canada and America.

Both Mawson and Geddes would feel rather short-changed by the philanthropist. They were, though, sufficiently enriched by the experience to suggest working together in the future. A collaboration that, alas, was never to be fulfilled. Nevertheless, the project and Mawson's close contact with as innovative a natural scientist as Geddes pushed him in a new direction: towards town planning, rather than mere park-making.

Town planning, along with radium and the teddy bear, became quite the smart topic for polite supper-table conversation. In 1903, the very same year that Mawson and Geddes were hatching schemes for Carnegie, the First Garden City Ltd had been established, with the aim of creating a completely new kind of city on 4,000 acres at Letchworth in Hertfordshire. This 'Garden City' was to be constructed as the physical manifestation of a concept outlined by the peripatetic Ebenezer Howard.

Born in 1850 in London to lower-middle-class parents, Howard had left school in his teens to become a clerk in a city firm. But always more of a daydreaming Billy Fisher than a head-down Bob Cratchit, he went through several jobs before emigrating to the United States in 1871. Seduced by the romance of frontier life, the next spring he followed a group of friends to a homestead in, by pure coincidence, Howard Country, Nebraska, some 120 miles from Omaha. As a City of London slicker with no practical farming skills, he made a dreadful plainsman. Within a year, he'd moved to Chicago and was back in 'the much more familiar world of short hand typing', as one biographer wryly observes.

But if he did buckle down to stenography from now on, his new surroundings only helped feed his biddable imagination. In Chicago, whose motto from the 1830s onwards was *Urbs in Horto* (City in a Garden), he first read the transcendentalist writings of Ralph Waldo Emerson and became aware of the spiritualist movement, attending a lecture by the famed American medium Mrs Cora Richmond. On a more material plane, the city was in the process of being rebuilt following the Great Chicago Fire of 1871, and this too was to have a huge influence on Howard. The conflagration had naturally brought the matters of fire precaution and safety to the fore, especially after a further blaze just three years later. With it came new thinking about urban design, and the so-called 'commercial style' of taller blocks in non-flammable materials (terracotta a big winner) was one phoenix to rise from the ashes. For reasons that are not clear, Howard returned to London in 1876, so he missed the latter stages of this development. But he must still have caught a whiff of the optimism that came from the idea of beginning, bigger and better, from scratch.

Given Howard's subsequent interests, it is also unlikely that he would not have heard of Riverside. Started before the fire but delayed for nearly a decade due to lack of funds, this was a purpose-built

Chicago suburb devised by our old friends Frederick Law Olmsted and Calvert Vaux. It was envisioned as a sylvan retreat where 'the conveniences peculiar to the finest modern towns' would be combined with 'the domestic advantages of a most charming country'. Howard, if later denying any direct influence, would proffer a not so dissimilar combination of town and country in his notion of the Garden City. Equally, the 'green belt', which would in time become one of the most influential features of Howard's Garden City concept, seems to have been foreshadowed by the commissioners of Chicago's Lincoln, West and South Parks, who, though working separately, shared a dream of creating a 'unified ribbon of green that would encircle' their city as early as 1869.

A further possible debt to Olmsted and Vaux was his decision to call the five-and-a-half-acre garden in his eventual plan the Central Park – intended to be at the dead centre of things, it was to be surrounded by public buildings, with a Crystal Palace serving as an arcade for recreation in poor weather and as a space for shops, picture galleries and the like.

Still, more than a decade and a half would pass following his return to London before Howard conceived of his Garden City or committed any ideas about it to paper. In the meantime, he earned his crust much as before, typing stuff up, working as a parliamentary record keeper and pursuing various esoteric interests on the side.

In 1879, for instance, he joined the Zetetical, a metaphysical debating club that met in Hampstead and counted the future Fabians George Bernard Shaw and Sidney Webb among its members. It was also a club that didn't entirely discount the possibility that the earth might be flat. Spiritualism, meanwhile, continued to be a passion for Howard, who presented two papers on the topic to the Zetetical the following year. That same year, he again encountered Cora Richmond, who on this occasion told him he had 'a message to give to the world'.

As it happened, it was another American spiritualist, George Dickman, who would ensure that Howard's message reached the world the best part of a decade later.

Before then, though, Howard was to fall in with the likes of the pioneering evolutionist Alfred Russel Wallace at the left-leaning Brotherhood Church in Hackney and under the influence of another message, outlined in *Looking Backward: 2000–1887*, a utopian socialist time-travelling fiction by the American Edward Bellamy. The novel – a sensation on its publication in 1888, selling in the millions and translated into as many as twenty languages – is related by Julian West, a wealthy Bostonian afflicted with insomnia. True to his class and general effeteness, he seeks a suitably complicated solution to this ailment. He hires a mesmerist and chooses to hole up in a purpose-built basement to enjoy hypnotically induced shut-eye, as you do. However, owing to an unfortunate turn of events, involving a fire and an unreliable minion, West sleeps on and on in his subterranean lair, only to be discovered, immaculately preserved, some 113 years later. And the AD 2000 where he finally steps, blinking into the light, is one where war, private property and money have been abolished and public-spiritedness has overcome selfishness. Hardly the worst world to wake up to.

Boston at the turn of the millennium is a clean, airy, modern city, comprised of 'broad streets, shaded by trees and lined with fine buildings for the most part not in continuous blocks but set in larger or smaller enclosures'. Every quarter contains 'large open squares filled with trees', and lined with statues and fountains that glisten and flash 'in the late afternoon sun'. The city is part of an industrially efficient, state-run society, one where technology has advanced enough for music to be beamed into people's homes by telephone and where heat and light are supplied solely by electricity. More importantly perhaps, the nation guarantees to nurture, educate and provide 'comfortable maintenance' for every single one of its citizens 'from the cradle to the grave'.

Howard later stated that while reading Bellamy he had been 'transported by the wonderful power of the writer into a new society' and saw, for the first time, the practical potential for a whole 'new order – an order of justice, unity and friendliness'. He was so taken with the book that he petitioned the publisher William Reeves to put out an edition in England. Its printing was secured only after Howard personally obtained 100 advance orders of the book for Reeves. To those hundred, hundreds upon hundreds more were rapidly added, and in 1890 a group of the book's most fervent British readers founded the Nationalisation of Labour Society (NLS) to promote Bellamy's ideas. Within two years its members, among whom was Howard, were actively discussing how a 'Bellamyite' colony might be created – their aim being to set up a community where 2,000 people could live and work in self-sufficient socialist harmony.

What such a community might look like and how it might work on a nuts-and-bolts, or bales-and-pitchforks, level by then increasingly preoccupied Howard. In February 1893, he gave a talk at a meeting of the NLS in which he presented in public for the very first time a basic outline of what would become the 'Garden City' – a phrase Morris is credited with coining.

Here it is worth mentioning, or clarifying, that Bellamy's own version of a future society, if green and leafy, appears decidedly urban.

It puts its trust, quite implicitly, in technology, becoming positively boosterish when peddling its own special brand of machines-will-save-us utopianism. The state in Bellamy's model society is, in turn, omniscient, infallible, and all powerful. It's not so much a nanny as governess, wet nurse, cook and headmistress rolled into one. Even in its day, socialists as much as Tories detected more than a slight whiff of totalitarianism about Bellamy's nation state.

To William Morris, for example, the whole thing stunk to high heaven. His own science fiction, *News from Nowhere*, was written in response to Bellamy's book, among others.

As we have seen, being the good proto-environmentalist that he was, Morris swapped the authoritarian technopolis for a rather more tabard-friendly age to come. Howard, by all accounts, shared many of Morris's reservations about *Looking Backward*. But seemingly he either judged a less free, if more equitable, society a price worth paying, or just chose to overlook some of its more dictatorial aspects and went on tirelessly talking up the book, forever pressing copies of it into the hands of friends, strangers and any potential converts to the cause.

Howard would go on refining and spreading his vision of a Garden City, and in 1898 Cora Richmond's prediction that he had a message to give to the world came a little closer to realisation, thanks to George Dickman. As the Managing Director of Kodak in Britain and a fellow admirer of Cora Richmond, Dickman could be said to have spent his personal and professional life summoning up the absent, the dead: both through the medium of photography and by regularly patronising the kind of medium likely to set glasses moving, tables shaking and ectoplasm manifesting in dimly gaslit parlours. If the future was not usually his to see, he saw enough of it in Howard, who had just finished drafting a manuscript entitled *To-morrow: A Peaceful Path to Real Reform*, and lent him £50 to get it published.*

The book appeared in 1898, and spiritualism accounts for one of the finished product's most striking visual elements: the diagram of three magnets that occupies the opening pages. This illustration is so eye-catching and so frequently reproduced that today it regularly floats free of the text it was originally intended to introduce. It features one magnet that lists the pros and cons of town life, a second that does the same for the countryside, and a third that reels off the rosy stuff that Howard's new combo, a town-cum-country city, will

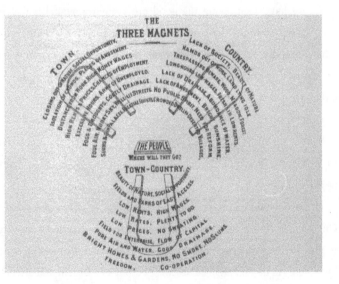

* Morris is absent from the roll call of sources that Howard liberally quotes in his book. Quotes from, and references to, Ruskin, Herbert Spencer et al. stud the text like cloves in a ham. But the Garden City, in many respects, feels more like an attempt to realise Morris's utopia than Bellamy's and a subsequent book, *The Garden City Movement Up-to-Date*, by Ewart G. Culpin, secretary to the Garden Cities and Town Planning Association, published in 1913, featured a lengthy quote from the wallpaper maker as its foreword, entitled 'A Prophet's Plea for Garden Cities'.

obviously offer. Magnets loom rather large in spiritualist theology and literature. John Murray Spear, for instance, who claimed the deceased Benjamin Franklin as an other-worldly confidant, believed that the minds of the living and dead flowed into one another through 'a grand, universal sea of magnetism'. In the 1850s, Spear retreated to a wooden shed at the top of High Rock hill in Lynn, Massachusetts, where he attempted to construct an 'Electric Messiah' powered by zinc magnets and copper coil that he believed would usher in a new utopian age.

That machine failed, but Howard, relying on his three magnets sketched in pen and ink, was no less ambitious, if perhaps marginally more worldly. He hoped the ideas he put forward would spark 'the spontaneous movement of the people from our crowded cities to the bosom of our kindly mother earth, at once the source of life, of happiness, of wealth, and of power'.

What he outlined was a detailed working plan for a new 'social city'. One that by design would provide 'workers of whatever grade' with a place to live and work that was a 'healthy, natural, and economic combination of the town and the country'. The land would be owned by the municipality, with income from rents used collectively to fund social services and old-age pension funds. The city he described surrounded a central park and was divided into six districts covering only 1,000 acres of a 6,000-acre site. The outer 5,000 acres were to be given over to an agricultural ring administered as a trust in the interests of the community, with farmland and cow pasture and general greenery ensuring it always remained garden-like and also limiting urban sprawl. But Howard was always to claim his plans, if detailed, were only ever 'suggestive' of what might constitute a 'Garden City'.

When the book, slightly revised, was reissued under the new title *Garden Cities of To-morrow* in 1902, Howard cited Adelaide as a potential model. This South Australian city had grown by leapfrogging over its original parklands, effectively creating a metropolis in a park that was far greener than its European or American contemporaries. By this point Howard's concept had a significant audience. The years between the two editions had seen the formation of the Garden City Association by Howard himself and the staging of two conferences, attended by the likes of George Bernard Shaw and the philanthropic Quaker industrialist Edward Cadbury, which considered the best means of putting the Garden City dream into action.

The eventual price of doing so at Letchworth would involve the intervention of socially responsible men of business like Cadbury along with Howell Idris and Aneurin Williams, and the jettisoning of some of Howard's most progressive ideals, among them communal government for the city, though not the central principle that the land be held in trust and profits be ploughed into paying for communal services. But once the scheme was up and running in 1903, Howard was gently nudged into a non-executive role. However, he was paid a stipend to tour and lecture about Letchworth on behalf of the company – which was quite possibly just a ruse to keep him onside, and out of the way.

The men tasked with building this new Jerusalem were Raymond Unwin and Barry Parker, both dyed-in-the-wool Arts-and-Crafters. Unwin was a Yorkshire-born engineer and former secretary of the Manchester branch of Morris's Socialist League. He was also a close friend of Edward Carpenter, the poet founder of the Sheffield Socialists and openly gay nudist, who, as an apostle of sandal-wearing, derided shoes as 'leather coffins'. Parker, born in Chesterfield, Derbyshire, had attended the South Kensington School of Art in London, but returned to the North to complete studies in interior design and architecture. Both he and Unwin were socially minded,

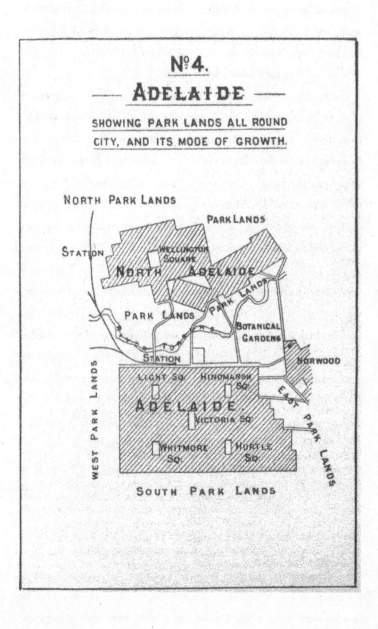

Nº 4.

ADELAIDE

SHOWING PARK LANDS ALL ROUND
CITY, AND ITS MODE OF GROWTH.

NORTH PARK LANDS

PARK LANDS

STATION

WELLINGTON
SQUARE

NORTH ADELAIDE

PARK LANDS

PARK LANDS

BOTANICAL
GARDENS

TO
STATION

NORWOOD

LIGHT SQ.

HINDMARSH
SQ.

ADELAIDE.

VICTORIA SQ.

EAST PARK LANDS

WEST PARK LANDS

WHITMORE
SQ.

HURTLE
SQ.

SOUTH PARK LANDS

signed-up advocates of housing reform, the simple and vernacular style, and leading lights in the Northern Art Workers' Guild. They had gone into business together in Buxton in 1896, not long after Unwin had married Parker's sister, Ethel.

In 1901 they published *The Art of Building a Home* – a near-companion piece to Mawson's book, *The Art and Craft of Garden Making*. This How-To for Arts and Crafts houses helped spawn a million Tudorbethan suburban semis in the decades to follow. The next year, the philanthropic chocolate manufacturers Joseph and Seebohm Rowntree employed the pair to design a model village for their factory workers on the outskirts of York, christened New Earswick. It was shortly after this that they were asked to submit a plan for Letchworth by First Garden City Ltd.

The 3,818-acre site, they discovered, was hardly a clean slate as it was bisected by the Hitchin to Cambridge branch of the Great Northern Railway and they had to take account of some pre-existing roads. What they devised was a group of interconnected villages – Unwin lauded the medieval village, as many an Arts and Crafts man did, for its combination of function, form and social cohesion – around a civic centre that was organised along a substantial mile-long axis to the railway station. This was modelled on Wren's unrealised post-Great Fire plan for the Exchange in London. There were distinct divisions throughout between the residential, social, shopping and manufacturing areas, with factories and workshops banished to the outskirts. For the residential streets the pair used irregular patterns, introducing the odd cul-de-sac, and went in for curvilinear road layouts. Amid plenty of trees, they dotted sparse groups of gabled cottagey houses.

In the end, and in order to make Letchworth financially viable, the company had to invite outside housing associations to join in its development. And while Unwin and Parker were able to stipulate the types of dwelling built there, their original master plan was diluted by the Garden City's incremental and sluggish growth. Unwin would duly depart to work on another new 'Garden City' settlement in North London, Hampstead Garden Suburb, before the first stage of Letchworth was finished. Significantly, the major feature was a corridor of green space named Howard Park in tribute to Ebenezer; it remains a public park to this day. But for Howard himself, Letchworth was a disappointment. The scheme, he confessed, had 'shrunk into' something 'somewhat smaller and humbler' than he had first pictured in his imagination. But he refrained from public criticism and took up residence there in 1906.

T. H. Mawson had visited Letchworth in the previous year. By now he was deep into the town-planning era of his career. In 1905 he would, for instance, make a very successful contribution to one of the most admired exercises in philanthropic place-making: the Port Sunlight model works and garden village on the Wirral. This sprang from the Congregationalist, paternalistic soap-maker William Hesketh Lever, who wished to see his factory workers employed and housed in decent conditions. Banishing dirt was his business, and if he couldn't keep his own staff clean and on the straight and narrow, off the lash and off the grimy rain-lashed streets of Liverpool, it was arguably a poor show for his product. And that was Sunlight – the first branded, mass-manufactured soap on the market. Mawson was involved in Port Sunlight's landscaping, suggesting alterations in 1905 to its original layout and drawing up plans for a hospital, school and public library.

Mawson's association with Lever was to prove a particularly fruitful one. Four years after his work at Port Sunlight, the 1909 Housing and Town Planning Act was passed, which gave local government the authority to develop new housing schemes. Within months of its appearance on the British statute book, the first world conference on town planning was held in Vienna. Mawson attended, and on his return Lever donated money for the establishment of a specialist Department of Town Planning at the University of Liverpool. Mawson would lecture there from 1911 onwards, the year that his book on town planning, *Civic Art*, was published.

At that time he also received a commission from Bolton – Lever's birthplace, and a town for which he'd already designed the Lever and Hall i' th' Wood Parks – to reimagine its centre. Horrified by the cramped back-to-back housing but unable to do much about the store of outlying ugsome factories that formed its perimeter ring, he thought big. Included in his proposals was a museum on a hill, purposely imposing, designed to push the aspect of the factories deeper into the background, and an oversized central arcaded boulevard that would aerate the urban space and connect it, atmospherically at least, to the countryside.

In the elegant line drawings by his main draughtsman, Robert Atkinson, the whole package looks impressively bold, if slightly overcooked. As is often the case with architectural illustration, the people are tiny inky black figures that haunt the picture like shadowy crows pecking about for corn (or eyes), dwarfed by the grandiose magnificence of the buildings. But in keeping with the Garden City ethos, there were to be gardens, pocket squares and playgrounds in the centre, with nearly every street heavily tree-lined. In one of Atkinson's pictures of a particular avenue, two twin rows of trees are so plump it looks like two giant caterpillars from an Atomic Age B-movie have strayed into Edwardian Bolton, the munching-up of industrial buildings their main priority.

A special feature of the plan was the outer ring road, an import from Vienna of the Ringstrasse, which indicates the increasing internationalism of Mawson and town planning as a whole in these tentative early days. And it says much about Mawson's global outlook that in 1913, when advising Exeter on 'the future' of its policies for 'town improvement within a period of a hundred years', he suggested that this Devonshire metropolis, not lacking in spindly medievalist details, should build a railway station along the lines of the then newly opened, epic Beaux-Arts-styled Grand Central Terminal in New York.

But Exeter, like Bolton in the end, would pass on Mawson's plans. Another never fully realised project was just on the outskirts of Cardiff. It began in 1905, as Mawson was visiting Letchworth, when he was hired by John Cory, the head of a prosperous Welsh ship-owning and coal-exporting clan, to lay out a 55-acre garden at his estate in Dyffryn, Glamorganshire. This in turn led to an invitation to build a garden village, a place where residents and workers could find 'peace and contentment', as Cory put it. Provisionally named Coryndon, in its promoter's honour, this was later changed to GlynCory Model Village.

The aim of GlynCory, as Mawson subsequently wrote, was 'to provide at an accessible distance from the restless activities of the large seaport town of Cardiff, a quiet retreat where, in forgetfulness of the stress and strain of business, lovers of country pleasures' might 'find suitable homes'. Conceived in the shape of a fan, radiating out from 'a strong and massive' church, the village was to have a tree-lined central avenue with a stream running down the middle of it, high-end villas and more affordable terraces 'in happy combination and repose in their fitting and restful settings', a concert hall, recreation grounds, a public garden, working men's clubs, co-operative shops and, as 'the greatest inducement' for a 'good class of resident', a golf course.

As it was, the First World War put the kibosh on this place of 'peace and contentment'. Only twenty-four houses were completed by 1914, and what progress was made after the war – which included the building of a school and some rather unlikely residential properties in a cod-Spanish-Moroccan vein – ground to a halt when South Wales took a direct hit in the slump of the late 1920s.

* * *

Like practically every other subject of the British or Austro-Hungarian empires, Mawson was professionally and personally touched by the war. Only three years earlier, with the gardens for Schloss Heesen in Hamm, Prussia under his belt, he had been nibbling a little strudel and drinking coffee in Vienna, as confident as anyone in the global forward march of planned 'garden cities'. But he seemed particularly cursed. In 1913, for instance, and with appalling timing, the Andrew Carnegie-sponsored Peace Palace in The Hague ceremoniously opened, the gardens and grounds of which he'd designed.

Much more devastating was the death of one of Mawson's sons, James Radcliffe Mawson, at Ypres on 23 April 1915. A student at the École des Beaux-Arts in Paris, he'd been expected to join the firm as a horticulturalist. In letters home from the front, he urged his family to do all they could to support the returning wounded. Within six months of James's death, Mawson, heeding his son's words, launched a campaign for the establishment of model industrial villages for disabled soldiers – places where they might live, and earn a living, in tranquil surroundings. Industrial here means, in a sense, industrious; the main idea was that the soldiers would not be idle and therefore would not be a drain on charity or the state.

Such a post-service settlement was later sent up by Noël Coward in an unsettling sequence in his otherwise jingoistic musical, *Cavalcade*, where blind veterans weave baskets beneath fluttering Union Jacks. There was certainly some opposition to the idea of special villages for ex-servicemen on the grounds that they might separate former soldiers from ordinary society. But Mawson took on the doubters. In 1917 he published a book entitled *An Imperial Obligation*, in which he laid out the case for 'Industrial Villages for Partially Disabled Soldiers & Sailors', which led to the creation of the Westfield War Memorial Village near his native Lancaster, its houses, rather less sensitively, named after major First World War battles, and its roads after leading military commanders. (Haig Avenue is one.)

During the Great War itself, parks and green spaces obviously had practical roles to perform, not all of them especially savoury. Among the most unsavoury was the use of Alexandra Palace as an internment camp for 'male enemy aliens of military age'. Since 1900, and by an Act of Parliament, North London's commercially unsuccessful answer to Paxton's Crystal Palace complex in Sydenham had been placed in the hands of a trust, which was required to make the palace and its park 'available for the free use and recreation of the public forever'. 'Forever' would be suspended for the duration of the conflict, and the park fenced off from the public with barbed wire and patrolled by armed guards. The great hall and other buildings on the site were used to house up to 3,000 internees, who slept row upon row on plank beds. Their numbers were made up of new German exiles, many fleeing their native land to avoid conscription, and English-speaking, middle-aged long-standing émigré residents. Some, like the distinguished artist Georg Sauter, had lived in Britain for over twenty years. This later demographic were especially nonplussed about being bunked up with just-off-the-boat Fritzs in not entirely sanitary conditions. Sauter's son Rudolf, nephew and secretary to the author of

The Forsyte Saga John Galsworthy, was also interned with his father at Ally Pally. He would later recall that the buckets in which soup was served were then used for washing the floors, and that in foggy weather the doors were not opened for days at a time and the stench 'became unbearable'.

Sauter Jr would leave a visual record of the camp in a series of paintings depicting its sleeping quarters, wash tents and mess kitchens, images that revel in the physical and mental limitations of internee life; each picture a study of claustrophobia, monotony and boredom. Sadly, much of Sauter's output was lost in a fire and there is no evidence of a supposed daring raid on the camp one night by a passing Zeppelin. Though completely discounted today, it was once commonly accepted that an airship had, under cover of darkness, taxied down to the terrace, where a band of waiting internees piled aboard, and flew away before the guards knew a thing.

Until his death in 1917, the camp commandant was Lieutenant Colonel R. S. F. Walker, a retired military officer and keen sportsman, who as a youth played football for Clapham Rovers and was a star of England's earliest national team. And in the absence of aerial excitements, hoofing a ball about the park, something Walker took great pride in encouraging, proved among the most popular activities undertaken by the internees. A highly competitive mini-football league lasted until severe food shortages in the final stages of the war led to a reduction in rations – one presaged by the replacement of beef with horse on the camp menu. The resulting diet leaving most too undernourished to play.

For the less sporting, there were concert parties and a dramatic club. But what kept most of these men busy during their incarceration was tending the 400 gardening plots cut into the park's lawns, flower beds and greens. This had begun as a means of keeping internees busy;

AN
IMPERIAL
OBLIGATION
Industrial Villages.
for
Partially Disabled
Soldiers & Sailors

by making prisoners somewhat self-sufficient, it was hoped, they would prove less of a drain on the nation.

Eventually, though, this carving up of parks into allotments was extended to civilian life when, in December 1916, the Board of Agriculture was granted new powers under the Defence of the Realm Act to requisition land for cultivation. Local authorities were required to turn waste ground, commons, heaths, public parks, ornamental gardens and vacant building land over to farming. Oats and wheat were grown in Heaton and Debdale Parks in Manchester. Hampstead Heath was ploughed up and planted with potatoes, and allotments were dug in the football pitches at Hull's East Park, Clapham Common, Victoria, Battersea, Bermondsey and other parks up and down the land. The polo field at Wimbledon Park became a piggery. Even Kew Gardens was not spared, with the edible taking precedence over the exotic in its greenhouses.

As in the next war's 'Dig for Victory' campaign, ordinary people were invited to do their bit by pitching in with fork, shovel and watering can. In Lloyd George's judgement, 'hundreds of thousands' of city dwellers 're-discovered the thrill and wonder of making things grow. A new fraternity made itself felt among these amateur cultivators from classes once widely sundered, who found themselves neighbours in the allotment field.' There had developed 'a kind of brotherhood of the big potato'. On suburban railway platforms, he maintained, bank managers had proudly pulled 'monstrous' tubers out of their briefcases, holding them aloft to elicit the admiration of their fellow passengers and challenging pin-striped rivals to produce specimens of greater size.

Meanwhile, with the threat of death near omnipresent, sexual passions often ran high. As did Fleet Street's fear of unbridled lust and the increased liberty wartime conditions now afforded women,

many enjoying life at work and in uniform and the freedom to dine out and roam about on their own at hours previously deemed unacceptable in polite society. Newspapers reported that young ladies from supposedly decent homes had been infected by 'khaki fever', so shameless were they becoming in their pursuit of soldiers. The Salvation Army went on a drive to reclaim 'unruly girls' whose numbers, they stated, were 'daily increasing owing to the abnormal conditions'. Mrs Helen Swanwick of the Women's International League, despite seeing it as the 'natural female complement to the male frenzy of killing', was not prepared to tolerate this khaki fever, and gathered bands of like-minded matrons and spinsters to form purity patrols to combat the outbreak on the streets of London. The streets provided rich pickings, and League members were not afraid of barging into brothels or accosting pimps in back-alley walk-ups. Yet there was equally fertile hunting ground in the bushes and long grasses of the capital's parks. Frequently marching into the deeper recesses of Hyde and Richmond Parks, in their blue uniforms and felt hats, armed with umbrellas, whistles and a strident tone of voice, they shamed couples out of their grass-stained amorous encounters, sending privates back to their barracks, once-perky tails limp between their legs, and persuaded seduced waifs and out-and-out tarts to refasten their stays.

Priapism of another sort was unavoidable elsewhere in public parks with the installation of defensive artillery guns. In Victoria Park in East London, the suffragette Sylvia Pankhurst addressed anti-conscription meetings in the shadow of such weaponry. Soon enough, these gained neighbours in the form of rows of runner beans and cabbages. Park landscapes throughout the war and across Britain rapidly acquired a contrary mix of vegetable fecundity and destructive firepower.

One of the earliest, and perhaps most potent, illustrations of battle-station Britain was seen in 1915, when the lake of St James's Park was drained – for some, as much of an affront to regal London as losing the ravens from the Tower. However, it was feared that the water would serve as an obvious pointer for aerial bombardment of Whitehall, so it was siphoned off and the lake filled in with a row of grey, two-storeyed concrete buildings. Conveniently close to the Admiralty, they were used to house offices for the Shipping Controller and his staff.

But while the topography was certainly changing, bands continued to play in most parks in the capital. And well they might, since the London County Council had only just equipped Battersea and Brockwell, Clissold, Finsbury and Southwark Parks with 'facilities for dancing in connection with the band performances'. Still, the council had to disband its own crack group of musicians for the duration of the war as the players enlisted or were conscripted. The band was never to reassemble again, as it turned out. In fact, probably due to the loss of brass players and drummers to the services, the park concerts that did continue throughout the conflict frequently consisted 'chiefly of vocal items provided by small Pierrot troops'.

Those fixtures of coastal resorts, as essential an ingredient of the Edwardian seaside as Mr Punch, cockles and a turn on the pier, Pierrots were first imported from French pantomime in the 1890s by the banjo player and impresario Clifford Essex. Essex simply lifted their clownish get-up (white make-up, ruff-necked tunics, bobbly hats and baggy pants) for his busking musical ensemble, wowing crowds at Henley Regatta, Ryde and Sandown on the Isle of Wight, and launching a craze for pale-faced crooners on British beaches that lingered until the 1950s. With their Gallic roots and seaside associations, though, these shows must have given London parkgoers pause for thought. No matter how cheering their songs, favourite cockney watering places such as Southend had been on the receiving end of Zeppelin raids, while across the Channel slaughter on an unimaginable scale continued in the fields of France.*

Peace, when it came, was signed in a park of sorts, at the Palace of Versailles and in full view of that most elaborate garden. This peace, it was hoped, would augur an end to all wars, and in the aftermath of it all, the town planners and park-makers would carry on trying to build a happier, greener world.

---

* On the fiftieth anniversary of the outbreak of the Great War, Joan Littlewood chose to dress the cast of her satirical musical *Oh! What a Lovely War* in Pierrot costumes for its opening theatrical run in Stratford.

CHAPTER 7

At Swim Model Boats

While peace was supposed to augur an end to all wars, ensure future prosperity and reconfigure the world along fairer lines, immediately after the Great War the picture in Britain, as elsewhere, was mixed in the extreme. On the one hand, there was a desire to return to things as they had been before the horrors of the conflict. The Austro-Hungarian Empire was done for and good riddance, London porter might be as pale and weak as water these days and, to add insult to injury, the pubs might now continue to shut in the afternoons for the foreseeable future. But old standards and old ways of being, some argued, had to be maintained for the good of the country. Otherwise a revolution, like the one in Russia, could well ensue.

But there was a counter-current to this. The public were now confronted with the sight of the maimed, blinded and shell-shocked returning from the trenches. Indeed, parks began to make special accommodation for these returning wounded, one of the most poignant additions after the war being a blind persons' recreation ground at Heaton, the first of its kind to be instituted in any British municipal park. Meanwhile, at the request of the Ministry of Agriculture and as part of a scheme to help them gain employment, 140 disabled soldiers were taught horticultural and agricultural skills at Carrington in Manchester, the municipal nursery where plants were grown for all of the city's parks and recreation grounds. Elsewhere, the war's devastating effects were visible in the complete absence of young men of a certain age in some towns and villages, their names written in stone on the war memorials in market squares and parks. The result was that some of the living felt they almost had a responsibility to live as fully as possible and so a certain kind of reckless excess was one response to the carnage. Cocktails and the hectic, nervy, parties of the Bright Young Things; love woven into mad jazz patterns, suede shoes, beaded dresses – these were all affirmations of the sheer vitality of the life and youth so cruelly denied to others.

Parks were to mirror these seemingly conflicting currents in British society in the interwar years. While self-improving developments instigated under the Victorians flourished, so did more liberal and fun-loving scenes, and a gander at the nation's public parks found the British boating, running, playing hockey, bowls and golf, swimming, concert-going and dancing. And, crucially, it wasn't just the men who were having all the fun.

The early post-war period certainly didn't seem to fulfil the optimistic expectations that had greeted the Armistice. The global influenza pandemic that coincided with the end of the war is estimated to have claimed the lives of over 50 million people. There was also the issue of wide-scale unemployment in Britain.

In largely rural areas the war had actually helped stall decades of decline in farming, with wheat production in Britain up 60 per cent from before 1914. To ensure that productivity continued, in 1917 the government passed the Corn Production Act guaranteeing farmers against losses for the next five years and later fixing minimum wages for farm workers through an Agricultural Wages Board. But an increase in acreage eventually led to a glut on the market. With prices plummeting, the government was forced to abandon its subsidies and unemployment in farming and manufacturing across the nation rocketed almost simultaneously. By 1920 over a million were without work. A large proportion were veterans who'd returned home from the front only to find they were surplus to requirements on a civvy street that had no further need of riflemen outside of fairgrounds or pheasant shoots.

In Norwich, joblessness was judged so acute that the council convened a General Purposes Committee 'to consider and expedite all schemes of work which can be put in hand or facilitated with the object of relieving the unemployment' in the city. At that time some 7,000 people were classed as unemployed, with another 1,040 on short time and 1,500 married men and 1,200 single men registered for relief work. Another 500 were already engaged on Corporation relief work and a further 220 on what the local Board of Guardians opaquely termed 'test work' – some sort of means-tested allocation of odd jobs around the place.

One of the proposals run up the flagpole and saluted by the committee at its sessions was to expand and improve the provision of public parks. As with the Victorians when confronted with massive unemployment around the Queen's Golden Jubilee in 1887, this struck the committee as an ideal means of supplying work for those without gainful employment.

But more and better parks were also needed, as Norwich was oozing far and wide out of its ancient medieval burrow and even beyond its nineteenth-century satellites. Once-outlying villages like Earlham and Eaton were being absorbed into the city, as meadows fell to the suburban housing brickwork of the Coleman Road estate and its ilk. Bluebell Lane, whose main traffic had once been cows and geese, gave way to a Bluebell Road, a rather less floral artery of asphalt. This pattern was common around the country, as those with the means – and those

fortunate enough to be in work in this era in fact saw their wages rise, their hours fall and their spending power increase – chose to vacate older urban centres for outer boroughs and their off-the-shelf dream homes with decent plumbing and electric lighting. This drift from the centre was accelerated by local councils which, under government recon-struction plans, cleared slums and relocated their former inhabitants in newly built estates. Often these emulated the Garden City ideal and were in former areas of open country, such as Becontree in Essex, which from 1921 became home to London County Council's largest scheme.

The private motor car, the plaything of a few Mr Toads with enough spare change to pay for horseless horsepower before the war, and the more democratic petrol-engined taxi, coach and omnibus were perhaps the crucial catalysts in all of this. Where there had been 132,000 cars in Britain in 1914, there were 314,769 by 1922. Four years after that, the figure had more than doubled, to 778, 056, and would top a million in 1930. Redrawing the maps of villages, towns and whole cities as they shrank journey times and the sense of distance, the ever-increasing tyre tracks of motorised transport led to a good deal of inking in of gaps between once distinct places, both geographically and imaginatively. But especially between cities and their outer boroughs, which now began to merge.* As the cities spread themselves out, though, their populations did not diminish. Between 1921 and 1931, the percentage of the British population living in cities rose from 30.4 per cent to 31.4 per cent. Consequently, there were now calls for parks in areas outside the obvious city centre.

As in the wake of the Crimea a little over half a century before, among the other issues the First World War had raised was, once again, the fitness, or lack of it, of the ordinary British working population. Famously, some conscripted privates were as much as a foot shorter than their public-school-educated commanding officers and so weedy and undernourished that many quickly gained weight, and, among the youngest, even inches in height, on army rations.

Just as the Victorians had thought one solution might be to get the working man out into the park and playing structured games, in the aftermath of the Great War several leading figures from the military called on the government to provide funds for more open spaces for vigorous exercise and team pursuits. An increase in their provision was a matter of national security, in the event of another war, as much as national health, or so the argument went. Most notable in this campaign was Brigadier-General Reginald J. Kentish, a former commander and British representative on the International Olympic Committee.

---

* Road building would itself form another, and quite major, component of government works programmes in the interwar down times, particularly moving into the early 1930s.

In 1925, Kentish was to found the National Playing Fields Association and started lobbying for an 'Open Spaces Standard' of five acres per 1,000 head of population. Of those five acres, four were to be dedicated to physical recreation, with only a single acre left for ornamental grounds or gardens for shirkers, ex-conchies, the elderly and the infirm, and other miscellaneous flower-sniffers too lazy for competitive sports. These targets were never realised, nor even officially adopted, but they were widely cited with approval by MPs and town councillors on the stump. Further impetus, and actual hard cash, for the laying out of more playing fields was eventually to come nearly ten years later from the George V Memorial Fund, the late king having seen sports as generally an admirable thing. He was, for instance, a fan of tennis and personally boosted the standing of the game after the war by attending Wimbledon, with Queen Mary, in 1919. (At least, according to that version of history where nothing really happened without a regal seal of approval, one then faithfully relayed to the world at large by Fleet Street and adopted en masse by an ever grateful populace.)

Up and down the country, councils took the National Playing Fields Association's message to heart. In Manchester the council used up to 1,200 men from the local Labour Exchanges to help build new sporting facilities. In Norwich, the man tasked with making similar improvements was Captain Arnold Edward Sandys-Winsch. Born in Knutsford, Cheshire and describing himself as 'none too bright at school', Sandys-Winsch nevertheless won a scholarship to Cheshire Horticultural and Agricultural College in 1905. There he earned a gold medal for research into botany and entomology, and, after working for a time at the Royal Horticultural Garden at Wisley, completed his articles under T. H. Mawson and Sons – Mawson proving the foremost influence on his own park work. Already a territorial, he was 'called to colours' in June 1914, serving first in the Royal Field Artillery, then as a fighter pilot in the Royal Flying Corps and, finally, in the Army of Occupation.

In sepia photographs of him in uniform, oxygen-choking, high-knotted tie and snug-as-you-like khaki, Sandys-Winsch appears tight-lipped, with pale, watery, somewhat glassy eyes, a thin, straight nose but extraordinarily flared nostrils, and almost eyebrow-less, his possibly naturally curly hair tamed by the regimental short back and sides and a good dose of oil. Officer-class tall, he seems never to have lost his military bearing, remaining stiff-backed and, with staff and the public alike, always rather severe from the moment he signed on as Norwich's Parks and Gardens Superintendent a few months after being demobbed in June 1919 until he retired in 1953. A motorcycle rider in the mode of T. E. Lawrence – fearless, the wind in that oily hair, eyes shielded by goggles but head helmetless – he instantly cut a dash in a still sleepy East Anglian metropolis having to deal with the abrupt fallout from the war.

The city's General Purpose Committee demanded four new parks from Sandys-Winsch, and in line with the National Playing Fields Association, they wanted ample tennis courts, bowling greens and cricket pitches. He supplied them, designing the Eaton, Waterloo, Wensum and Heigham Parks between 1921 and 1933, all of which were laid out with the aid of unemployed labour. At Wensum, the land had been purchased by the city council in 1907 with the aim of building a swimming pool, but was then co-opted for a rubbish dump. From the spring of 1921, and labouring for over 122 weeks, twenty-five previously unemployed men levelled the ground and equipped the park with lush greens and a formal paddling pool, although this feature was ultimately appropriated by ducks. Similarly herculean efforts changed the 6 acres of waste ground at Heigham into a positively Olympian spread of tennis courts, bowling greens and 'space for casual unorganised games'; a rock garden was added, too, and a cast-iron pavilion originally hailing from Philadelphia. But Heigham, which opened in 1924, was modest in comparison with Eaton and Waterloo.

Eaton was certainly the grandest. The former gardens of an old manorial hall, it had spent the Great War as a training ground for trench warfare for soldiers bound for Flanders and Picardy. After that it played host to the Royal Norfolk Show, agriculture and livestock replacing infantry and war games. But other than that annual event, the site, long promised to the city as a park, was left largely alone, grass unkempt and going boggy, until new roads and housing reached its perimeter in the early 1920s. It was then that Sandys-Winsch was given the go-ahead by the council to make something more of it. The ratepayer's coin was once again to be augmented by substantial government employment grants, and Sandys-Winsch was able to assemble a crack company of 103 men. Construction of the park took over three and a half years, not far off the entire duration of the Great War itself, and was conducted as a well-drilled campaign. The final results would be epic, triumphal, clean-sweep, geometric, orderly to the nth degree. With spacious radiating avenues, a circular formal garden and a fountain, a domed bandstand and monumental quadrant pavilions in cream stone and neoclassical formation, it could plausibly have been mustered by the legions of Imperial Rome. A Maciste sword-and-sandal silent could have been shot on the terraces by the lake. Mussolini, you slightly fear, might have felt quite at home here in the 1920s, sitting on a bench, leafing through Dante, and recalling de Chirico's phrase, *Pictor classicus sum*. This was plain monumental where his mentor Mawson's Arts and Crafts-infused essays were merely extravagant.

Even the model boating lake, with its balustraded clubhouse fit for an Indian raja, seems so generous in size it might just be taken as parodying the sports it was intended for, making the wee craft appear tinier than ever. But perhaps its scale reflected the significance of this sport locally. A prominent Norwich clergyman, the Reverend John Callis, had first urged the council to build a model boating lake in a letter to the local press in 1908, stating that the hobby was a 'healthy interest' and one ideally suited to 'the potentially disaffected City youngster'. Whatever the validity of his claims for model boating as a cure for urban juvenile delinquency, the article resulted in a petition that received over 800 signatures and was presented to the city council with the support of several eminent citizens. Today, on every Sunday from Easter until autumn, you can still watch a miniature four-steam-turbine HMS *Norfolk* glide across the lake in her battleship grey, convincingly detailed with top deck, funnels and lifeboats, when the model boating club meets.

Intriguingly, the oldest continuous model boat club in the world is in London's Victoria Park – the Victoria Park Model Steam Boat Club dating from 1904.* Shortly after that its coffers were bolstered by a £1 donation by Horatio Bottomley, the Liberal MP for Hackney South. Bottomley was also the founder of the *Financial Times*, and a serial fraudster who narrowly avoided conviction for falsely inflating share prices in its pages. Subsequently bankrupted by debt, he had to stand down as an MP, but bounced back at the outbreak of the First World War when *John Bull*, his virulently anti-German patriotic newspaper, enjoyed an astronomic rise in sales. Trousering huge sums while speaking at dozens of recruiting rallies, and encouraging possibly thousands to step towards their deaths in the trenches, he was finally convicted and jailed in 1922 for promoting a bogus Victory Bonds banking scheme.

The boat enthusiasts of Norwich would have to wait much longer than their London counterparts, of course. They would have to sit patiently for twenty years after submitting their original petition back in 1908 until Eaton Park with its lake was opened to the public. It was perhaps just as well the lake was as capacious and grand as it was: the pent-up demand of Norwich boaters must have been immense after such a delay. Elsewhere in the park, other games had also been given serious room to flourish, with well-proportioned pitches for football and cricket, tennis courts and bowling greens. And given the generous outlay on such facilities and the general architectural pomp, it seems especially fitting that when Eaton Park was officially opened in 1928 it was high royalty, in the shape of the Prince of Wales – the future King Edward VIII – who cut the ribbon.

---

* Within six years of the club's founding, Victoria Park gained another (now lost) pint-sized attraction, when it received the gift of a miniature garden from the Mayor of Tokyo. Created by the Yokohama Nursery Company and first displayed at a Japanese–British exhibition at Shepherd's Bush, it measured nine by four feet and was mounted on a trolley that could be wheeled outside for people to admire it on fine days.

At the ceremony, the Prince, who'd earlier attended Royal Norfolk Shows on the same site, saluted Eaton Park as a scheme that provided 'a great slice of the country almost in the middle of a great city'. The Prince's presence at the opening of a park which aimed to improve the common lot along really quite Victorian lines is particularly interesting, given that he, in many ways, instantiated this interwar era's escape from Victorian and Edwardian proprieties in matters of manners, morals and style. Though, of course, not everyone got the chance to launch a transatlantic liner, dally with American divorcees or sleep with diplomats' wives after cocktails at the Embassy on globe-trekking state junkets.

Still, here was a man who would one day choose life over the stuffy duty of pre-war tradition, and swathes of the public were now seized by a similar spirit of *carpe diem*. A shift in social mores was beginning, and it was particularly evident in the new trends of concert-going and dancing. Whereas a waltz was the pinnacle of Edwardian foot-stepping and the foxtrot in the 1910s judged almost terrifyingly erotic, if not an outright aberration by some, peacetime dance floors pounded to young couples doing the Black Bottom, the tango, the Charleston and the Missouri Walk. American-style ragtime and jazz was now to see off German and Austrian oompah as the soundtrack for even high-society gatherings. In public parks, too, the craze for syncopation could not be ignored, and it began to affect the topography. For example, in 1921 and starting at Platt Fields, Manchester City Council began introducing new 'sunken' bandstands to its parks and expanding enclosures for dancing. In many parks the areas beside bandstands previously occupied by seats were simply colonised by eager dancers, much as Teddy boys would one day rip up cinema seats to frug to 'Rock Around the Clock'.

In 1921, the Hull councillor Archibald Stark and Mr Witty, the city's
Parks Superintendent, were considering calls from the public to install
a dance floor in the East Park, and went on fact-finding missions to
Woodhouse Moor, Wortley and Armley in nearby Leeds to inspect the
facilities there. At Armley, the floor in the park was 'of asphalt', and
thought likely to be 'very rough and destructive to boots'. Wortley's
was of concrete and 'better than Armley but not very smooth'. But
none of these park floors, they reported, had originally been intended
for dancing; they had just been adopted for the purpose by resourceful
Leeds folk. Admirable as the visiting councillors found this, Hull, they
argued, deserved better. If budget constraints forced them to abandon
plans for a wood and mosaic floor, they eventually spent £584 on laying
a specifically designed asphalt floor in the park in 1925. It wasn't perfect,
though the enjoyment of it, locals later remembered, far 'outweighed
the crudity of the surface'.

Full dance bands, like classical orchestras, did not come cheap
and just three years after the installation of its new dance floor the
East Park began experimenting with using gramophone players for

recitals and dance concerts.* Messrs B. Cooke & Son, a local iron-monger and scientific instrument maker, would go on to supply them with an 'Igranophone' player and four moving coil loudspeakers and a microphone for amplifying music. By 1929, the East Park had hosted forty-three 'Igranophone concerts'. The impeccably named Mr Marshall, 'one of the key men in the greenhouses', seemingly proved the most skilled operator of the new electric-amplification equipment. Equipment that with its cranking handle, needles and all too easily breakable shellac 78 r.p.m. records, probably really did need to be tended to as lovingly as any budding seed or hothouse flower. Accordingly, his rota was adjusted to accommodate his new duties, for which he was also rewarded with overtime rates. What local working musicians, or his colleagues, forced to cover his green-house shifts, made of this is not recorded.

However, not every innovation in park entertainment was accepted quite so easily. Forays into staging costumed concert party shows in some of Manchester's parks in 1921 were challenged by the trade body for proprietors of entertainment venues, who accused the parks department of muscling in on their turf and breaking rules that limited council expenditure to bands of instrumentalists only. After nearly two years of legal wrangling, the parks department was granted special powers under the Manchester Corporation Act of 1924 to stage such concerts, and singing and dancing by Dinky Doos-style troupes, each with a little Jessie Matthews to call their own, resumed. The presence of such female voices on stages and bandstands once dominated by all-male brass and military bands perhaps best sums up the democratic mindset of the more progressive municipals of this era.

* London was slightly ahead in this. In 1924, the LCC recorded that some eighty performances were made in its parks 'by mechanical means'.

It was really women, with their refusal to give up the liberty they'd enjoyed during the war, who made the most of these new parks and sports grounds. During the war itself, the Ministry of Agriculture had persuaded park departments to employ young women to take the place of male gardeners lost to the services. In 1916, at Heaton Park in Manchester, around fifty women were trained as gardeners over a six-week period and then sent on to fill vacancies at other parks up and down the county, retaining their positions until the men returned at the end of the war. If they lost those jobs in 1918, the war had shown that many of the spurious arguments previously advanced about the unfitness of women for certain kinds of work, or the hazardousness of athletic exertion to their heath, were palpably false. Much more disturbing for some was that, in comparison with many of the men who came back from the trenches, young women were often self-evidently in better shape, fitter and healthier.

Still, the post-war years would see the first bill enshrining female suffrage, the campaign for which had been waged with lively rallies in public parks, such as Sylvia Pankhurst's Women's May Day in Victoria Park in 1913, a demonstration that met with violent opposition from the police. Five years later, the Representation of the People Act granted women over thirty the vote, as long as they owned sufficient property. Universal suffrage, for women over twenty-one, would not come until ten years later. Elsewhere, British women's horizons and options were widened further by reading the likes of Marie Stopes's book on sex, *Married Love*, and by winning greater access to birth control. Meanwhile, parks were no longer merely a place for genteel promenading along set paths with a parasol. Like the Lyons corner houses, they were now places where emancipated women of all classes felt at ease to go alone. And, more importantly, to be left alone in, as the parks were, for the most part, safe civic spaces, patrolled during the day by keepers and gardeners.

There were, in any case, simply more lone women about. Another legacy of the war was what Fleet Street – in response to the 1921 census, which revealed that there were 1,702, 802 more females than males in the population – termed the 'Problem of Surplus Women': a problem it explored with sensitivity and tact in articles such as 'Two Million who can never Become Wives'. The eventual figure for this generation was about half that, with a million remaining unmarried and childless. But not all of these women regretted being left on the shelf, as Fleet Street might have put it. Far from it. Many middle-class women were relieved to be spared unwelcome matches, and legions, like the acquaintances of Muriel Spark's Miss Jean Brodie, chose to crowd 'their war-bereaved spinsterhood with voyages of discovery into new ideas and energetic practices in art or social welfare, education or religion'. For others, getting on with earning a living and remaining self-sufficient was enough. This was just possible for those who had positions as secretaries, teachers, governesses, superior domestics and nurses. Inequities in rates of pay and pensions (teaching, for example) didn't always make that easy, with men presumed to have a family to support earning more, even if they performed the same job.

In the late 1930s, Hyde Park witnessed a rally by the National Spinsters' Pensions Association for improvements to women's working and retirement conditions. The park was something of a hub of female solidarity in London, since it was usually crowded with nannies and their charges. According to Jonathan Gathorne-Hardy's book, *The Rise and Fall of the British Nanny*, they were at their zenith in the park in the 1920s and '30s – the era, incidentally, when P. L. Travers's first *Mary Poppins* book appeared. 'Thronging, drifting, sitting, rocking',

FRESH AIR
IN LONDON'S PARKS

Hyde Park   Kensington Gardens

Regent's Park   St. James's Park.

TRAVEL THERE BY

UNDERGROUND

they were, apparently, 'more numerous than the buffalo upon the plain, more talkative than starlings at a moot'.

Another hallmark of the age, perhaps in response to the ravaged flesh of those who had returned from the front, was a new cult of fitness and physical beauty. This revolved around taking exercise, eating healthily and living more hygienically thanks to the latest breakthroughs in medical and domestic science, which included the discovery of insulin and penicillin.* The Olympics were the ultimate embodiment of this new cult. And though Germany and Austria were barred, it was with potent symbolism that the first Olympic Games after the war were staged in Antwerp in 1920. From Flanders fields, the Games, by extension, implied, a fitter world had to arise. A world fit for heroes, sporting and military.

British sportswomen, however, would not represent their country at the Olympics until 1932, their male contemporaries and Brigadier-General Reginald J. Kentish (with his IOC hat on now) voting against their inclusion before then. For the most part, in fact, athletics remained something of a boys' club, and largely the preserve of chaps from the universities, the army, the civil service and the City. Illustratively, at Victoria Park in East London, the resurfacing and railing off of a pre-war cinder running track and the erection of decent changing rooms in 1926 attracted City boys, not locals – the financial men finding the park a convenient bus or train ride from Liverpool or Broad Street stations and the Square Mile. That same year these hearty fellows formed the Victoria Park Harriers at the Mitford Castle Tavern on Cadogan Terrace facing the park and right beside Victoria Park station. But the lads were to face some stiff competition from the recently established Women's Amateur Athletics Association.

---

* Though penicillin was discovered in 1928 it wasn't actually used to treat infections until the 1940s.

The arrival of such sporting organisations was symptomatic of the general expansion of leisure activities for women in the period. Thanks to smaller families and Marie Stopes's first family-planning clinic for 'married women' in Holloway in 1921, more manageable homes and the arrival of such labour-saving marvels as electric cookers and vacuum cleaners by Hoover and Electrolux, middle-class women, at least, had more time to devote to leisure interests: bridge, flower-arranging à la Constance Spry, and learning German, if Muriel Spark is to be believed. Or solving murders, if the fiction of Agatha Christie is to be believed too. And if Miss Marple is the archetypical querulous spinster, Christie's novels also teem with often quite butch sporting women. The gruff-voiced Emily Brewster in *Evil Under the Sun*, an avid rower described, distastefully by an author who herself enjoyed surfing, as 'a tough athletic type', is a classic example.

Although some private clubs excluded women, facilities in public parks were, at least in principle, open to all. It's worth noting that shortly after Rock Park, Llandrindod was taken into council hands in 1926, women bowlers are first recorded as playing on its previously private and male-dominated greens. The ladies formed their own club in 1933 – and just in time to compete in the World Bowls Association's National Championships staged that year in Rock Park.

In tennis, meanwhile, the 'old school brigade' might continue to dominate the All England Club and Wimbledon. That, certainly, was the opinion of Fred Perry, the son of a Labour MP who picked up the game on communal courts in the 'Co-partnership' Garden Suburb of Brentham in Ealing. At Wimbledon in 1930, Baron de Morpurgo, the Trieste-born tennis-playing aristocrat, was so outraged by being beaten by a working-class upstart like Perry that, instead of shaking his hand at the net, as gentlemanly protocol demanded, he slapped him in the face. But less silver-spoon-fed admirers of the sport – who from 1922 flocked to Wimbledon's new 14,000-seater stadium and from 1927 could listen to broadcasts of the championship from the BBC – were finding it easier than ever to play in local parks. By 1924, the parks department of the London County Council provided some 725 public courts. And whereas Manchester City Council possessed just 111 courts in its public parks and recreation grounds in 1918, ten years later their numbers had swelled to 418, of which 313 were 'hard courts' surfaced with shale. The firm of Grassphalte, who produced the 'Grassphalte Green Hard Tennis Court', supplied many local authorities with these courts.

Always considered one of the more 'respectable' forms of outdoor exercise for women, tennis also offered a way of mixing with eligible males decently. And in an era when some women were determined to not remain surplus, and staying trim had become a social asset, tennis boomed in popularity among the so-called 'bachelor girls'.

Up till now, golf had been another largely exclusive sport, endorsed by the Prince of Wales and his fast set in their tweeds and loud checks, and by the new aristocracy of American tycoons, heiresses and Hollywood movie stars. Here again, British public parks gave women and men access to the sport. While it had supposedly been played on Blackheath Common since the time of James I, in 1923 the Royal Blackheath Club and its pitch 'moved into private links in the neighbourhood'. Rather adorably, the LCC responded the following year, extending 'the facilities for playing the game to Clapham, Streatham and Tooting Commons'. And while the council maintained a golf course and clubhouse out at Hainault Forest, it also laid out putting greens at Battersea Park, Golders Hill and Lincoln's Inn Fields. Fees were a modest 3 (old) pence for a round of eighteen holes. Again in Manchester, the only public park able to accommodate a full course was at Heaton, but by 1929 the council had installed nine putting greens in other municipal parks across the city. And on Captain Sandys-Winsch's watch a public course was established at Earlham in Norwich.

On courses like these, the office worker or the mill girl with a rented putter could indulge dreams of being a Fairway Flapper like Edith Cummings. The first woman athlete to grace the cover of *Time* magazine, Cummings was the model for Jordan Baker in *The Great Gatsby*. Fitzgerald's party-going, 'incurably dishonest' professional golfer was rumoured to have 'moved her ball from a bad lie in the semi-final round'. Scott Fitzgerald's Baker is painted as a thoroughly modern Millie with a 'cool, insolent smile' and a 'hard jaunty body'. But perhaps the most telling detail of her thrustingly up-to-date-ness in 1925 is that she has 'slender golden' arms. For while dawns might have been golden in the Victorian era, arms were expected to remain shrouded in cloth, and the preferred colour of a woman's complexion was somewhere between wan and deathly pale.

Much as thinness was once a sign of poverty, and plumpness a badge of affluence, rather than their opposites today, the tan had been disdained as a mark of low social status. Peasants, farmers, fishermen, travelling tinkers and tramps had tans. They worked outdoors, exposed to the elements, and with their hands. But with industrialisation having removed workers from the land, the tan gradually lost its association with manual labour and by the turn of the twentieth century was being touted by the medical profession as a possible cure for tuberculosis. Dr Auguste Rollier, an exponent of 'heliotherapy', or sun therapy, opened a TB clinic in the Swiss Alps in 1903. In the new century, Northern Europe came to be seen as cold and repressive when contrasted with the more honest, sexually liberated and earthier cultures of the Mediterranean and further south. The adoption in the 1920s of the French Riviera, previously a wintering spot for affluent, if often unwell, English aristocrats, as a summer bolt hole by artistically inclined, wealthy Americans, nudged sun-seeking and the suntan into vogue and, consequently, with the aid of Coco Chanel, on to the pages of *Vogue*.

Although having to contend with slightly chillier conditions, this cult of the sun found plenty of disciples in England. It invariably went hand in hand with bathing of the more aquatic kind. This despite *Vogue* warning its readers in 1923 that 'swimming' had 'a way of increasing the girth in an amazingly short time'. Swimming's popularity with women, however, received a boost in 1926, when the American Gertrude Ederle, crowned Queen of the Waves by the press, became the first woman to swim the English Channel.

In the public parks, men and boys had long been free to use the bathing lakes, but for women and girls, access had been limited – and where they were permitted access they were restricted to set hours and gender segregation was rigorously enforced. As indeed it had been on most beaches at seaside resorts into the Edwardian age.

In 1902, the London County Council had agreed, 'as an experiment', to allow women the sole use of the lake at Parliament Hill, Hampstead, on Wednesdays, 'subject to their wearing costumes approved by' the Amateur Swimming Association. In the following year, the council was asked to consider allowing bathing 'by both sexes all day at all bathing places subject to proper costumes being worn', but concluded that 'it would not be desirable at present to extend the existing facilities for bathing by men and women'. The municipality would gradually thaw on this issue, with women and girls by 1924 only forbidden to bathe at Clapham and Plumstead Commons, and mixed bathing in the Serpentine in Hyde Park, with new shore-side facilities named in honour of the Labour politician George Lansbury, permitted for the first time in 1930. Yet the council continued to obsess about what people could and could not wear, with the Amateur Swimming Association acting as the arbiter of acceptable costumes in London park pools. And their strictures didn't just apply to women.

Minutes from an LLC meeting in 1935 record a dim view being taken of a suggestion, from an organisation calling itself the Men's Dress Reform Party, that male bathers should be allowed to 'wear slips only at all times' (slips, presumably, swimming trunks). But a year later, they seemed to have relented somewhat, voting to allow men to 'bathe in short costumes in mixed bathing'.

In the end, technology helped soften the social attitude to mixed swimming. Costumes in the latest machine-knitted wool, such as the figure-hugging one-piece jobs produced by Jantzen, who marketed 'The Suit That Changed Bathing into Swimming', may have been skimpier than earlier outfits, but they made uninhibited movement far easier for women. High-waisted trunks for men, fashioned in similarly state-of-the-art materials, allowed the fellas to show off their athletic prowess without loss of decorum in company – though the LCC, obviously, reserved judgement on that.

But perhaps most important of all was the arrival of an entirely new breed of swimming pool, the achingly modern, if not outright *moderne*, lido. As a Pathé news film from 1934 put it, the lido 'added a new word to our language and a new recreation to our habits'; it noted, over images of skimpily clad bathing beauties, that people might now understand why 'lido had supplanted Ludo'. Largely sculpted in concrete as gleamingly white as a *Titanic*-sinking iceberg, their architectural form made swimming en masse appear almost clinically hygienic. Sir John Betjeman, for instance, reviewing the new concrete Empire Swimming Pool in Wembley by the architect Sir Owen Williams in 1934, astutely judged it as embodying 'what we stand for: machinery, mass production and physical health'.

Indeed, their art deco lines were so streamlined and futuristic that some of these open-air pools looked as if they'd crash-landed from a space adventure. And quite possibly one starring the Olympic bronze-medal-winning swimmer turned actor Buster Crabbe as Flash Gordon or Buck Rogers. A large percentage of lidos were built by the corporations of seaside towns (Hastings, Saltdean, Morecambe, Blackpool, New Brighton, Southend, Worthing), in a slightly coals-to-Newcastle fashion. Though that perhaps underlines their perceived superiority over a common-or-garden sea, where only thirty years earlier women wishing to preserve their decency had still entered after being wheeled down to the shore in a box.

But the London County Council, especially after Herbert Morrison assumed leadership in 1934, was among the most vigorous promoters of their creation in metropolitan public parks. This was part of

Morrison and the Labour Party's three-year 'Health for London' plan, which aimed to produce 'a London with fields right round it, with more parks and playgrounds and swimming pools than any other city in the world'. Brockwell Park, Tooting Bec, Victoria Park, Parliament Hill, London Fields, Kennington, Southwark Park, Charlton: the LCC catalogue, which finally ran to thirteen lidos in total, reads like an especially wayward bus route, but red-brick and shiny new concrete outdoor swimming facilities were now within easy reach of the capital's inhabitants. Commenting on the 200-feet-long pool in Victoria Park, which opened in 1936 and was capable of accommodating a thousand people, Dick Coppock, chair of the LCC's Parks Committee, spoke of bringing 'the seaside to East London' and maintained the lido was 'as good as Margate'.

But while the waters of the lido might run cool and still, more troubling political currents were being felt in Victoria Park. That June and July, Sir Oswald Mosley, a former Tory MP and Labour Cabinet minister turned leader of the British Union of Fascists, held rallies there. Figures vary from a few hundred to the hundreds of thousands touted by deluded neo-Nazis, but best estimates maintain that about 5,000 Mosleyites attended these fascist meetings. On both occasions his blackshirts faced spirited opposition from members of the Independent Labour Party, trade unionists and Jewish and communist organisations, and police on horseback had to intercede to keep the two groups apart. Following these rallies, Mosley announced his intention to lead a march of uniformed BUF members through the East End and 'the heart of the Jewish quarter' on Sunday 4 October. Their route from the Royal Mint to Shoreditch – where the blackshirts had their headquarters, and where their leader would stand for parliament for the very last time in the 1966 general election – was to skirt Victoria Park itself. But on the day, its progress of goons, newly costumed in black military-cut jackets, grey riding breeches and jackboots, was halted at Cable Street in Aldgate, where 'a crowd seized materials from a builder's yard and began to construct a barricade' using 'corrugated iron, barrels, coal, and glass ... and even pulling up paving-stones'.*

---

* An official statement by Scotland Yard and the Metropolitan Police implied that clement weather was to blame for the lively scenes across the capital, recording that: 'A Fascist assembly was held in the East End to-day, and largely owing to one of the finest days of the year, many people were attracted to it, including a large number of women and children.'

Two days later, Mosley was in Berlin, secretly marrying Diana Guinness née Mitford, the cousin of Winston Churchill, at the family home of Nazi propaganda chief Joseph Goebbels. Adolf Hitler, the guest of honour, gave the couple a photograph of himself in an eagle-topped frame as a wedding present. The couple were to spend the war behind bars, but not before one final appearance. On 5 May 1940, shortly before they were interned in Holloway Prison, Mosley gave his last public speech for the duration of the war at Victoria Park – a call for peace, no less. Film footage of the event, some nine months into the fight against Hitler, captures a depressingly large group of followers greeting him with fascist salutes as he moves under a canopy of trees. But public parks were now to give their all to yet another world war.

CHAPTER 8

A Patch of Air

The setting is London, 1942, Regent's Park, the first Sunday of September, and it is the opening of Elizabeth Bowen's novel *The Heat of the Day*. Bowen had been here before in her fiction, beginning another book, *The Death of the Heart*, published just before the war, in exactly the same location. Reflecting on the attraction of living near Regent's Park – which she did, residing at 2 Clarence Terrace NW1 for close to twenty years and throughout the war – Bowen once wrote that it seemed 'something out of (or in) a book' and that 'it did never wholly emerge from art'. Conversely, since *The Heat of the Day* contains a thinly veiled portrait of her own lover, Charles Ritchie, who claimed that Regent's Park was 'a landscape of love' for the couple during their affair, it could be said that her art never wholly emerged from life either. Which is not to its detriment by any means. The realities of a bomb-shabby Blitz-era London, personally experienced and deeply felt, supply the latter novel with its great verisimilitude.

In the first few pages of the book, published in 1948, the park is drawn on the cusp of autumn, with leaves on the turn, the light of a sunny cloudless day on the brink of going down. For the last few precious hours, this park, a dreamy realm of rose gardens, lawns and avenues, drifting leaves, quivering gnats and dissipating cigarette smoke, has provided 'the solution of somewhere to be' for the city's lonely and lost. As well as the bored and the amorous. A concert is now under way by a Viennese orchestra, perhaps the last of the season. Its repertoire of waltzes, marches and gay overtures is familiar and soothing, with its echo of earlier, more carefree times – if a haunting reminder of a whole Mitteleuropean civilisation then being blasted to hell and trampled under jackboots. The park at this moment, though, is said to be 'hourless': the music creates the illusion of a suspension of hostilities, even if the presence of Czech soldiers in uniform offers evidence to the contrary.

The war is revealed throughout the book by just such little additions and subtractions, with the absences as omnipresent as anything else. It is a city of missing buildings, the recently dead and those serving overseas. At a fruiterer's shop, a placard for the 'Dig for Victory' campaign sits on the shelves where produce should be. But Bowen's portrait of the park being used just like a park, regardless of the war, was true enough away from fiction. The apparent ability of Londoners and the inhabitants of other major British cities raided during the Blitz to blot out elements of the turmoil around them is never less than astonishing. As early as October 1939, for instance, edicts instructing the nation to carry their gas masks at all times were already being ignored in the capital. To do so was becoming so passé that that month one London park keeper complained he was jeered at by some cheeky urchins for carrying his. Statistics on commuters at Westminster Bridge bear this out, the 71 per cent of men and 76 per cent of women recorded as carrying gas marks shortly after war was declared in September falling to just 24 per cent and 39 per cent, respectively, by that November. In a diary entry for 31 August 1940, George Orwell records that an opinion was 'spreading rapidly that one ought simply to disregard the raids except when they are known to be big-scale ones and in one's own area', and by his calculation about half of those strolling about Regent's Park that day completely ignored the siren.

Orwell and his wife Eileen, by then living rather modestly in comparison with Bowen, in rooms in Chagford Street not far from the park, were woken later that same night by 'a tremendous crash said to be a bomb in Maida Vale'. It was, of course, impossible to avoid the war. Indeed, in a piece entitled 'London, 1940', Bowen wrote achingly about Regent's Park being penetrated by the war at the start of the Blitz. During an early German assault, an unexploded bomb landed just inside its perimeter gates, 'making a boil' in the tarmac of the roadway. With the park subsequently locked to the public, Bowen was left to peer in through the railings, and watched dahlias blaze out their colour, leaves fill empty deckchairs and water-fowl, used 'to so much attention, mope round the unpeopled rim of the lake'. One morning, however, she spotted a small boy on a bicycle who had managed to find a way in and was cycling around whistling 'It's a Happy, Happy Day'.

This defiantly cheery tune, issuing from the lips of a child who refused to be denied entrance to the park, whatever the dangers, was immediately picked up by the six soldiers digging out another bomb nearby. In the distance, Bowen could nevertheless hear disposal teams detonating incendiaries removed from a remote hinterland of the park. The pathos of a scene that combined absurd good humour and potentially horrific destruction led her to conclude she had 'no feelings to spare'.

Orwell's diaries provide, if by hearsay, further details of Bowen's unexploded Regent's Park bomb, which, he wrote on 27 September 1940, was 'said to be the size of a pillar box'. His own interests in the comings and goings of Regent's Park were not arbitrary. Having joined the district's Local Defence Volunteers, the forerunner of the Home Guard (the real life Dad's Army of those excluded by age or physical infirmity from giving their military all elsewhere), he was involved in drills in the park. In her wartime memoir *It Was Different at the Time*, his friend and future lover Inez Holden describes her spirits being raised by the sight of a ragtag squad of Home Guard volunteers in Regent's Park one misty day in August 1941. She does not record if Orwell was among the ranks, but does note that a middle-aged man wearing pince-nez was playing a harmonica, others were singing and that two of the company 'looked very young', and the whole thing felt like 'a mirage'.

The home-guarding Orwell, in one particularly grumpy diary entry of June 1942, admits despair at the lack of direction from high command with regard to his platoon's well-intentioned attempts to dig a series of trenches in Regent's Park 'in case airborne troops' landed there. With memories of the Western Front still raw, such trenches in the capital's public parks and in other major cities were often among the first works undertaken following the outbreak of war. Sections of Hyde Park were excavated to a depth of 40 feet in the opening months of conflict, and the kind of deckchairs Bowen observed accumulating leaves in the locked Regent's Park were banned on the grounds that they might impede the access of military vehicles. Rumours, like weeds, were another thing that spread in the Blitz, and the story that the Hyde Park trenches were intended to serve as makeshift graves after raids proved surprisingly persistent – a company in Willesden supposedly supplying the park with cardboard coffins. Hyde, like Regent's Park, also suffered bomb damage, though seemingly no direct fatalities, unlike Victoria Park, where an old man and a small boy were killed while out walking. One blast in Hyde Park, in an area known as the Dell, uncovered a water conduit for the old Palace of Whitehall dating back to the days of Edward the Confessor.

Demand for sand to fill hessian-sack defensive bags led to diggers turning a section of Hampstead Heath into 'a miniature Cheddar Gorge' by the autumn of 1939, in the words of one contemporary observer. Hampstead's newly exposed geological forms, in their opinion, offered a rich vista of 'warm lines of ochre, orange and red'.

Along with excavations, parks were made battle-ready by additional defences. St James's Park was studded with brick and cement blocks intended to inconvenience hostile tanks. But its lake – unlike during the previous war – was only partially drained, as civil defence officers argued that the water was an essential resource for firefighters. The Pen Ponds at Richmond Park, however, were drained, supposedly to prevent German seaplanes landing, though they surely always had the option of the nearby Thames.

Of all the acres of Britain obliterated during the Luftwaffe's bombing campaign, perhaps no city suffered such a single catastrophic assault as Coventry on the night of 14 November 1940. A significant centre of manufacturing, its car plants and aeronautical factories had rapidly been turned over to the production of munitions, armoured vehicles, and planes for the RAF. But despite its importance to the war effort, the city was relatively poorly defended, and when the Germans came on that cloudless November night, a full moon shining (the raid was meticulously planned to coincide with the lunar cycle when there would be more light to guide the bombers, and codenamed Operation Moonlight Sonata), not a single plane was brought down by its anti-aircraft guns. After thirteen hours of continuous bombing over 75 per cent of the buildings in the city were destroyed. The ancient St Michael's Cathedral was a hollow wreck with only part of its tower left standing. Emissaries from the Mass Observation organisation who visited Coventry the following day described the city as being in a state of collective nervous breakdown. Firefighters and policemen, often powerless to do much to improve the situation, were attacked while attempting to perform their duties. The 50 per cent fortunate enough to retain their homes were without gas, water or electricity.

Just a few days earlier, the annual Remembrance Day commemorations for the First World War had gone ahead at the city's Memorial Park, which had opened in 1921 as a garden of remembrance for the lost. Remembrance Day would be observed throughout the war, and during the 1939 commemorations there must have been a despondent atmosphere, as eleven days earlier Coventry Corporation had announced its intention to plough up 2 acres of land in the park – fairground and flower beds to be superseded by plots for growing food. (Most of that growing, as detailed in an article in the *Coventry Telegraph* headed 'Doing a Man's Job', would eventually be done by one of the Corporation's new 'lady gardeners'.)

More of a mark on the park's topography was made in early 1941, when, too late to do anything about Operation Moonlight Sonata, sixty-four permanent rocket guns were installed, each manned every night for the next two years by eight platoons. Meanwhile, the pavilion was converted into a radar station.* Coventry, of course, wasn't alone in gaining such artillery, and was a little late to the party. London parks had had their hulking great anti-aircraft guns from the outset. The sound of the city's battery was so familiar that, in the vein of exiled German birdsong expert Ludwig Koch on the BBC, Harold Nicolson, then heading the Ministry of Information, set down his attempts to identify the different gun sounds of the parks in his wartime diaries. 'There is,' he wrote, 'the distant drumfire of the outer batteries. There is the nearer crum-crum of the Regent Park guns. Then there is the drone of aeroplanes and the sharp impertinent notes of some nearer batteries. FF-oopb! they shout. And then in the middle distance there is the rocket sound of the heavy guns in Hyde Park. One gets to love them, these angry London guns.'

Love them or not, they became as familiar to Londoners as the chimes of Big Ben, which though silenced for two years in the previous conflict, continued to bong as bombs rained down. But these guns weren't always Londoners' friends. For instance, the installation of a new type of rocket launcher in Victoria Park in the spring of 1943 is widely believed to have helped cause the worst civilian catastrophe of the war: the Bethnal Green Tube Disaster. Construction of the station had begun in the late 1930s as part of a new eastern extension of the Central Line, but with the outbreak of war it was halted, and the still Tube- and trackless tunnels were adopted, initially against Whitehall mandarins' wishes, as a shelter by the people of the East End. Able

---

* After the war, stones from the ruined cathedral would subsequently furnish the park with the material for a new rockery, itself ringed by freshly planted memorial trees.

to accommodate some 5,000 people underground, the Tube station eventually grew into a miniature subterranean town, with a hospital, a library, a canteen, chemical toilets and its tunnels lined with thousands of bunk beds. Theatrical shows and even wedding parties were staged down there. For locals the drill had become as familiar as Harry 'I'm Henry the Eighth, I am' Champion's music-hall act.

On the night of 3 March 1943, and with warnings of a potential Luftwaffe bombing run, hundreds processed to the Tube station and made their way underground as usual. At 8.17 p.m. the air-raid siren sounded, bringing more people to the station. Once there, they had to negotiate its single entrance and the nineteen steps that led to a landing stage. There were then a further seven steps to reach the ticket hall and the escalators, which led to the platform and tunnels 80 feet below.

Whether there were enemy aircraft in the area remains a matter of official dispute, but at 8.27 p.m. an anti-aircraft unit stationed inside Victoria Park, roughly half a mile away from the Tube, started firing rockets into the sky. It was using a completely new type of Z-battery ammunition that had never been fired in the area before. According to Alf Morris – then a twelve-year-old schoolboy, present at the Tube station that evening – there was 'a great whoosh' unlike anything they'd heard previously. Morris recalled people started screaming, 'It's a bomb!'

Panic broke out, and in the frenzy to get underground a woman carrying a baby and her bedding apparently tripped on the steps down from the ticket hall to the platform, triggering a domino effect of people falling on top of one another. Morris, pinned to a concrete wall, was lucky enough to be pulled to safety, but in the ensuing melee 173 people, mostly women and children, died of asphyxiation. It is a bitter irony that the park which was created to provide East Enders with a patch of healthful green on their doorsteps should be implicated in this disaster.

From October 1939, the government had been issuing kits for Anderson shelters free of charge to all households earning less than £250 a year. Named after Sir John Anderson, the then Home Secretary, these shelters were designed to resist a 50kg bomb. But they could only be installed in homes with a garden large enough to accommodate them, something few Bethnal Green residents possessed, hence their reliance on the Tube station. Herbert Morrison, former head of the LCC and Anderson's successor in Churchill's wartime Cabinet, would also give his name to a shelter – the Morrison, an iron-and-wire mesh table-like contraption that could be used inside more modest homes. He also stepped up the building of other public shelters in public parks and recreation grounds, some of brick and lime, but others of the trench-and-concrete-tunnel variety, such as those installed at Edmonton's Jubilee Park.

While additions were being made to the parks, other elements were vanishing. Whereas Bowen had been able to peer through the railings at the out-of-bounds Regent's Park in September 1940, such spiky decorative ironmongery – once memorably described by Jonathan Raban as 'giving the Empire teeth' – was already receiving its call-up papers elsewhere. The Braintree and Bocking Public Gardens gener-ously sacrificed to the munitions works an exquisite set of encircling light-wrought railings provided for the park at its founding in 1888 by local manufacturer Francis Henry Crittall. Crittall, whose Essex firm would go on to establish the first steel plant in America (in Detroit in 1907), and whose name became synonymous with a type of steel-framed window used in ocean-liner-inspired modernist houses, had not only supplied the railings, he'd also sorted out the food for the park's opening banquet. The Crittalls, somewhat unusually, dividing their high-Victorian energies between engineering and catering for 'ball suppers, wedding breakfasts, garden parties and public luncheons'.

However, a pair of Crittall's park gates escaped the drive for scrap metal at the Braintree and Bocking Gardens (though they would, in time, fall to post-war improvements). For some reason, this seems to have been quite common practice during the war – fences going to scrap, but gates left standing. Following the removal of all the railings at Manchester's Alexandra Park, for instance, the gates were again left untouched. This appears to have left the watchman with something of a dilemma – one he solved with compelling jobsworthiness.

As the *Daily Express* reported on 20 June 1940, despite the fact that the railings had gone to the Armoury melting pot the previous week, and the park was therefore effectively open to all, at all hours, the watchman doggedly continued to pound his nightly three-mile beat. A chain of hefty keys in hand, he carried on scrupulously locking each and every one of the six pairs of gates now left standing on the fringes of the park, as lonely as unclaimed dancers on the floor of a Mecca ballroom. As he informed the paper's reporter, he intended to keep locking the gates until he received 'orders to stop'.

Such I'll-do-as-I've-always-done-ism was not the reaction of Manchester's press, which chose to put a much more positive, and even progressive, spin on the banishing of barriers. In an article in the *Manchester Evening News* on 25 June 1940, headed 'The Parks All Go Continental', it was argued – somewhat bravely, since less than ten days later Marshal Pétain had signed on as the Nazis' puppet premier of France's Vichy government – that there was a 'Continental air about Manchester nowadays'. In the heart of the city, it went on, people could 'walk from one pavement right across the roadway and sit in Whitworth Park without hindrance'. With Paris occupied, ditto Belgium and Holland, the would-be *flâneurs* of Chorlton-on-Medlock could, the *Manchester Evening News* seemed to think, finally saunter like Baudelaire on the Place du Carrousel.

Genuine continentals in Britain were, alas, faring rather less well. Back in 1939, the Home Secretary, Sir John Anderson (he of the shelters), had urged Parliament 'to avoid treating as enemies those who are friendly to the country that has offered them asylum'. But the *Daily Mail* – which in 1934 had published a 'Hurrah for the Blackshirts' – was six years later declaring that 'In Britain, you have to realise, every German is an agent'. A better-safe-than-sorry policy was inaugurated, and by the end of June 1940 some 27,200 'enemy aliens' had been interned. The Olympia in Kensington, the Royal Victoria Patriotic Asylum on Wandsworth Common and the Kempton Park Racecourse were among the staging posts used to process internees, some of whom were placed in a partially completed housing estate in Huyton near Liverpool before being dispatched to camps on the Isle of Man. Eleven thousand internees were eventually shipped to Australia. In tit-for-tat moves, deplored by Orwell in his diaries, 1,376 German prisoners were chained up in Canadian internee camps in response to the manacling of 2,500 Allied prisoners, mostly Canadians, by the Germans at Dieppe.

While the Oval cricket ground was requisitioned as a prisoner of war camp and Lord's was used as an aircrew receiving centre – the pecking order between these two bastions of English cricket perhaps illustrated by their respective roles during the conflict – part of Heaton Park in Manchester was given over to an RAF embarkation and training centre. New recruits to the officer corps were able to avail themselves of three new clay pigeon shooting ranges. Like so many other municipal greeneries, it was armed with barrage balloons and an anti-aircraft gun, but in keeping with its top-flight (and indeed top-secret) role in the RAF, it also had sentry boxes and park buildings, used to house a Navy, Army and Air Force Institutes (NAAFI) store and a squadron clubhouse, the latter enjoying a visit from the American bandleader Glenn Miller.

But for most parks, it was the passing, in 1939, of two pieces of legislation, the Emergency Powers (Defence) Act and the Cultivation of Lands (Allotments) Order, that inaugurated the most significant change of their use during the war. The former empowered the Ministry of Agriculture to take possession of farms and control food production and the latter gave local authorities the right to seize unoccupied land for cultivation. In combination with the 'Dig for Victory' campaign, these Acts saw swathes of parkland become farmland, just as in the previous war but on a much larger scale. Plymouth Hoe was hoed for potatoes. Vegetable plots would appear in the moat of Tower Bridge. Hyde and Battersea Parks gained piggeries. Eleven acres of Primrose Hill were put under cultivation, and thirty in Bushy Park. Even the flower beds beneath the Albert Memorial in Kensington Gardens were dug up for peas, runner beans and Brussels sprouts.

The suggestion that the Royal Parks, prior to that, might not have been doing their bit was raised in the House of Commons in April 1940. And it was left to the Liberal MP William Mabane, Parliamentary Secretary at the Ministry of Home Security, to rebuff such criticisms. He responded bullishly, stating that there were already 'extensive arrangements' for 'growing food in the Royal Parks in London'. By his calculation some 'sixty-three acres' had already been set aside for allotments and 80 acres were 'under cultivation for oats and root crops'. In addition, a proportion of the greenhouse space was 'being used for cultivating tomatoes, lettuce'. And 'French beans, potatoes and other vegetables' were 'to be grown in some of the flower beds'. But he cautioned against 'making too drastic a sacrifice of the flowers', believing horticultural beauty no less important to public morale than vegetable-growing.

In this he was supported by Cecil Henry Middleton. Known simply as 'Mr Middleton' to the thousands (if not millions, now that some nine million Britons held radio licences) who tuned into his weekly BBC Radio programme *In Your Garden*, he was the accepted voice of the 'Dig for Britain' campaign. As the consultant horticulturalist to the 'Boots the Chemist' chain, lending his name to their range of gardening products, and with a weekly column in the *Daily Express*, whose readership exceeded seven million, Middleton's words carried weight – occasional dropped Hs and all. So when he informed the public, as he did on numerous occasions, that 'an allotment' was 'like the army', they listened. And acted accordingly, even if – like Mr Geer of Woolwich, a contributor to the Mass Observation wartime diary project – you were lumbered with a section of Plumstead Common that was 'a stony desert' beside a barrage balloon, from which nothing, no matter how long or what you dug, watered and hoed, appeared willing to grow. Then again, Middleton also reassured the population that the first month 'was the worst' but after that they'd start to enjoy it.

But Middleton, like Mabane, retained his love of less edible flora, stating that 'even a Dig for Victory show' was 'a poor affair without its flowers'. Providers of much-needed foodstuff, allotments were also encouraged for keeping chins up. Those who were unable to engage in active duty could at least remain busy, and there was no finer way for a ration-ravished and bomb-weary population to get fit than engaging in physical labour for the common cause, or so the propaganda went. The Ministry of Health rammed the message home in a pamphlet entitled *How to Keep Well in Wartime*, which included advice on preventing muscles 'becoming set'. Headed 'Muscles are Meant to be Used', it suggested that readers should use their weekends to 'walk, cycle, swim, dig, row a boat and enjoy it'. If trenches, the draining of the odd lake, bomb craters on

pathways, bombs generally, and concrete enemy-tank excluders prevented some who were intent on avoiding their muscles 'setting' from undertaking all of these prescribed activities in certain parks, most parks did continue to offer all the facilities for such sporting exercises. And now, should the mood grab you, you could shovel some earth and plant a marrow, too.

While they were busy encouraging the population to stay fit, there were obviously plenty of things that the Ministry of Health and the government didn't want the population doing in this period. Talking carelessly, for instance. In person or on the telephone – Bowen, in *The Heat of the Day*, mentions, just in passing, a public phone box that carries a sign telling potential users to refrain from telephoning. And in parks, there was the problem of sex. Though the weather might be far from welcoming in England, and the parks' greenery less plentiful for rolling around in than before the war, lust, it seemed, liked nothing more than bombs raining from the sky, enforced darkness and rail-less public parks. That civilian clinics alone reported over 70,000 new cases of venereal disease in 1942 gives some indication of the general level of rutting (and ignorance of sexual hygiene) flourishing behind blackout curtains and inside Anderson shelters.

With a floating population of Allied servicemen of all nationalities, sex was sold by seasoned professionals and rank amateurs alike. In London, some Soho streetwalkers reported working fourteen hours a day to accommodate the demand after the Americans arrived in the capital. Indeed, the number of recorded prostitutes rose during the war; but this statistic is no doubt skewed by the fact that, for single women who did not wish to serve in the armed forces (and in this war some 460,000 of them did), giving your profession as prostitute was one surefire way to avoid the call-up. Fearing that they would bring moral degeneracy and disease into the ranks, the military top brass barred sex workers from the forces. Under this ruling, many an urban bar-room broad and nightclub hostess chose to tick that box rather than endure time on a farm or in khaki. And who can blame them, really?

Meanwhile, in the opinion of the London gangland racketeer Billy Hill, during the war 'good-time girls became brazen tarts' and 'ordinary wives became good-time girls'. Perhaps accordingly, prices for sexual favours varied enormously – from a pack of Wills, a pair of nylons and a port and lemon to upwards of £2 – American airmen supposedly retorting 'I want to rent it, not buy it', when quoted rates in the region of the latter figure. It was the Americans who coined the name 'Hyde Park Rangers' for the girls who solicited in and around that particular London park.*

---

* Back in 1925, no less than Sir Basil Thomson, the distinguished former Assistant Commissioner of Scotland Yard, was arrested for committing an act of indecency in Hyde Park. He was apprehended with a woman called Thelma De Lava, who was alleged to have been 'manipulating his person' at the time of the arrest.

One Canadian officer interviewed for a report by the Public Morality Council claimed that the areas around Green Park and Hyde Park at twilight were 'a vast battle ground of Sex'. Where Trixie and Fifi stood in Piccadilly and Soho doorways, surreptitiously illuminating their faces with small torches to attract night-time trade, the park girls (shall we call them Rosemary, Heather or Willow?) used directional whistles to 'communicate with servicemen' in the dark. Having hooked their tricks, a few caresses in the gloom was all it would take for an experienced girl (or boy, for that matter) to surmise the man's rank, nationality and wealth from insignia or an epaulette on their uniform. Fees adjusted accordingly in the wake of that information, of course. An inebriated officer, unsteady on the lawn, was obviously in for quite another type of rolling entirely.

But prostitutes throughout the war often had as much to fear from their johns as from the Luftwaffe. London ladies of the night were stalked by the so-called Blackout Ripper and countless other more anonymous murderous men: paperless deserters, impersonators of RAF officers, public-school sadists, aggrieved cuckolds, gangland thugs, repressed homosexuals, and the Gordon Cummins of Fleet Street fame who all killed women, sometimes with impunity, under cover of aerial assaults, in light-less parks, dim back alleys and one-bar gas-fire illuminated tenement rooms. In the so-called Wigwam case of 1942, Joan Pearl Wolfe, murdered by her lover August Sangret, a Canadian soldier

---

Thomson, the author of *Queer People*, a memoir about his intelligence work during the First World War, which included interrogating the exotic dancer turned spy Mata Hari, claimed that he was merely undertaking research for a new book on vice. This excuse proved to no avail. Found guilty and fined £5, Thomson opted to live mostly in France in the wake of the scandal but did go on to publish several more books. What methods he undertook for researching those later volumes are, alas, unknown to this author.

partially of North American Indian origin, was actually *buried* in a park, Hankley Common, near Godalming, Surrey, where she'd been camping out in a makeshift tent of her killer's devising.

Meanwhile, with opportunities for men and women to stray enhanced by lengthy periods of separation, the line between whoring and merely making the best of things before being blown to pieces could be thin. Keeping mum, as the propaganda posters wisely advised, about the company husbands and wives kept while they were parted became close to second nature for a population on the fiddle with clothing coupons and smoking knocked-off fags. Indeed, hunger for love and sex runs through *The Heat of the Day* like the seam of a black-market nylon. As Bowen puts it in the novel, in a London whose streets were glittery as ballrooms with broken glass, and where the air was hazy with brick dust after raids, 'Nature tapped out with the heels on the pavement an illicit semaphore.' For her protagonist, Louie Lewis, the twenty-something only child of Kentish parents who have perished in a coastal bombing attack, Regent's Park is a place to fill in empty weekday evenings after dreary work at a factory. And on Sundays, with her husband Tom stationed abroad, eager airmen and the mound in the park under the ilex serve as a substitute for the hollow in the sheets of their marital bed. Since Tom brought her to the park and to the same spot, she regards these infidelities as acts of piety, her frolics practically rituals to conjure him, or at least their former Sunday frolics, into being.

For Bowen herself, the park was personified by her adulterous lover, Charles Ritchie. Writing to Ritchie in January 1950, she maintained that it had 'become you to me'. However, walks through what she termed 'the gentle tract of their happiness' seem to have been their preferred activity there. In fact, it is quite hard to picture Bowen, an

Irish aristocrat, with a fine long nose and black hair as sleek as a seal, and rarely photographed without pearls, ever rolling on the grass.

An activity equally frowned upon by the wartime government was travel. As petrol was rationed, only essential travel was condoned. When *In Your Garden*'s Mr Middleton was bombed out of his home and had to live with relatives in Northamptonshire, the BBC refused to grant him extra coupons to cover the additional distance he had to travel to and from their studios. Which, given his role as the booster for the Dig for Victory campaign, seems remiss of the Corporation or the authorities, if not both. Though perhaps it merely shows how little petrol there was to go around.

Indeed, the government tried its best to discourage holidays of any form that involved a journey. Getting away from it all – a luxury afforded to the few before the 1920s and '30s, anyway – was deemed a drain on national resources. In 1940, the Ministry of Labour dreamt up an alternative: Holidays at Home. The scheme's ethos, communicated via a series of circulars distributed around Britain, was to encourage local councils to lay on special events in the parks and public gardens in their area in order to dissuade leisure-seekers from sloping off elsewhere and using up valuable fuel. In its infancy, it appears hardly to have been a roaring success. Home Intelligence reports from June and July 1941 wryly commented that Holidays at Home were 'honoured more in the breach than in the observance'. And despite troop deployments and barbed wire on the beaches, many traditional holidaying spots such as Brighton and Blackpool did surprisingly well that summer and throughout the war, with performances by, among others, Tessie O'Shea, Frank Randle, Jimmy Clitheroe and Jewel and Warriss carrying on much as before.

But there were councils, some in landlocked regions, who pulled out all the stops for Holidays at Home. Huddersfield was one. Its Parks and Cemeteries Committee was singled out for special praise by the journalist and later Labour MP J. P. W. Mallalieu. In his book *Passed to You, Please*, Mallalieu wrote that 'men' – and seemingly it was only men – 'who live and work in Huddersfield ... know what Huddersfield people want'. As a result, he was proud to report that these knowledgeable sons of West Yorkshire had devised a crowd-pleasing three-week programme of sports, games and donkey rides in the local Greenhead Park, along with concert parties, military bands, yacht contests and open-air dancing.

Like many others, Greenhead was by then lacking its railings – and its gates – but Mallalieu's plan of entertainments proved popular, and on one Saturday that summer apparently as many as 30,000 people crowded into the park. According to Mallalieu, throughout that brief season, ordinary Huddersfield folk 'dropped into holiday clothes, walking about the streets in open neck shirts and flannel ... children played in the fresh air and sun of the park, well looked after by voluntary helpers, so that their mothers could have even more of a rest than they would have done at the seaside'. The cost, he maintained, was just £500 to the ratepayers; in contemporary terms, that would work out at a still modest £25,000. The council went on to hire donkeys to replicate the seaside atmosphere of Skegness, and even poached a county cricket club from across the Pennines to play exhibition matches.

The historian Chris Sladen, in his study of the scheme nationwide, points out that the local council in Sheffield, praised for supplying extra chairs in its parks, paid the distinctly capitalist amusement-ground and holiday-camp entrepreneur Billy Butlin to act as a consultant for their Holiday at Home season – an act which somewhat undermined Mallalieu's 'red flag holidays for all' thesis. Butlin, so notoriously exacting that he often personally went through swill bins at his holiday camps to determine which items on that day's menu were being rejected, also muscled in on a money-grabbing deal on a swingback ride in Sheffield that year, to boot.

But, for the most part, less capitalistic forces largely prevailed. The fruit-juice-drinking and sandal-wearing fraternity – disciples of Edward Carpenter & Co. – pitched in, with ambassadors from the English Folk Dance and Song Society advising on sing-songs, dance classes and traditional revels in public parks. The borough of Barnet, for instance, staged an Olde Worlde Fayre and concert in aid of Anglo-Soviet Friendship. The success of such Holidays at Home gatherings resulted in a distinctly out-of-character editorial in *The Times* on 13 August 1943, which argued for the continuation of such civic festivities after the war, as a means of reviving the 'Merrie England of yore'.

More modern, even transatlantic, entertainments were to be enjoyed at Coate Water in Swindon, where there were bathing beauty pageants by the public pool and a young Diana Dors walked off with a prize for recitation at one Holiday at Home shindig. American servicemen stationed nearby gave demonstrations of baseball and basketball for sports-loving Swindonians.

Perhaps the most comprehensive Holidays at Home programme was staged in the capital's parks by the London County Council. Although it ceased to publish its annual guide to open-air entertainments during the war, minutes from meetings show that the park committee was determined that, as far as possible, events should continue. In direct response to the Ministry of Labour's Holidays at Home circular, the council allocated an additional £4,000 to the parks entertainment budget for July and August of 1941. Extra concert parties, shows and games were arranged, with, among others, the Amateur Swimming Association and the London Water Polo League pitching in on galas in park lidos. Victoria Park, Blackheath and Clapham Common were also on the receiving end of the then apparently ubiquitous Old Worlde Fayres.

The next year the LCC's budget was upped again and the Holidays at Home season was expanded to run in London parks from June until September, its offerings now far more adventurous. The highlight for many was the visits by the Sadler's Wells Ballet Company to Victoria Park that August. The opening performance was attended by the Home Secretary, Herbert Morrison, as well as the Russian Ambassador and his wife. Though typical English summer weather rather put the damper on things, 11,000 people still went along. Remarkable, really, that such festivities went ahead in a park still scored by underground bomb shelters, allotments and pigpens, and eight anti-aircraft ack-ack gun bases; its eponymous nearby railway station and the lodge at the Bonner's Gate entrance were charred ruins. In due course, a prisoner-of-war camp for Germans and Italians would be established in the north-east quarter of the park near the old Harriers running track. Its internees, according to one local resident, were 'easily identified' behind the fences because they 'had big yellow circles sewn onto the back of their clothes'.

The Sadler's Wells Ballet journeyed to Brockwell Park the following year, while Victoria Park was treated to a performance of *Il Trovatore* by the Carl Rosa opera company. These highbrow shows weren't to everyone's taste, however much those later Italian internees might perhaps have delighted in Verdi. The Bethnal Green Trades Council complained that such entertainments in Victoria Park 'did not meet the desires of the district', afflicted as it was by the fallout from dockland bombing. But at the end of the 1942 season, one and a quarter million people were calculated to have attended at least one LCC Holidays at Home event. Across fourteen parks, the council had mounted close to 500 concerts, 250 concert parties and over a hundred open-air dances. Given this wave of activity in 1942, it's perhaps little wonder that *The Heat of the Da*y begins with such an immense sense of foreboding about the approach of autumn that year, when Regent's Park's bandstand and open-air theatre would again fall silent as the nights drew in – and darker than ever, thanks to blackout restrictions.

Up in Coventry's Memorial Park, meanwhile, in a city where thousands were now without homes, the Holiday at Home package was as lively as anywhere. The Home Guard mounted gymkhanas. Children folk-danced. Their parents jived to the strains of the South Staffs regimental band playing 'The Chestnut Tree' and 'Boomps-A-Daisy'. Licensed and unlicensed refreshments were available. And, perhaps prophetic of the boom to come, a beautiful-babies contest was staged in the park in August 1943.

There was a new sense of optimism in this city which had suffered such devastation at the hand of the Luftwaffe. And now, less than four years after Operation Moonlight Sonata, the local council published 'Preparing for a Brighter Future', its plan for rebuilding the city. This document revealed that the city's parks department had already purchased over 2,000 'decorate trees' and that these had been planted in the Memorial Park until such time as they could be redeployed in the shiny new Coventry that was expected to arise from the ashes in the not-too-distant future.

Back down in London, what might be called the green shoots of recovery had also started to appear in 1944. That summer, London Transport was maintaining that the capital had 'never presented a gayer appearance, with 13 open-air dancing locations', and '13 different open-air entertainments'. But this of course coincided with the arrival of the lethal pilotless V1 rockets, or doodlebugs, which came as a depressing blow, especially after such a lengthy lull in the bombing of the British mainland. The Germans soon graduated to the V2, but as their fortunes in Europe came tumbling down, the doodlebugs began to subside, Hyde Park being the recipient of the last rocket to hit the capital, on 20 March 1945: it landed just inside the park near the Marble Arch. Graham Greene, staying nearby, heard 'a huge crash, followed by a terrific rumble and the sound of glass going'. After that there was silence. The rocket attacks officially came to an end just a week later.

By then the barrage balloons in Regent's Park had been lowered for the final time, the Home Guard disbanded, and the capital's 25,000 part-time firefighters dismissed. By 3 May 1945, the paths and grass of St James's Park were already being dug and re-sown and wooden railings erected to prevent people stomping about the new plants before they'd had a chance to grow. Similar barriers reappeared around private squares and gardens – 'So the lawful citizens of the square can make use of their treasured keys again,' Orwell groused, 'and the children of the poor kept out.'*

Around the same time, London County Council expressed the hope that all of the allotments in its playing fields and parks would be gone by the end of 1945. And that summer, for the first time since the outbreak of the war, an ice-cream van was stationed outside Battersea Park, the ban on ice-cream manufacturing having been lifted only the previous November. The war was well and truly over.

The appearance of just such a frosty comestible could however, at a stretch and with the benefit of hindsight, be seen as rather an unfortunate augury of the icier relations between former wartime allies which would define the era to come – the return of railings to the parks themselves a foretaste of the iron curtain to fall across Europe, though that would probably be taking things a little too far. Then again, given the popularity of parks as meeting places for spies – at least in movies like *The Ipcress File*, where seemingly no state secret or abducted nuclear scientist could be traded without a meeting on a park bench or bandstand between agents of opposing ideological powers – it might not be so far-fetched after all.

---

* Only a few months later Orwell was also to sniff a desire among such great and good for a return to pre-war establishment know-your-place authoritarianism in the arrest of five people outside Hyde Park. These individuals had been selling pacifist and anarchist newspapers but were charged with obstruction. He highlighted their case in his essay 'Freedom of the Park' published in *Tribune* in December 1945.

CHAPTER 9

Post-war Playgrounds

As the victorious Prime Minister of the wartime coalition government, Churchill had expected to romp home in the first general election after the war. But in July 1945 Churchill was summarily dismissed, with Labour and Clement Attlee enjoying a landslide victory on the back of their promises to create a welfare state, and with it a more equitable society. They were faced with an uphill battle. In the aftermath of the war, recovery certainly did begin, but large areas of Britain's urban centres still lay in ruins, with bomb sites, like some demob suits, lingering on for decades to come. The last ones in London, for example, were not filled in until the early 1970s.

Even before the war was over, the question of what to make of the ruins was raised. As early as January 1944, the *Architectural Review* had proposed turning into permanent gardens of remembrance seventeen of the forty-five churches in the City of London that had been severely damaged by enemy action. This churchyard plan enjoyed the support of T. S. Eliot, Julian Huxley, John Maynard Keynes and Kenneth Clark, who were among the signatories of a letter to *The Times* dated 15 August 1944. Further flesh was put on the bones of the scheme in *Bombed Churches as War Memorials*, a book edited by W. R. Matthews, the Dean of St Paul's, and published the following year, in which the gardener 'Miss Brenda Colvin' and architect Jacques Groag supplied plans for churches including St Vedast Foster Lane, Christ Church, Newgate Street in the City, and St Anne's Church, Soho.

They envisioned these former places of worship becoming 'open spaces giving glimpses of green against the livid grey of pavements and buildings, affording places of relaxation and retreat from the bustle of traffic, where the City worker could 'eat his lunch under a tree or rest for half an hour against a fragment of sun-warmed masonry'.

Outside London, the book suggested, Coventry Cathedral and St Andrew's, Plymouth might be similarly converted (the latter city's park pavilion having also been lost in the Blitz). Historic examples such as Tintern Abbey and Raglan Castle were cited in defence of leaving buildings in a state of romantic decrepitude. The book was heavily illustrated, with superb black and white line drawings shaded with patches of vivid colour by Barbara Jones. Their distinctive palette quite wonderfully suggesting the potential of these ravaged sites to be transformed from hollows of charred brick and stone, monochrome and intensely melancholy, into inviting polychromatic pocket squares of flora.

Debate about the shape and form of such public memorial gardens was intense. In 1943 the Institute of Park Administration published recommendations for *Post-war Planning and Reconstruction*. In it they considered memorial 'rest gardens'. They believed it 'conceivable that the public opinion will desire to perpetuate in some tangible form the memory of those who pay the Supreme Sacrifice during the war'.

But, the Institute argued, 'War Memorials should be made to contribute toward the well-being of the living.' Open spaces, they went on, should be 'considered as a form of preventative medicine' and their provision 'calculated to go to the root of the question of public health'. Despite these fears that sedentary contemplation might be given precedence over such preventative medicine, several of the churchyard memorial gardens were made, with Christ Church, Newgate Street and Coventry Cathedral among them.*

Induced by the onerous terms of repayments on American loans for reconstruction, Britain was faced with a period of austerity, and in September 1949, at the height of the financial crisis, the pound was devalued from $4.03 to $2.80. Britain was having to come to terms with its new standing in the global geopolitical pecking order. In 1951, the signing over to the Americans of an ancient common at Greenham in Berkshire for their use as a strategic airbase spoke volumes. A Forest of Arden for centuries, it had been haunted by 'poachers, cowherds, botanists and cloudspotters' and genteel picnickers until its requisitioning by the RAF in 1941.

In 1951, the effects of austerity were manifest at the opening of the Festival of Britain. Whereas Paxton's Crystal Palace before its removal to, and eventual ruination at, Sydenham had been the locus of an immensely grand and international affair, the Great Exhibition's 100th-anniversary successor was to be more insular and national. Still, when the idea of an exhibition was first mooted in government circles in 1946, romance and an overwhelming respect for the history of 1851 (no matter that Prince Albert had been German) meant Hyde Park was named as the ideal location. The LCC's confident predictions about everything returning to normal in the wake of the war had not quite been borne out, but Hyde Park was one of the few central London parks that had been cleared of wartime accoutrements. A round-up of prostitutes across the capital that January even removed some of the women whose nocturnal whistles had added to the gaiety

---

* In a further twist on the parks and ruins theme, much of the 'miniature Cheddar Gorge' dug when sand was excavated at Hampstead Heath for the war effort was eventually filled in with the masonry and contents of bombed-out houses.

of the park during the blackout. The site, it seemed, had everything going for it. But to deprive people – in particular, civil servants from the neighbouring government buildings – of a chance to stretch their legs of a lunchtime was duly judged unconscionable ... by government civil servants.

In the hunt for alternative park sites, an intergovernmental committee alighted upon Osterley in outer West London, after finding that the Exhibition Hall at Earls Court and Olympia had been booked already. At Osterley there were 300 acres of parkland arranged around a neoclassical stately home that had once belonged to the Earls of Jersey. Lying off the Great West Road and connected to the city centre by the Piccadilly and District lines, its suburban location was less of a problem than the potential price tag of £70 million to the taxpayer.

Scrabbling around for somewhere else, somewhere cheaper – this being the age of austerity – the marshes at Woolwich Arsenal were suggested. As were Trent Park in Cockfosters, Hampton Court – even Sydenham's Crystal Palace Park and the Museums of South Kensington. Battersea Park was another name that continually cropped up in discussions, but again the difficulty of installing what was described as 'recoverable standard shedding' for exhibition venues caused it to be crossed off the main list too.

The solution was found in an area of damp slum tenements and riverside wharves on London's South Bank, earmarked already by the LCC for a new concert hall and ripe for regeneration. Part of its appeal was the vista of the Thames, its advocates reminding doubters of Paris's last exposition, of 1937 – a world fair of scientific and technological wonders whose exhibits beside the silvery Seine had included Picasso's masterpiece, *Guernica*, commissioned for Spain's official pavilion. Its proximity to Waterloo station also put it, as Miss J. Tyrwhitt of the

Association of Planning and Regional Construction pointed out during one committee meeting, close to 'the London of Shakespeare, the London of Dickens'.

The festival was not restricted to what Evelyn Waugh denounced as the 'monstrous constructions' on the South Bank. There were hundreds of events across the country. A festival ship, *Campania*, laden with exhibition paraphernalia did the rounds of ports and naval towns. Two thousand bonfires were lit up and down the land on the opening night alone. Shakespeare's plays were performed in his native Stratford and a Dickens pageant assembled with as many soot-stained urchins and top-hatted patriarchs as could be mustered in the grounds of Rochester Castle in Kent. Regency dinners were eaten at the Brighton Pavilion for perhaps the first time since the Regency, while Mystery Plays were performed in York in the open air and in the greensward of the ruined St Mary's Abbey for the first time since 1572. The festival was also excuse enough for some civic improvements. Municipal garden flower beds were planted in imitation of the Britannia's head emblem, and topiary trimmed into shapes of the Lion and the Unicorn. New parks and playing grounds were laid, for example in the village of Trowell in Nottinghamshire, whose new fields were christened with a game of cricket 'played in the dress of a century ago'.

When it came to the festival's official park, time was wound even further back, as a spanking brand-new pleasure garden and funfair were installed at Battersea Park. Gerald Barry, former editor of the *News Chronicle* (the herbivore paper of choice back then) and the festival's planner-in-chief, conceived these as homage to the pleasure gardens of the eighteenth century, offering fun, fantasy, music and fireworks. (But not, we can suppose, the drunken revelries, pox-ridden courtesans and pickpockets that did for the originals eventually.)

'Here, in part of this park,' Barry explained, 'we shall lay out gardens and lakes where there will be many opportunities for various kinds of entertainment, from bands and dancing to the more rollicking attractions of the traditional fun-fair. There will be restaurants and cafes here, too, and illuminations at night. What we have in mind is not just a fun-fair – though there will, as I say, be that, in one corner of the gardens – but something more spacious and leisurely – something new for London – or, perhaps, I should rather say something old, something going back to the spirit of Vauxhall Gardens.'

There were some other similarities between the two. Like Vauxhall, a purely commercial enterprise, the Festival Pleasure Gardens and Fun Fair were to be 'self-financing' and would charge an entrance fee. This was largely to overcome objections from the likes of the *Evening Standard*, which ran an article opposing the gardens with the header 'Spend the money on St Thomas' Hospital'. And unlike the South Bank festival site, where advertisements were eschewed entirely, the pleasure gardens' designer, James Gardner, had to seek sponsors to pay for many of Battersea's features and entertainments. Foreshadowing the branding synergies of our present era, Nestlé sponsored the crèche, the Worshipful Company of Brewers the three beer gardens, named after the lost pleasure grounds of Cremorne, Ranelagh and Vauxhall. Sharp's Toffees backed the Punch and Judy shows, which, given their depiction of domestic violence and assaults on babies and policemen, might find rather more difficulty in attracting corporate coin these days. The tonic water and minerals firm Schweppes lent its name to a grotto, and the Lockheed Hydraulic Brake Company a mermaid in bronze. The Dublin-based stout-maker Guinness paid for a highly elaborate 25-foot-high clock.

Constructed by Hatton Garden clockmakers Baume & Co. Ltd, the clock was loaded with mechanical marionettes styled after the toucans and ostriches in Guinness's advertising. These sprang cacophonously into life at various hours of the day and night. The company also produced Festival Guinness, a special limited edition Double-Extra Stout to tie in with (or cash in on) the Festival of Britain, though its availability in pubs in the capital was hindered by a veto orchestrated by London's own brewers.

Those wishing to eat or drink in Battersea had six restaurants to choose from, three of them 'buffets' or self-service jobs, then considered chicly modern and appealingly democratic, dispensing with snooty serving staff and allowing diners to pick their own meals. In addition there was a dance pavilion, a wine garden, a tea shop, snack bars, tuck shops and kiosks selling nuts, toffee apples and all the indigestible teeth-rotting stuff found on seaside proms.

The funfair, judiciously located as far east of the 'posher' Chelsea side of the park as possible, was also to bring some genuine Coney Island, or at least American, rides to south-west London. Seven transatlantic rides were purchased on a government-funded shopping expedition, the showmen's pockets stuffed with an almost unbelievable (for 1950) £30,000. Such largess from the post-war Labour administration resulted in questions being asked in the House by Tory MPs and had the *Daily Mail* frothing at the mouth that money could be found to buy American fairground equipment while rationing still remained on certain common goods. But their protests were in vain. Battersea would have its Skywheel, its Bubble-Bounce and Flyo-Plane. Not to mention the Big Dipper sourced from Sutton Coldfield, and dodgems and moon rocket from Southsea. Americana of a kind that might just have met the approval of Winston

Come to / the

FAIR

Come to the Festival Pleasure
Gardens—come to the flowers
and the lakes and the fountains—
come to the Fun House, the Grotto, the
Miniature Zoo—come to the bands and
illuminations—come to the eating and
drinking and dancing—come to the shops,
the theatres, the fireworks!

IN LOVELY BATTERSEA PARK

Open: weekdays 10.30 a.m. to 11.30 p.m.
admission 2s. (children 1s.)
Sundays 12.30 p.m. to 10 p.m.
admission 1s. (children 6d)
by train, underground, bus and water-bus from the
South Bank Exhibition and all parts of London.

FESTIVAL / PLEASURE GARDENS Battersea Park, S.W.11

Churchill – since he referenced the Mississippi River in his famous
Battle of Britain speech – was represented by a Dixieland paddle
steamer with an 'Old Kentucky' barrel organ.

More parochial, but arguably much more enchanting, was the Far
Tottering and Oyster Creek Branch Railway. The invention of *Punch*
cartoonist Rowland Emett, this was a fantastical pen-and-ink steam-
train line, with high-funnelled Stephenson's *Rocket*-style engines and
beleaguered station employees, which had first appeared in the pages

of the magazine and was expanded into a book in 1949. Now, at the park, it was transformed into an adventure ride. Here, six years before Disneyland, with its Mark Twain steamboat and costumed minions waving four-fingered gloved hands at crowds, was a collection of adored – albeit by rather fogeyish middle-class types – cartoon characters coming to life.

Punch's then editor, the cartoonist Cyril Bird (who drew under the pen name Fougasse), used its pages to mock a modernist sculpture commissioned for the festival from Henry Moore; somewhat ungratefully, given that the magazine had the kind of living advert in the form of the Far Tottering that the likes of Guinness had to pay for. In a cartoon published on 27 June 1951, a stick-figure couple on the South Bank – the man inked with a flip-brim hat and carrying his coat over his arm, the woman with a shopping bag – are pictured heading away from a plinth bearing a thin reclining figure with a hole in its stomach. Beneath them a caption reads: 'That reminds me, dear – did you remember the sandwiches?'

There was a Moore or two to see in Battersea, as an open-air sculpture exhibition was another of the park's festival attractions. Fleet Street hacks, even more waggish than Fougasse, wrote of members of the public confusing the artworks with amusements from the funfair. But regular visitors to Battersea were familiar enough with the concept, as the park and the LCC had put on the very first open-air sculpture exhibition in Britain three years earlier. Pieces by Rodin, Matisse, Jacob Epstein, Barbara Hepworth and Henry Moore had been displayed in the park for the edification of the local community, who were believed to be as starved of beauty as they were of food (and for the probable enjoyment of the pigeons, too). In 1951, forty-four pieces occupied the park's subtropical garden and alongside Rodin, Hepworth, Epstein and Moore again, there were works by Giacometti and Eric Gill.

Despite all this the Grand Vista was arguably the most captivating element of Battersea's festival additions. It was a wide terrace flanked by ribbed arcades, topped by white wire figures of men and women, and had shallow steps leading down in the Venetian manner to ponds, fountains and a rectangular lake, behind which was a lacy screen. This scenery, and it was close to stagecraft, was the work of the artists John Piper and Osbert Lancaster, with a flower garden by the inventive horticulturalist Russell Page. Throughout the festival, it supplied the backdrop to performances of high-wire acrobats and twice-weekly firework displays. On what were called Carnival Days, those who wore fancy dress got in for free.

But the gardens and funfair at Battersea were to be plagued with difficulties. Work on the park ran late, and the funfair opened eight days after the main festival, just in time for the Whitsun weekend, largely because showmen, itchy for punters' pounds, shillings and pence, were unwilling to countenance any further delays. It was three weeks before the Pleasure Gardens itself was ready to invite the public to amble about its tree walk or dance with a costumed stranger in a tented pavilion made up of over 15 tons of fabric. The location itself was partially to blame. When excavations were made for the gardens, it soon became apparent that the original park was really just verdant dressing on top of a reclaimed riverbed; heavier than usual rains caused the site to flood so badly that workmen nicknamed it 'Batter Sea'.

Cuts to budgets, changes to members of festival committees and government cabinets, arguments over a cricket pitch and tarmac, a strike, and a contractor accustomed to building wartime airstrips all conspired to make the road to the park's opening as twisty as the rails on the funfair's Big Dipper.

Political commentators have argued that the Festival, conceived as a 'tonic for the nation' to celebrate the end of the war and show that the country was back on its feet after the grim years of deprivation and gruelling shortages, arrived electorally just too late for the Labour government. Michael Frayn, reflecting on the Festival in 1963, felt it was 'the last, and virtually, posthumous work' of the liberal do-gooders, gentle ruminants, and signers of petitions of the radical middle classes. Herbert Morrison later described the Festival as 'the people giving themselves a pat on the back'; sadly, not all the people returned the favour when it came to the ballot box that October. Labour secured more votes than in their 1945 landslide, but lost on seats to the Conservatives.

If these gentle ruminants had prevailed after the war, they were, Frayn argued, all but exhausted by 1951. The 'Carnivores' – made up of upper-class and Grantham-shopkeeper-stock Tories, Evelyn Waugh and the cast of the Directory of Directors – sensed weakness and, intent on ending a period of egalitarianism they viewed as having been extremely detrimental to their interests, now pounced without mercy at the earliest opportunity, and Labour would not see power again until 1964.

Famously, Churchill's very first act upon regaining the premiership was to order the scrapping of the Skylon, the futuristic sculpture erected on London's South Bank as part of the Festival. Shaped like the kind of rocket ship Dan Dare, the *Eagle* comic's intergalactic Biggles, would pilot in his weekly battles with the Mekon, this was Atomic Age optimism cast in steel. With its near neighbour, the flying saucer-like Dome of Discovery, the Skylon came to define the Festival in the popular imagination, then and since, as a celebration of Britain at its most forward-looking: a things-can-only-get-better, electricity-will-be-too-cheap-to-meter, and a no-tabletop-need-ever-be-dirty-again-with-wipe-clean-Formica nation. Churchill loathed it. His hatred of the Skylon even extended to rejecting an offer from the American property mogul and huckster William Zeckendorf. The one-time owner of the Chrysler Building and the developer of much of Los Angeles wanted to buy it, along with the Dome of Discovery, and have both of them shipped to the States to serve as tourist attractions in California. In a rare example of the half-American passing up dollars in hand, Churchill preferred to send them to a breaker's yard instead. That decision was all the more telling since in January 1952 the Prime Minister undertook a grovelling state visit to America with the aim of renewing the 'special relationship'.

The Tories, then, dusted down their bulldozers and unleashed their wrecking balls on the South Bank almost as soon as the last Festival-goers had been ushered out of the Dome of Discovery, scratching their heads as they went, perhaps wondering what had become of the socialist utopia these buildings suggested was imminent. Battersea Park, though, was largely left alone, the 'Brighter Half' of 'the Big Show', with its commercial deals, evidently posing less of a threat ideologically to the incoming government.

Its funfair, with an entrance fee of 6d, joined the Tower of London and Buckingham Palace as a tourist destination; but, unlike them, was patronised as much by Londoners as visitors from out of town or over-seas. Where fairgrounds in other London parks tended to be fleeting, seasonal affairs, with bone-shaking amusements mostly still confined to coastal resorts, Battersea offered permanent thrill-a-minute rides and a touch of escapist glamour in a grey and – until the passing of the Clean Air Act in 1956 – dirty old town. It lasted over twenty years. More punters were pulled in with yearly Star Galas sponsored by the *News of the World*. As newsreel footage from the early 1960s shows, these involved lengthy autograph sessions with famous names from the big and small screen – Shirley Bassey, Benny Hill, Harry Secombe, Mike and Bernie Winters, the bloke in *Zulu* who wasn't Michael Caine, all filmed mingling with the public and scrawling their famous names in little autograph books held in front of them by eager fans. Larking about for the cameras in one segment, they pose next to the Crazy Cottage fun house, on its roof a neon sign that announces 'Colour Television'.

Its eventual arrival – and test transmissions were to begin in 1964 – wouldn't, obviously, do newsreels any long-term favours. The new Television Tower, where the BBC would beam its colour broadcasts from in future, was to be erected in Crystal Palace Park. Rising high up above the park's neoclassical Italian terrace with its fireweed-infested steps and broken statues, this gleaming totem of technological ingenuity could hardly have wanted a better setting in which to look technologically ingenious. Its message was simple. The future, glimpsed on the South Bank by the Skylon and the Telekinema (the Festival's cinema that dazzled visitors with 3-D movies and TV shows), was here.

And if that television tower changed the landscape of one specific park, televisions themselves would, over time, change parks. The first great national event of the era was the coronation of Elizabeth II in 1953 – the first coronation service to be televised and, for many, the first event they'd ever seen on television. An estimated 27 million people in Britain watched her being crowned at Westminster Abbey. Aside from people jamming themselves into neighbours' sitting rooms, there were large-scale gatherings with a million and a half watching in local ball-rooms, town halls and churches that had been granted collective licences to screen the ceremony. Three thousand people bought tickets to see it on a big screen at the Festival Hall on London's South Bank, and there were similar screenings at the Odeon Leicester Square and in Billy Butlin's holiday camps in Filey, Skegness and Clacton. Passive viewing, even undertaken communally, was not the whole story, of course.

Thousands gathered in Hyde Park to watch the coronation procession, eager to catch sight of the Queen and her coach, as fleets of marching bands from around the Commonwealth filed past the park to herald the arrival of this new Elizabethan age. There were street parties and pageants in provincial municipal parks, too. Seeking to conjure some of the spirit of the first Queen Bess, in Saltwell Park in Gateshead members of the local am-dram society donned doublet and hose, tight bodices and bonnets to put on a 'Merrie England' show. Maypoles were danced around on Ripley's Village Green and dragons fought at Wallsend's Coronation Fayre. In Rotherham, Muglet Lane Recreation Ground was renamed Coronation Park in honour of the occasion, and even in a county that takes some pride in plain, not to say blunt speaking, this new moniker was judged an improvement. Meanwhile, down in Wembley, all the borough's parks were treated to new teak-hewn 'Coronation seats'.

Within two years of the coronation, it was calculated that 42 per cent of households in London Transport's catchment area – which included Wembley – had television sets. That increase was perhaps more down to the ending of restrictions on hire purchase by the Conservative government in July 1954 than to the Queen's big day out, but a sea change in the country's leisure habits was taking place: one that would have consequences for public parks.

With the arrival in 1955 of commercial independent television, there was even a chance to flip between two channels: a carnivorous alternative to the does-you-good Reithian BBC of herbivores, which emerged in the form of ITV, with its adverts and game shows. Television viewers, while they could avail themselves of sets in pubs, working men's institutes and the odd sporting clubhouse in a park, mostly watched at home and with their immediate families or friends. And that home would increasingly be theirs alone, either privately owned or rented from the local authority, and more likely than ever to be in the suburbs.

Post-war town planning had been directed at drawing the population out of dilapidated and congested city centres. In 1946 the New Towns Act designated the creation of eleven new towns, and the Town Development Act of 1952 sought to modernise populous older cities; slums were cleared and made more liveable, with fewer people and less industry. It was hoped that a million people could, for instance, be encouraged to leave London. While established shire towns were to be improved and expanded to accommodate the urban overspill, the New Towns were a blank page where planners' dreams of separating homes from industry and pedestrians from traffic could be realised, amid skilfully landscaped zones for factories, shops, leisure facilities and housing. Or so the thinking went.

The Conservatives, after assuring voters they would not dismantle the welfare state, came into government on a promise to build 300,000 new homes a year – 100,000 a year more than Attlee's post-war administration had managed until then. 'Housing is the first of the social services,' the party's 1951 manifesto maintained. Four years later, they were able to seek re-election boasting that their 'Party's pledge to build 300,000 houses a year was derided by our opponents as impossible to fulfil. In fact, nearly 350,000 were built last year, and at least as many are likely to be built this year.' And despite preferring to promote the idea of a property-owning democracy, housing minister Harold Macmillan was to preside over a heroic increase in council housing, allowing local authorities free rein to borrow to build.

However, as critics have rightly pointed out, in his rush for quantity, quality was occasionally sacrificed. Some of the worst examples of shoddy, system-built tower blocks appeared during his tenure both as Housing and, later, Prime Minister. As did philistine planning atrocities like the destruction of the Euston Arch, Macmillan remaining supremely indifferent to its fate while the public, as well as Pevsner and Betjeman, struggled to preserve it. Holding a 'bonfire of controls', the Conservatives were to unleash a welter of speculative development, with shiny new office blocks, housing estates and shopping precincts mushrooming.

In the suburbs and outside London, the architects and planners of new housing estates were usually obliged, or expected, to incorporate communal lawns or recreation grounds in their schemes. And by and large, decent landscaping was the norm, with estates equipped with pocket parks boosting a football pitch and/or cricket nets, a slide and a couple of swings, canopied by electricity pylons and penned in by housing and shops, but where dreams of becoming the next Denis Compton could still be indulged.

Inspired by the Swiss-born architect Le Corbusier's Ville Radieuse (or Radiant City), the high-rise urban council estates that arose rapidly after the passing of the Housing Subsidies Act in 1956 – which gave local authorities greater subsidies to build higher – aspired to the ideal of creating 'towers in a park'. Many achieved it, and there are numerous examples of thoughtful landscaping in inner-city estates, Alison and Peter Smithson's brutalist Robin Hood Gardens in Poplar, with what they called a 'quiet green heart' at its centre, among them. But too often all that was supplied was an expanse of undernourished turf or an asphalt sports pitch at the foot of a block of flats. A report by the National Playing Fields Association in 1954 entitled *Playgrounds for Blocks of Flats* was damning, stating that 'only in very rare cases' had 'architects been asked to give serious consideration for playground space for flats' and that 'no serious attempt' appeared 'to have been made to ascertain the point of view of mothers with young children'.* In J. G. Ballard's 1975 novel, *High Rise*, the character Richard Wilder, a priapic documentary filmmaker, is of the same mind. Commenting on their luxury tower block, he opines that 'the trouble with these places is that they are not designed for children. The only open space turns out to be someone else's car park.' At Benwell in Newcastle, the council did make space for children, installing in 1963 a new playground of an almost Brutalist design that dispensed with conventional swings and roundabouts in favour of a brick maze and a model train for children to climb on made entirely from concrete – these fixtures mirroring the rebuilding being undertaken across the whole city.

However, other significant green spaces were maintained as part of these new developments. Seven of the first New Towns – Basildon, Bracknell, Crawley, Harlow, Hatfield, Hemel Hempstead and Stevenage – were located in a ring outside London, and in accordance with proposals put forward by the architect-planner Patrick Abercrombie in his Greater London Plan of 1944, between them and the capital was the Green Belt – a lung of fallow ground, supposedly to be preserved as 'a pleasant amenity'. Herbert Morrison had

---

* In a later report from 1961, however, the National Playing Fields Association wrote glowingly about the corridors of the new Park Hill estate in Sheffield, designed by Jack Lynn and Ivor Smith. Though hardly green, the concrete floors of these enclosed, 10-feet-wide 'streets in the sky' could, they believed, easily serve as traffic-free playgrounds for kids.

imagined something much like it back in the 1930s, but more as a vast encircling country park for Londoner day-trippers.

Since finally passing into law in 1955, however, the Green Belt has largely acted as a kind of here-be-no-houses brake on the city's sprawl. And in the same period, the first ten National Parks were formally designated, saving areas of outstanding natural beauty from the incursion of all this new brickwork.*

As the economy began to improve, rebuilding and rehousing schemes continued to escalate at what today seems a quite extraordinary clip. At Stevenage, the first of the designated New Towns (begun in 1946), the verdure of the landscaping was a prominent and much-touted element of its design. In Harlow New Town, masterplanned by Frederick Gibberd, each neighbourhood was interspersed with what he called 'green wedges' and there was a series of parks all designed by the landscape architect Sylvia Crowe. But the inclusion of a purpose-built sports leisure centre in the plans of the former was a pointer to future thinking about parks and recreation grounds in general.

And sports was becoming front-page news. In 1954, the British runner Roger Bannister broke the four-minute mile and the World Cup Final was televised live for the very first time. Less rosily for British soccer, the England football squad was to suffer its second comprehensive drubbing in a matter of months at the hands (and far swifter feet) of a team from communist Hungary. Having already beaten a side that included such footballing greats as Stanley Matthews 6–3 at Wembley the previous November – becoming the first overseas club ever to defeat the national side at home – the Hungarians went on to thrash

---

* These were Dartmoor, the Lake District, the Peak District and Snowdonia in 1951, the Pembrokeshire Coast and the North York Moors in 1952, Exmoor and the Yorkshire Dales in 1954, Northumberland in 1956 and the Brecon Beacons in 1957.

England 7–1 at the newly built Népstadion (People's Stadium) in Budapest. These defeats were as crushing for the nation as for the side, lounge-bar philosophers seeing uncomfortable correlations between the loss of Empire and loss of England's footballing invincibility.

In Hungary and across the Eastern Bloc, these victories were lauded as proof of the superiority of the Communist system. Only two years after the Soviet Union's first appearance in the Olympics, sport was already deemed an essential weapon in the Cold War – which may partially explain why the London County Council chose, also in 1954, to finalise plans for a brand-new sporting complex in Crystal Palace Park. Its remit upon acquiring the park three years earlier had been 'to use the Crystal Palace for purposes of education and recreation and the furtherance of commerce, art and industry'.

In its commercial days, the park had been a true sporting mecca, hosting the FA Cup Final between 1895 and 1914. Speedway, which, like greyhound racing, had been a hugely popular spectator sport in the interwar years, continued there with stops and starts until the early 1970s. But in the wake of the Great Fire of 1936, its athletic facilities had shrunk dramatically. The new National Recreation Centre was designed by the Architect's Department under Leslie Martin, the guiding light behind the Royal Festival Hall, and seems to have been commissioned by Sir Gerald Barry, the impresario-cum-organiser of the Festival of Britain. Martin would be gone from the LCC by the time the Centre finally opened in 1964. But the building – clean, modern, in wood and concrete, possessing lots of communal areas in an almost open-plan design reminiscent of contemporary offices – certainly shares the optimistic internationalist leanings of his Festival Hall.

At the very moment when Britain was waking up to the fact that it was no longer quite the master of all the games it had written rulebooks for, this sports centre was conceived as a nationalistic project. Barry set out the case in patriotic terms that ignored the role, say, of the Ancient Greeks, stating boldly in one LCC report that:

It may perhaps seem remarkable that the British nation which invented and bequeathed to others most of the forms of sport which are now enjoyed throughout the Western world, should have no central home for sport of their own to which their own athletes and those of other nations can look as a focal point.

But in wishing to create a home to hothouse athletic talent, the Centre had a distinctly Soviet aura about it. The command-economy countries of the period, as their trophy cabinets were to show, devoted considerable resources to specialist training camps to almost battery-farm sportsmen and women of every stripe.* Britain might have Roger Bannister and the four-minute mile in the sack and Everest whipped – if by a New Zealander and a Nepalese – but a totting-up of the Olympic baubles after Helsinki in 1952 implied a certain malignancy in the field of track events. Australia and Czechoslovakia walked off with more gold, silver and bronze than Britain did that year. The National Recreation Centre was therefore deemed necessary to stop the rot and keep the reds under the bed at bay too. The health of the nation, in every sense, was at stake.

With a National Health Service now caring for people from the cradle to the grave, the government had a far greater handle on the well-being, or lack of well-being, of the country. Health was a real

---

* Bulgaria under Communism, for instance, was allocated model boating as its designated sport. Its lake facilities, to this day, remain the envy of UK clubs, like that at Victoria Park, which compete in the World Championships there.

government issue, one with a ministry, and a minister, to look after it. And one thing they will have noticed was that people were becoming less active. With the end of rationing in 1954, austerity was rapidly superseded by a never-had-it-so-good affluence for millions. There was virtually full employment, and with wages rising by 34 per cent between 1955 and 1960, Britain entered what *Queen* magazine referred to as 'the age of Boom' (that title proving prophetic as, ultimately, things didn't end too well – though arguably nowhere near as badly as the neo-liberal Right would have us believe). But while the sun shone, new homes were furnished with HP-purchased sofas and new fitted carpets, refrigerators, washing machines, electric cookers and, as we have seen, TVs. The home itself became an entertainment all of its own. Millions of Britons in the middle of the twentieth century were of a mind to spend their spare time at home, now they had one.

Trips to the cinema or to see a show and having a drink or two in the pub were fast replaced by a night in front of the telly with a can of beer. People could spend the day pottering about their own garden, following tips from Percy Thrower of *Gardeners' World* – the avuncular parks superintendent for Shrewsbury whose astonishing display of fuchsias in the city's otherwise war-weary Quarry Park had caught the eye of a passing BBC radio producer in 1946.

Meanwhile, technology was further mechanising areas of work, and there was an accompanying rise in white-collar and retail professions, so a growing proportion of the national labour force was engaged in less physically demanding jobs – though such roles might, admittedly, often prove less hazardous to health in other respects. With high employment and buoyant wages, people finally had the cash to avail themselves of the calorific fine German wines, Dutch lagers, Black Forest gateaux and high-end, low-tar cigarettes – the regal-sounding

Pall Malls, Embassys and Marlboros – they had been denied during the long period of austerity.

One of the most visible indicators of the increasing prosperity was soaring car ownership, which rose by 250 per cent between 1951 and 1961. Four wheels being judged far better than two legs, politicians and planners responded by reconfiguring whole towns, cities and villages to accommodate their progress. In what might seem a curious contradiction, the country was becoming both more mobile and more domestic. At weekends now, the whole family was likely to pile into the Austin 800, tartan blanket and wicker basket full of Spam sandwiches packed in the boot, and drive out to somewhere scenic. In 1955, they could, if they so wished, motor to Britain's first garden centre in Ferndown, Dorset. Three years later, the opening of the Preston bypass even provided a motorway for them to picnic beside.*

Urban parks were no less of a draw for motorists. By the end of the 1950s, traffic jams were a common sight at the gates of Victoria Park in East London. On fine Sundays, its drives were quickly choked by rows of encircling cars, the air filling with fumes and the sound of furious Vauxhall Cresta owners, gunning their engines and swearing under their breath, as they failed to find a space to park. Weekday commuters, some former East Londoners who'd been re-housed further out after the war and drove to and from the new suburbs and estates in Essex, used the park driveways as a shortcut. Congestion and boys racing newly purchased Sunbeam Tigers and Austin-Healeys became such a problem that in 1967 the park resorted

* Its foremost backer, Ernest Marples, the Minister for Transport and former director of his own road-building company, was a keen runner and started most of his working days with a lap around Hyde Park.

to permanently closing its main gates to prevent cars from entering. The old roadway was then replaced by paths for athletes, cyclists and roller-skaters.

Aware of this less active population, the government pushed ahead with schemes like the National Recreation Centre and encouraging greater participation in sports at school. Free schooling for all had been extended to the age of fifteen by the Education Act of 1944, which also prescribed free milk and required local authorities to provide playing fields for all schools. Rooftop playgrounds were a common solution in city schools, especially in London. But meanwhile many public parks, including Victoria Park, where a new athletics pavilion was built in 1963, also responded to government campaigns for greater participation in sports by adding or refurbishing their running tracks. Indeed, as Britain was a country acclimatised to group activity by the war, with millions belonging to a trade union and working for large-scale paternalist employers or nationalised industry, and of course inspired by the sportsmen and women they were now able to watch so easily on television, membership of park sports and social clubs was probably at its height in the 1950s and '60s.

Another feature of the boom years was the soaring birth rate, which reached its post-war peak in Britain in 1964. Parks quite possibly contributed to this breeding bonanza. A survey conducted by Mass Observation in 1946–7 found that 'a notably high proportion of marriages' arose 'from chance encounters' and that while 25 per cent of couples were introduced through friends or family, and others at work, 10 per cent met 'at dances, on holidays, or just in the park'. In any event parks were compelled to add extra play areas, some replacing older ornamental gardens or flower beds. A cynic, of course, might suggest that more children's facilities were added to parks to warn courting couples of the eventual consequences of their love-making and so restore the birth rate to more manageable levels.

In Kennington in 1960 a new playroom, children's toilets and children's gymnasium equipment were added to the park, while at Bishops Park in Fulham a year later, a former bowling lawn was converted into a 'Toddler's Green' for the under-fives. And reflecting the thinking of contemporary child psychologists and educationalists, its committee also mooted giving over another area of the park to 'free play' – though they were stymied by other demands on the space. Talk and chalk might still be the order of the day in most state schools, with their timetables learned by rote, corridors not for running in and 11-plus exams crammed for in almost military fashion, but as the 1950s rolled into the 1960s, the new decade brought with it 'comprehensive' education, fresh theories and legislation on child development and learning by play. Indeed, in 1959 the United Nations' Declaration of the Rights of the Child had declared play a universal right, stating that children should have the 'full opportunity for play and recreation' and that 'society and the public authorities' had to 'endeavour to promote the enjoyment of this right'.

Acting on this, the London County Council would appoint dedicated 'Play Leadership Chiefs' in all of its parks. Pat Turner, working in this capacity, was horrified on starting his shift one day in 1964 to meet 'ten howling babies in their prams' abandoned outside Brockwell Park's playground. Turner found their 'young attendants' playing inside and decided to provide a place where mothers could take their infants 'to play while they, themselves, relaxed'.

A Brockwell Park hut was promptly co-opted for the first 'One O'Clock Club', this meagre space stocked with enough used toilet-roll spools, egg boxes, Copydex glue, glitter and poster paints to satisfy the most eager devotees of *Blue Peter*, but also offering room for 'mothers to sit and chat'. The concept was such a success that it was adopted across the capital's parks and numerous One O'Clock Clubs remain in place to this day.

Before becoming a 'play chief' Turner had run one of the earliest 'junk' – or 'adventure' as they became known after 1953 – playgrounds: the Lollards in Lambeth. Constructed on the site of a bombed school, its chief promoter was the formidable landscape architect and children's rights campaigner Lady Marjory Allen of Hurtwood. Stopping over in the then recently liberated Copenhagen while working for UNICEF in 1946, Allen had been taken to see Emdrup, which she believed was 'the first waste-material playground in the world'.

Initiated a couple of years earlier and under the nose of the Nazis by the Danish landscape architect Carl Theodor Sørensen – who'd first put forward the idea of setting aside areas where children might 'play with old cars, boxes and timber' and argued that play should be directed by the youngsters themselves rather than park architects – it was nothing short of a revelation to Allen. She resolved to create a similar playing ground on her return to London, and the Lollards, by some accounts already claimed by the local children anyway, was the result. It garnered lavish coverage in *Picture Post* in 1946. The black and white photographs published there were of urchins in ill-fitting hand-me-downs, mercilessly severe short back and sides haircuts, over-sized shorts and knitted tank tops, enjoying themselves on climbing frames constructed of salvaged wood and scrap metal.

Such images fitted in perfectly with the 'make do and mend' ethos of that time. But the underlying philosophy of letting the kids do it for themselves was more suited to the age to come. In the following few years, and with the backing of the National Playing Fields Association, Allen established a further ten adventure playgrounds around London, including Camberwell and North Kensington, and two outside the capital, usually on bombed or waste grounds leased cheaply or loaned by the local authorities and staffed by sympathetic council-employed wardens. Before the Lollards was redeveloped and a new school built on the site in 1960, Turner, who serenaded visitors with passages from classical overtures on a violin, encouraged the kids to camp out on the site, cooking their own food on open fires. They were also invited to dig vegetable patches and expand its stock of rope-swings and Heath Robinson-style contraptions with discarded planks and tyres sourced locally.

Allen dismissed standard municipal playgrounds as 'bleak as barrack squares and just as boring' but the adventure playground, if in a somewhat tamer form than she liked (mud and the freedom to dig up the ground or light a fire were among her prerequisites), was rapidly adopted in often quite traditional public parks across Britain from the late 1950s on. One modelled after the Lollards opened in nearby but rather more stately Kennington Park in 1958. The pop-physiological language used by a contemporary commentator to describe the one installed in Victoria Park in East London is particularly telling. The writer salutes the adventure playground there for enabling children to 'express their abundant energy and imagination'. And it says as much about how speedily social attitudes changed that the staff at such playgrounds were by the late 1960s billed as providing the 'kids with a degree of non-authoritarian guidance'.

Not unlike David Cameron's rather more short-lived plea to hug a hoodie, it was accepted that a little more love and a little less stop-that and keep-off-the-grass might prevent children and newly invented teenagers from running completely wild and ruining parks for everyone. Play parks and adventure playgrounds – like youth clubs with their skiffle contests watched over by kindly vicars in comfortable jumpers – were perceived as a means of conquering the phenomenon of juvenile delinquency. A phenomenon that Fleet Street had elevated to a threat to the foundations of society. But that society – especially in the aftermath of the *Lady Chatterley's Lover* trial, the Profumo scandal and the first Beatles LP – was by now younger, eager for change, and far less deferential to established authority in all its guises. The age of Boom would become a boon time for protest songs, anti-nuclear arms rallies and satire. Park keepers in their peaked caps or brown trilbies, with their litter-spiking sticks, whistles and rulebooks, became easy figures to ridicule.

From the early 1950s, the *Beano* comic acted as a weathervane for this sort of insubordination. Dennis the Menace, the striped-top-wearing and bog-brush-haired tearaway created by Davey Law, first appeared in the comic on 15 March 1951, and his debut strip, set in a park, revolves around the mischievous tyke's attempts to subvert 'Keep Off the Grass' signs. And the Menace, aided from 1968 by his dog Gnasher, was over the next four decades frequently pitted against Parky Bowls, a compelling jobsworth of a keeper.

Another premonition of the park as a potential playground for newly liberated and counter-cultural activities, however, is James Broughton's 1953 short film, *The Pleasure Garden*. Shot by the German-born cinematographer Walter Lassally in the ruins of Paxton's overgrown Crystal Palace Park, in the film the park becomes the backdrop to what Broughton called a 'mid-summer afternoon daydream'. Broughton himself was a bisexual and moneyed West Coast American. A proto-Beat, he was a poet and experimental film-maker who had come to Europe in the early '50s, after being dismissed from military school for a gay affair and dropping out of Stanford University because he could afford to. He found the British 'more eccentric and repressed' than he could possibly have imagined. *The Pleasure Garden* can almost be read as a personal attempt to sexually liberate this nation's supposedly uptight population. A sort of 'turn on, tune out and cop off' for a people for whom hot-water bottles and chilblains Broughton presumed were still enough of a night-time complication.

Once the titles have receded, a young woman in a Victorian black velvet cape skips up to an angel-tombstone statue, and with a piped voice, schoolmarmish and shrill, enquires: 'What is your pleasure, please – your favourite pleasure? Would you expect to find it in the open air, in a more or less public park?' And what unfolds over the course of the next thirty-nine minutes is a kind of Manichaean battle for pleasure – an antecedent of the clash between, say, the animated Beatles of *Yellow Submarine* in Pepperland and the Blue Meanies. On the one side are the puritans headed up by Col. Pall. K. Gargoyle, a prudish park keeper in an undertaker's top hat, frock coat and dark glasses intent on converting the garden into a cemetery. Played with suitably querulous, if buttoned-up, exasperation by John Le Mesurier, Gargoyle wanders from outrage to outrage. Breaking up a pair of male wrestlers on the grass, naked aside from some rather snug briefs, he mutters, 'This is indecent and put something on.' Pinning up penalty notices left, right and centre, he exclaims 'Disgraceful, distasteful', while actually nailing fig leaves on to statues' nether parts. Ranged against him is an assortment of lovelorn oddities in the park, several in antique-shop clobber and all in search of emotional and physical fulfilment. Most remarkably for a film of this age, these oddities include two men and a young woman who are unearthed from the bushes – the girl when grilled by Gargoyle on the precise meaning of this ménage simply shrugs, telling him that the boys are 'together', resulting in Gargoyle's furiously thumbing a park rulebook to select the appropriate by-law to deal with this particular misdemeanour.

The film picked up a gong at the 1954 Cannes festival, in the now sadly defunct category of 'Prix du filme de fantaisie poétique'. Its main guns were aimed at killjoys and – not dissimilar to Ealing comedies of the same vintage – the fun-sapping edicts of bureaucratic officials and self-appointed pillars of the community. The sort of aldermen and justices of the peace, misty-eyed for Empire, whose ire was stoked by Lord Beaverbrook's *Daily Express* – which enjoyed the sales and status of today's *Daily Mail* as the paper of choice for the aggrieved shire dweller – and for whom the return of a Conservative government under Churchill was viewed as a godsend.

But their time, it seemed, was over. In his recent memoir, *An Encyclopaedia of Myself*, the critic and documentary maker Jonathan Meades reckoned that the 1950s and early '60s, were, perhaps, the last golden age of the bogus majors. No snug bar, hotel lounge, local council office or minor public school, in his opinion, was free back then of an ex-service type, neat of dress, self-importantly clinging to their rank and ever willing to share the benefit of their man-of-the-world experience. The termination of their reign came some time between the anti-nuclear-missile Aldermaston march and the arrival of Action Man, when they became plain risible and characters fit only for sitcoms like *Fawlty Towers*.

Spared national service and the Vietnam war, British teenagers of the 1960s duly adopted uniforms of their own. Some of them, like the duffel coats of the 'ban the bombers' and the parkas sported by scooter-riding mods, drew from and subverted these old majors' military wear. By the latter half of the 1960s, though, a new aesthetic of nostalgia became fashionable, perhaps subconsciously fed by the sloughing off of most of the remaining pink bits of the Empire and the often crass modernisation of town and city centres, where wrecking balls were claiming once-grand Victorian stations, music halls and shopping arcades in the name of progress. Bright young things of the burgeoning hippie movement were donning old policemen's capes and guardsmen's red jackets picked up from the antiques market on the Portobello Road, or neighbouring 'happening' vendor of Victorian apparel, I Was Lord Kitchener's Valet. This ironic military dandyism proved a fleeting fashion, speedily replaced by a more earnest cheesecloth and the head-to-toe denim that has enjoyed numerous reiterations and revivals since. Arguably the most lasting document of this antique style's heyday is the Beatles' 1967 LP *Sgt. Pepper's Lonely Hearts Club Band* – the fab four appearing on the record's gatefold sleeve in the shiny finery of the eponymous fictional band. Its front cover, a peerless assemblage by Peter Blake of the group surrounded by a selection of their heroes, with models by his then-wife Jann Haworth and waxworks from Madame Tussauds, has become so familiar as to be arc-welded into the collective consciousness.

Perhaps less well known is that in Paul McCartney's first imagining, he pictured the Beatles on the sleeve 'in a park up north somewhere and it was very municipal, it was very council'. As he told his Boswell, Barry Miles, in *Many Years from Now*: 'I had the idea to be in a park and in front of us to have a huge floral clock, which is a big feature of all those parks.' Querying something that has puzzled parkgoers ever since their initiation in the opening decade of the twentieth century, he and his fellow Beatles contemplated exactly 'why', as McCartney recalled, 'they do a clock made out of flowers'. Their conversations, perhaps inspired more by the kind of grass rolled up and smoked than the variety mown for cricket pitches, roamed over the idea that these clocks never moved, just grew; 'time' was therefore rendered 'non-existent' and the floral clock 'frozen'.*

It is a Mr J. McHattie, the chief superintendent of parks in Edinburgh, who is usually credited with first introducing floral clocks to Britain in 1903. The idea of a kind of herbaceous calendar can be traced back to the Swedish botanist Carl Linnaeus, but McHattie is believed to have felt compelled to bring floral clocks to the Scottish capital after seeing models at a gardening exhibition in Paris. From Edinburgh these extraordinary confections of the organic and the mechanical – working, if often only hour-handed, timepieces embedded in living, growing flower beds – spread rapidly, becoming by the interwar period a mainstay of Britain's public gardens, and especially in the major northern municipalities and in popular seaside resorts, like Morecambe and Bridlington.

---

* Parks would be responsible for some of Paul McCartney's best and worst creative conceits. It was while out walking his dog Martha on Parliament Hill Fields with the band's biographer Hunter Davies that the phrase 'It's Getting Better', which a one-time session drummer had used all the time, floated into his head, resulting in the song of the same name. On the other hand, a day filming in 'a park in Denver' with his Super 8 camera laid the seeds for the *Magical Mystery Tour* movie ...

In the event, 'the municipal environment' was deemed 'no longer appropriate' for the Beatles and frozen time metamorphosed into a guitar, when the Clifton Nurseries in St John's Wood failed to deliver quite enough flowers for 'even a small floral clock' to the photo shoot at Chelsea Manor Studios on Flood Street.*

However, the Beatles' work with parks was not done. Three weeks after the album's release, the underground newspaper *International Times*, whose editors included Barry Miles and financial sponsors numbered one Paul McCartney, published an article headed 'In Their Hearts They Know We're Right: Play in the Parks You Must You Can', which recounted an event that they chalked up as 'a rare victory' in the 'never-ending battle to wrest the usage of our public parks away from the people we pay to maintain them'. It reported that members of the Exploding Galaxy, a commune established on the Balls Pond Road, Islington by the performance artist David Medalla, had succeeded in staging one of their impromptu dance dramas in Regent's Park. Their show had attracted the attention of 'the inevitable park fuzzman', who subsequently returned with an 'SS type (jackboots, helmets, guantlets [*sic*], etc.)' and, later, ten policemen. Despite the support, apparently, of 'several school teachers and several housewives', the former taking down the officers of the law's names and numbers, the group was forced to move on to Primrose Hill to avoid arrest.

The article wound up with a sort of dos-and-don'ts manifesto for hippie park frequenting. Littering was a complete no-no and the

---

* Another so near and yet so far park-related album sleeve was Jimi Hendrix's *Electric Ladyland*. Hendrix had wanted to use a photograph, taken by McCartney's future wife, Linda Eastman, of himself and his band, the Experience, larking about beside the Alice in Wonderland statue in New York's Central Park, but was overruled by his record company.

playing of radios and tape-machines was, it suggested, best avoided. But park keepers, it argued, had 'got to learn to relax and remember that parks are not just for looking at' and that kids were 'citizens'. Those who were 'molested by park attendants' were advised 'to go to a nice square' who could speak their language. Make sure, the piece advised, that keepers were left in no doubt that they were infringing the rights of ordinary citizens who'd paid for the park and were as entitled to enjoy it as anyone else. Finally, it asked its readers to remember that 'the park's fuzz aim' was to make their living 'off the park with as little work as possible' and that 'hating beatniks' usually only came 'second'. For all of the free-and-easy, let's-do-a-dance line, there's something rather Thatcherite about this we-paid-for-it-with-our-taxes rhetoric and impugning of public-sector workers.

The following year park authorities appear to have become more forgiving of beatniks. Or certainly the more entrepreneurial pop-band-managing ones – because with the aid of the Ministry of Works, the 'ever-idealistic' rock promoters Blackhill Enterprises were able to orchestrate the first proper free concert at the Cockpit in Hyde Park on 29 June 1968. Memories of this and subsequent gigs in the park, given the passing years and certain substances ingested by organisers and attendees, are inevitably patchy. Some claim to have attended a more spontaneous event in the selfsame park involving a flatbed truck and a PA system powered by electricity siphoned off a cable for ornamental lights. Others are less sure if this was the same gig, or a different one somewhere else entirely. But much like David Hemmings in Michelangelo Antonioni's cinematic dissection of Swinging London, *Blow-Up*, unsure whether he's witnessed a murder in Charlton's Maryon Park and if a mimed tennis game hasn't acquired a corporeal reality, distinguishing fact from fiction was never one of the psychedelic '60s' strong points. Quite the reverse, usually.

The DJ John Peel, whose late-night underground music show *The Perfumed Garden* on Radio London soundtracked the Summer of Love, on one occasion playing *Sgt. Peppers* in its entirety, definitely attended the Hyde Park concert and filed a glowing report of the day. Peppered with flower-power imagery and full of phrases such as 'the blessed drifted and around them music hung in the air and touched the trees', it makes somewhat toe-curling reading in the twenty-first century. Bearded strummer Roy Harper's 'free songs' are said to have 'wheeled and danced in the sun like butterflies' while Jethro Tull apparently 'played with fire and brought out the first rays of the sun'. The sounds of Pink Floyd fell around 'with the touch of velvet and the taste of honey'. Far out, obviously. Hints of the slightly more saturnine Peel treasured by the nation do surface in a few dry asides – the Serpentine, he notes, sounding rather more tongue-in-cheek than ingenuously wide-eyed, 'is a great name, should you have overlooked it'. But this is the hopeful hippie who felt at ease writing, 'Were there any notes of sadness and misunderstanding in the park? I hope not' and wondered if those walking by the Cockpit today might not 'feel the power of a magic hour ... still hanging there'.

Whatever the actual quality of the event, its novelty certainly ensured that Peel never forgot it, and later, when such idealism had fallen out of fashion, he recalled it no less fondly in his memoir *Margrave of the Marshes*:

I always claim that the best outdoor event I've ever been to was the Pink Floyd concert in Hyde Park, when I hired a boat and rowed out and I lay in the bottom of the boat, in the middle of the Serpentine and just listened to the band play. I think their music then suited the open air perfectly. It was – it sounds ludicrous now, it's the kind of thing that you can get away with saying at the time and which now, in these harsher times, sounds a bit silly – but I mean it was like a religious experience, it was that marvellous. They played A Saucerful Of Secrets and things. They just seemed to fill the whole sky and everything. And to coincide perfectly with the lapping of the water and the trees and everything. It just seemed to be the perfect event. I think it was the nicest concert I've ever been to.

But while love may have abounded among these flower children, a more fractious side to the late 1960s was indicated by the need for Pink Floyd to give assurances to the Bailiff of the Royal Parks and the Ministry of Works that none of the park's bins would be kicked in. Such acts of wanton vandalism, the straights in suits informed them, were becoming a persistent problem. Only the previous September, Bishops Park in Fulham had been ravaged by rival football fans after a Fulham and West Ham match. Shrubs and railings were torn up in the affray and football supporters subsequently barred from entering the park on match days. Up in Newcastle, meanwhile, the Town Moor and Parks Committee looked into granting its park keepers the power of arrest and recruited more active men who might be willing to 'tangle with young toughs' who 'ruin plants and playground equipment'.

At Hyde Park, the hippies, having left the bins untouched, were invited back. And by the following June, 150,000 signed-up members of Peel's 'hairy smiling army' flocked to see Blind Faith, Donovan and the Third Ear Band. Those numbers were impressive enough to persuade Mick Jagger, who as an ex-student of the LSE always had a head for figures, to offer the services of the Rolling Stones for another free concert a month later. In the event, the Stones in Hyde Park concert turned into a memorial for their erstwhile guitarist Brian Jones, found drowned in the swimming pool of his Sussex pile two days before the gig. In a documentary about the concert filmed by Jo Durden-Smith for Granada Television, the event has the air of a garden fete. Though one with an estimated 250,000 people in attendance. 'Nearly three times as many as the immortal cup final at Wembley', in the calculation of compère Sam Cutler, who also dispenses advice on heat exhaustion and points out the locations of toilets and places for lost children to congregate. That he doesn't, in the end, announce the winner of a raffle comes as a genuine disappointment. Meanwhile, Charlie Watts can be seen handing out apples and oranges through the window of a backstage caravan; it could be a picnic on a lay-by.

Only the presence of groups of Hell's Angels in storm-trooper helmets, their denims and leathers adorned with swastikas and iron crosses, suggests the potential for something a little more threatening. But even here, their menacing get-up is shown to be more bark than bite. Employed to police the crowds, a task they attend to with a mixture of geeky earnestness and the dithering ineffectiveness of a dozen *Dad's Army* Corporal Joneses, these wild ones seem pathetically weedy, if anything. Gawky of frame, pasty of complexion and crooked of teeth, they stand much as Cliff Richard to Elvis when compared to their hog-riding American peers. (Which, given the events of Altamont a few months later, was perhaps no bad thing.)

Away from the stage and the throngs of long-haired, short-haired, skimpily and over-dressed old mods, old rockers and newer

hippies – quite a number of whom choose to sit out the Stones' act in the comfort of striped deckchairs or lying comatose on the grass – life goes on as close to normal. Bowlers in neatly pressed slacks roll their woods on greens, cavalry officers on horses trot along driveways, and rowing boats, ducks and coots float on the Serpentine. Orderliness seems the order of the day, extending right up to the end of Durden-Smith's film, where a distracted-looking old lady with cotton-wool white hair in a cardigan and meringue-like hat is caught walking through a bunch of hippies, most of whom are frantically attempting to tidy up. At which point the park itself looks only marginally more litter-strewn than the streets of the King's Road, which appeared briefly earlier on.

The Stones themselves, breadstick thin and edging towards glam in gender-bending eye make-up and big girls' blouses from the trendy boutique Mr Fish, were debuting Mick Taylor, their replacement guitarist for Jones. And if in pre-show interviews Mick Jagger appears just too Tiggerishly excited at the prospect of playing in the park to be in mourning, the singer took to the stage and read two stanzas of Shelley's poem *Adonais* as a tribute to their fallen founding member.

On its completion, the band's little helpers appeared with boxes full of hundreds of white butterflies, which they released into the air. Many, though, had already died in the heat from inadequate ventilation. Some butterflies failed to get far beyond the front row, accidentally crushed by stoned teenagers swaying to 'Honky Tonk Woman'. But more than enough lived to flutter off deep into the park – where they went on to cause immense damage to the flowers and vegetation. It was an ominous sign of things to come, for all concerned, really.

CHAPTER 10

When the Sun Cries Morning

Who in all honesty would choose to venture into the park of 'Down in the Park' by the Tubeway Army? Of an almost funereal pace, its languor emphasised by phasing-effects on the plodding drums and a recurring mini-Moog synthesiser line that sounds like cars passing on a rain-sodden dual carriageway, the park of the song is a dystopian nightmare. A space menaced by 'rape machines', where androids called Machmen kill undesirable humans as a spectator sport. In 1979 its composer, Gary Numan, a twenty-one-year-old former forklift-truck driver and fan of the science fiction of J. G. Ballard, Philip K. Dick and William Burroughs, was in little doubt that such a reality was imminent. In an interview with *Smash Hits* published to coincide with the release of the accompanying album, *Replicas*, he maintained that the human race was heading for extinction as boys and girls were becoming 'physically unisex'. Soon enough 'everyone would wipe each other out' anyway, as gang fights were 'going to get completely out of hand', they'd be 'gang battles with guns' and everyone would 'just get destroyed'. The machines, he concluded, wouldn't need to take over, there'd be no one 'there to stop them'. As his interviewer, Ian Cranna noted, Gary's was 'not a pleasant vision' but it was a timely one. Even if some of its more apocalyptic elements largely, and thankfully, failed to materialise.*

---

* For contrast, try 'A Walk in the Park' by the Nick Straker Band, also released in 1979. An upbeat floor-pleaser made with very similar synthesiser kit but to

Numan had recorded the album over two months in Gooseberry, a budget cellar studio popular with reggae and post-punk acts like Black Slate, Public Image Ltd and the Slits, located below a dentist's in Soho's Chinatown, during the bitter winter of 1978/9 – the coldest January since 1963. The album's creation was therefore accompanied by weeks of frost, freezing fog, hailstorms, sleet and snow. And perhaps more notoriously, streets and public parks all around Britain piled high with uncollected rubbish, council bin men and refuse collectors – along with gravediggers and crematorium staff, school caretakers, oil depot, rail and transport workers – having come out on strike as part of action advocated by the National Union of Public Employees and others for better wages and conditions. The conclusion of this Winter of Discontent – as the press, reviving some of the rhetoric that had swirled around Ted Heath's no less troubled Conservative administration in the early 1970s, called it – was a vote of no confidence in James Callaghan's Labour government. In the resulting general election on 3 May 1979, Margaret Thatcher came to power. Numan's single 'Are "Friends" Electric?', the second from the *Replicas* LP, was released the following day and rose to the top of the singles chart, while the LP topped the albums. No correlation, obviously. But a love of cars and a certain bleakly mercantile view of human relations – Thatcher famously noting that the Good Samaritan of the Gospels needed money to be altruistic and Numan that in the near future friends might be hired – was common to both.

On the album's sleeve, Numan stands inside a bare room illuminated by a single unshaded light bulb. His face, impassive, is plastered with

---

a notably different end, it extolled the unwinding qualities of shady glades on troubled minds and, unusually for a disco number, advocated the need to get straight.

Pan Stik, his hair bleached to an arc-light white; he wears black jeans and a silky black shirt and tie. The look is sufficiently monochromatic to win any 'come dressed as a pint of Guinness' contest. Numan stares at an old-fashioned sash window, slightly open, to his left. In its top pane, a night sky is lit by a crescent moon. And in the bottom half there are what could be trees, fencing and a gateway, over which, in neon-lit letters, 'The Park' is spelled out. The sign in this tableau certainly possesses the gaudiness of an amusement arcade. But the overwhelming impression again is of somewhere unimpeachably sinister and nocturnal, like Batman's Gotham. Which perhaps explains why 'Down in the Park' itself was picked to appear on the soundtrack of *Times Square*, a 1980 teen-pop punk movie about two runaway girls on the still-mean streets of New York. The film, shot on location, today stands as a document of a Big Apple whose deliquescing tenements and fly-blown streets were inhabited by slouchers and loungers, hustlers, dipsomaniacs, junkies and released mental patients, and when its parks were a byword for crime and danger.

Central Park had witnessed its first murder back in 1872 – and was to see plenty more in the following century, with a particular spike around the centenary of that initial slaying. But a survey undertaken by the park association of resident New Yorkers in 1963 had already found that 'fear' was 'the overriding thought in most people's minds about parks in New York City'. They were forced to conclude that New Yorkers were actually 'afraid to use their parks'. This despite the fact that between 1955 and 1964 there hadn't been a single murder in Central Park. And for half of that period, a dress code that banned the wearing of bathing costumes and even halter tops was enforced; Olmsted's exacting standards, it seems, were being upheld. Viewers tuning into Barry Gray's pioneering TV talk show in 1959 would not, however, have been left with that impression. Gray informed his audience that if they valued their lives, and didn't want to be 'killed or mugged', they should 'keep clear of Central

Park, especially after nightfall'. Central Park was, in his opinion, 'a happy hunting ground taken over by the dope-happy hoodlum, the homosexual, the exhibitionist, the potential murderer'; 'one great open-air cesspool'.

Gray may have been misrepresenting things, but his vision soon seemed prophetic. The next decade would see the greenswards play host to landmark anti-Vietnam and civil rights demonstrations, and the first 'gay-in' after the Stonewall riots, and therefore come to embody the relaxed liberality of the city. More conservative New Yorkers, the wealthy dwellers in expensive apartment blocks on Fifth Avenue and Central Park West, were less enamoured of this influx of 'ruffians' to '*their* park'. But this was as nothing compared to the very real and increasing dangers lingering in the park. Indeed, between 1960 and 1970 crime was to rise four times faster in the park than in the rest of the city. Ironically, perhaps, it was only after this period, when crime had worsened in the city as a whole, that Central Park gained its truly fearsome reputation as a no-go area – much as a genteel rural village, a country house or supposedly egalitarian Sweden can provide a more striking backdrop for a murder mystery, so stories about crimes in the park enjoyed a far higher profile in the press during the early '70s. In 1973, for example, the *New York Times* devoted extensive coverage to three homicides in Central Park, while 1,676 other murders across the city as a whole attracted nothing like the same column inches. Television dramas and movies, such as 1974's *Death Wish*, starring Charles Bronson as a pacifist architect turned vigilante who guns down a junkie stick-up artist in the park, perpetuated the idea that this was an urban jungle best avoided, particularly after dark. Even actors doing Shakespeare in the Park in broad daylight were not safe – or so Woody Allen encouraged people to believe, with the character Rob in *Annie Hall* recalling that he got mugged 'playing *Richard the Second*', two guys with leather jackets stealing his leotard.*

In the midst of this, the city was teetering on the edge of bankruptcy, and the cost of maintaining the parks, when put against keeping hospitals, schools and fire stations open, was deemed an unnecessary expense. To save money, New York's park department's budget was cut by 60 per cent between 1974 and 1980, and after the resolution of the city's fiscal crisis of 1975, it would lose more than half its permanent and seasonal work-force. An alarmed investigation into the city's parks, published in the *New York Times* in May 1977, reported that they were 'in an advanced state of deterioration'. More than 500 parks and playgrounds were being tended to weekly by a mobile team of rangers, who could do nothing to stem the tide of vandalism or the piling up of trash that turned many into rubbish dumps. Beer cans filled the ponds in Central Park, whose lush Sheep Meadow, deprived of the care and irrigation formerly lavished on it, was left to become as dry as a dust bowl.

Across the Atlantic, in Birkenhead, the park that had inspired the creation of Central Park was not faring much better. A decline in manufacturing, the contraction of the British shipping industry and the development of containerisation for cargo brought the closure of docks and high levels of unemployment to the Wirral and Merseyside in the 1970s. And Paxton's park was to become something of a punchbag for those frustrated, angry or alienated by an emerging economic order that seemingly could find no place for them.

Like Central Park and other New York parks, its plight was also worsened by the actions of the local authorities and national

---

* Garth Risk Hallberg's doorstopper 1970s-set New York novel, *City on Fire*, continues to perpetuate the myth to this day, the plot of this 2015 book turning on a shooting in Central Park.

government. In the early 1960s, the Birkenhead Corporation nursed ambitions to redevelop the whole area, and unfurled plans to replace all the villas and terraces surrounding the park with 'closely spaced blocks of multi-storey flats'. By all accounts, some of its members viewed the Victoriana of the park and neighbouring streets with distaste and were not especially sorry when vandals finally started to chip away at some of the former's more floridly nineteenth-century elements. However, even they were soon taken aback by the savagery and scale of the damage inflicted on the park. On 4 October 1972, the *Birkenhead News* reported that vandals had 'badly wrecked' the Swiss bridge, punching holes through both sides of it, and smashed up the iron bridge. The estimated cost of the damage was put at £26,000, and as the Corporation was unwilling, or unable, to meet the price of repairs, the bridges were closed and the islands they once reached left to grow wild. In the following year, the two lodges at the Grand Entrance, where Olmsted had been greeted by milkmaids, were described in council meeting minutes as 'eyesores'. Their windows broken and their walls daubed with graffiti, they would only fall further into dilapidation after a £40,000 renovation plan was rejected out of hand in a time of power cuts and three-day weeks.

And on it went. Cars were abandoned and set alight in the park. A wooden pavilion erected by the Field Lawn Tennis Association just before the First World War was torched by arsonists. In 1977, sculptured columns and decorative stonework in the Boothby Ground area of the park were smashed to smithereens. A photograph of the aftermath of the devastation has a park keeper in horn-rimmed glasses and full Sally Army peaked cap holding a chunk of broken masonry, his face a picture of utter incomprehension. This attack at least brought the poor condition of the park to wider public attention, and it was now declared a conservation area. But that couldn't halt the vandalism, nor its patronage by the wageless and those seeking to forget economic or personal vicissitudes by other means. On 25 September 1978, the *Liverpool Daily Post* stigmatised it as a refuge for 'drunks and dossers' and by 16 March 1981 the paper would claim that 'pram mums' were avoiding the park for fear of being attacked. That same year, its showcase conservatory, a greenhouse that tipped its hat in homage to the park's great creator, had to be demolished, simply to prevent it from being destroyed by those who were doing it harm on an almost daily basis.

Birkenhead Park may have been dealt an unusually bad hand, but many other public parks in Britain were beset by much the same problems. In Norwich, Captain Sandys-Winsch's Waterloo Park similarly lost its bowls pavilion to a fire started by malicious pranksters. Mother nature too seemed to be conspiring against parks. The arrival of the *Ophiostoma novo-ulmi* fungus, or Dutch elm disease, on logs imported from America in the late 1960s was to have devastating consequences for British trees. To date, some 60 million elms are estimated to have been killed. But in the early 1970s and in the initial epidemic, the loss of grand avenues of elms in many parks seemed to augur a looming ecological catastrophe. If previously the meat and potatoes of science fiction, scientists were now growing ever more vocal about dangers to the environment.*

---

* In John Wyndham's apocalyptic novel, *The Day of the Triffids* (1951), the eponymous walking, carnivorous stinging plants menace London's parks in the wake of the freak meteor shower that blinds almost the entire world's population. 'I had noticed several lumbering across Hyde Park, and there were others in Green Park,' the book's sighted narrator, Bill Masen, records at one point. 'Very likely they were ornamental, safely docked specimens – on the other hand, maybe they weren't.'

Urban parks were also disadvantaged by particular bits of British legislation. The creation of the Countryside Commission in 1970, which made government grants available to country parks, was iniquitous to say the least, denying funds to its city-slicker peers. On top of that, the adoption of recommendations in the Bains Report of 1972, which resulted in parks being folded into broader local authority 'recreational services' departments that also managed sports centres, swimming pools and museums and galleries, only diminished the money available to parks for basic upkeep. Parks with lidos were particularly badly hit by this arrangement, since a Sports Council's *Planning for Sport* report in 1968 had already pressed for the replacement of 'outdated' outdoor lidos with more 'efficient' indoor swimming pools. These were judged better suited to a nation feeling its way towards central heating and double glazing and just dipping its toe into package deals in the warmer waters of the Mediterranean.

Largely dating from just before the Second World War, many lidos, once so sleekly modern, were plagued with problems of vandalism and decay similar to those of the parks themselves. During that famously long and hot British summer of 1976, Parliament Hill lido was broken into and its changing-room cubicles reduced to timber, its windows shattered and the pool filled with broken glass. And that July, the lido made the national news when a fifteen-year-old boy, Enrico Sidoli, died soon after an altercation in its pool. Calling their safety as a whole into question, the tabloids painted a lurid picture of lidos as the haunt of thugs, their waters nearly as dangerous as the coast off Amity Island in the recent blockbuster movie *Jaws*. Parliament Hill survived the bad publicity, but in the next decade and a half, London alone would lose eight former LCC outdoor pools. In the early 1980s, the admittedly more *au naturel* Men's Pond at Hampstead Heath was in such disrepair and its waters were so shallow that a 10-metre diving board had to be removed to prevent acrobatic bathers from injuring themselves.

The problem of finding money for maintenance and staffing was compounded by a system where expenditure on parks and gardens was not included in the government's Standard Spending Assessment for local authorities. In effect, those wishing to fund parks had to find the money from somewhere else, and as the economy tanked that 'somewhere else' was increasingly hard to find. Financial necessity as much as fashion dictated that parks cut back on horticultural fripperies like floral clocks and flower beds – the latter in Birkenhead, and elsewhere, subjected to bovver-booted assaults in any case. Sowing them over with grass that needed only the occasional hoe and mow offered a double saving, since fewer staff were needed to attend to them. But having fewer staff about the place of course left the park vulnerable to further vandalism. Ordinary parkgoers missed their reassuring presence, and feeling less safe might forgo their usual jaunts around the cracked paths, wrecked shrubberies and incinerated bandstands. Leaving them, in turn, for the sole enjoyment of weirdos with nowhere else to be. It was a vicious circle, really, and one made even more vicious by the introduction of compulsory competitive tendering for all park maintenance contracts by Margaret Thatcher's Conservative government in the 1980s.

Believing the market to be the panacea for nearly all public institutional ills, this ruling forced local authorities to seek outside bids to run every aspect of their public parks, from cleaning and cafes to gardening and maintenance. Obtaining value for money, but allowing contractors to make a profit, was the mantra of the policy. And some councils, less wily about small print and the sharp-elbowed practices of a contemporary business world that looked in admiration at

Wall Street's Gordon Gekko, signed exceedingly poor deals. A common practice among many contractors, in the interests of minimising their expenditure and maximising their profits, was to keep only a skeletal force of often unskilled maintenance staff and deploy them in roving gangs – a practice cash-strapped New York had trialled in the mid-1970s, with no more pleasing results. Moving from park to park across a borough, these squads were supposed to blitz what desperately needed to be blitzed and undertake essential repairs and duties. Some were dedicated and extremely efficient but, by and large, only the bare minimum ever got done. The parks were devoid of officials for sometimes what seemed like days at a time. And the absence of permanent trained gardeners meant that the variety and quality of planting declined.

The less inviting the parks became, the more those with the means to do something else did something else. Especially with shopping becoming a leisure activity in its own right – one serviced by new out-of-town, American-style malls that were treated as destinations and promenaded through in a manner not dissimilar to the parkland walkways of old. And out-of-town businesses were increasingly to be found in parks of their own. Though of a kind with minimal greenery and mostly clustered off a corridor by an A road. With 70 per cent of UK households owning a car by 1994, and following the promotion of country parks in the 1970s and '80s, for those that could afford it the 'Sunday stroll in the local park' had, according to one contemporary study, been 'replaced by a car-based trip' to a country park, where visitors were 'likely to find car parking, toilets, interpretation centres, activities, gift shops and a more structured "experience"'.

An Audit Commission report from 1994 found that less than 10 per cent of the UK's urban parks had cafes or refreshment kiosks, and only 25 per cent still had toilets. With the recession of the early '90s dimming their lustre even further, the nation's parks had just about reached rock bottom, the *Observer* newspaper noting in 1995 that most of Britain's Victorian parks were 'decaying' and regarded as 'unsafe and uninviting by their users'. But fresh thinking, hard data and a little bit of luck were about to lead to a quite spectacular improvement in their fortunes.

CHAPTER II

Things Can Only Get Better

Historically, public parks were designed to improve their environment and raise the value of properties around them. But by the early 1990s that idea, in most instances, had been completely turned on its head, with many local parks perceived as having a negative impact on their surroundings. Donald Simon's assessment of New York in 1976 could just as readily be applied to swathes of the UK fifteen years later:

> For many people a park is no longer an amenity: It represents a threat to their safety and a liability to the value of their own property. In a quarter of a century, a long-established philosophy has been overturned. The image of a greensward decorated with a monument to a national hero or a playground filled with happy children has been replaced by visions of acres of weeds interrupted by vandalized statues, or playgrounds barren of any usable equipment occupied by the social dregs of the community.

But those visions, if lost for a while, were to resurface now in the early 1990s. The renewal of public parks came following decades of declining populations and deindustrialisation of cities. But the gradual repopulating of inner and fringe urban neighbourhoods – first by immigrants, and then artists, artisans and media types, and eventually by financiers and bankers, in the great game of gentrification – refocused attention on city green space. These new populations brought with them the notion of community, and green space was an intrinsic component of this. And so, here and there, in the very centre of major English cities, new kinds of communal gardens began to sprout up, often planted in brownfield sites and tended by local volunteers. Two significant forerunners in the 1970s and '80s were the William Curtis Ecological Park and the Camley Street Nature Park, created, respectively, on vacant land near Tower Bridge and King's Cross Station. Of course, once these areas became identified as communities they grew increasingly desirable, and the effect of such innovations as those first new communal gardens would often eventually price segments of that original community out.

Islington in North London was an early beneficiary, or victim, of this gradual gentrification, a process perhaps first intimated, as Jonathan Raban argues in *Soft City*, by the professional slummer George Orwell's move into Canonbury Square in the 1940s. Four decades later, and thanks to a campaign by environmentally minded locals, a defunct railway siding near Arsenal station was reborn as Gillespie Park, a wild garden and nature reserve. In 1991 its lush grasslands were enticing enough for the only common orchid in the entire borough to plant itself in the park. The following year an ecology centre for schools and the general public was opened there.

The park had originally faced opposition from some local residents, who were concerned that a wild garden on their doorstep would be a magnet for untamed vagrants and fly-tippers. Instead, the park had to fight off the attentions of avaricious property developers in the 1980s and the Tory Secretary of State Nicholas Ridley's attempts to divest the public of its unprofitable public spaces. But by the mid-1990s, parks and fresh brownfield green spaces such as Gillespie Park were coming to be recognised as economically useful tools in the voguish field of 'urban regeneration'.

In 1994, for example, a new park was laid out by the London Docklands Development Corporation on a parcel of derelict land at Limehouse. This was among the last creations of the LDDC, established in 1981 to redevelop some eight and a half square miles of docks, wharves, basins and warehouses closed and left to rot after the arrival of container shipping. Part of the re-landscaping of the whole area following the completion of the Limehouse Link Tunnel (the cut-and-cover roadway connecting Limehouse to the rising financial fiefdoms of the Isle of Dogs and Canary Wharf), the park was named Ropemakers Fields – this particular site famed in Samuel Pepys's day for the manufacture of rope for hoisting sails, lowering anchors and lashing cargo. And as befits a park also conceived as a complement to new luxury waterfront housing, it played heavily on that history. A rope motif was built into its railings and bollards, and a sculpture in copper by Jane Ackroyd – featuring a herring gull, beak wide open as if in mid-squawk, planted on a coil of rope – was installed.

Makers of anything other than money in the City would of course become thinner and thinner on the ground in that part of Limehouse in the coming decades. Out of either thrift or as a memorial to those industries obliterated and replaced with computer-generated office towers, shops, chain coffee-houses, bars, restaurants and off-the-chart on-the-grid apartment buildings, the park's bandstand was fashioned with cast-iron columns salvaged from warehouses at St Katharine Docks.

Meanwhile, talk about arresting urban decay, creating liveable cities and building sustainable communities burbled around town-planning conference rooms heady with the smell of whiteboard marker pens and cafetières. And such talk was no doubt also heard across the table in the bijou Upper Street eateries patronised by Labour politicians then on the brink of power. Certainly, the think tank Demos – as closely associated with the triumph of 'New' Labour under the leadership of a forty-two-year-old Tony Blair in the 1997 general election as the handbag house act D:Ream and their campaign anthem, 'Things Can Only Get Better' – were preoccupied by these questions, producing in 1994 a report on city parks in association with Comedia, the publisher and promoter of new theories about urbanism and the creative industries.

Park Life: Urban Parks and Social Renewal was the result of the 'observations of over 10,000 park users and interviews with more than 1,200' in ten different parks of all stripes. Many of its findings astounded even those running the parks. One of the biggest surprises was simply that far more people were using their parks than either government policy makers or their providers realised. Forty per cent of those surveyed claimed to visit their local park every single day. Slightly more men than women used parks, and there was one dog to every eight people. But those users represented a much wider cross-section of society in terms of age, ethnicity and income than users of most other public leisure facilities. The difference was particularly striking when parks were squared up to council-run or subsidised indoor sports centres. Whereas 70 per cent of parkgoers travelled on foot, 80 per cent of sports-centre users drove. Where those of all ages and in all manner of jobs (or no jobs at all) visited parks, sports centres were predominantly the preserve of the 18–45-year-old 'professionals' in IT and accountancy, recruitment and PR.

Councils, then, were effectively subsidising the most affluent members of their communities at the expense of the whole. Parks, the report was able to show, were cleaner, greener and better value for money. Reflecting on its research some twenty years on at his home, a flat overlooking Clissold Park in Stoke Newington, its co-author Ken Worpole remembered being floored by how counter-intuitive much of what they found seemed back then. For example, even the commonly accepted view that the home was private and the park public had to be re-evaluated. A number of young people they spoke to, Worpole recalled, stated quite categorically that they went to the park for privacy. 'They couldn't stand to be cooped up at home. There was always someone about, wanting to know what they were up to. It was too noisy and busy, with the television on and their sister's stereo, so they went to the park to be left alone.' With home today so full of technology, Worpole believes that in the modern age parks may have come to 'function much like churches once did', as places for 'solitude and sanctuary'.

As a case in point, another of the report's interviewees, a man from Hounslow, described the park as the only place he could relax. He could get fresh air in his own garden easily enough. But thoughts of 'things to do back in the house' constantly came to mind. The park, therefore, supplied a space for him to forget about everything else.

It also highlighted another common misperception: that young people liked nothing more than to 'run amok' in parks. In their surveys, Worpole and his colleagues found that most young people wanted 'almost exactly the same things as many elderly park-users – toilets, cafe, to be treated with a bit of respect, and somewhere, as often as not, to be quite sedentary, sit down, lie on the grass'. Equally important was that they needed 'to feel safe' and to that end actually welcomed a range of 'other people to be about'.

The report pointed out that, in comparison with other council leisure facilities, like sports and concert halls, parks were clearly much more open and versatile as venues. They could host an array of different types of event, sometimes contiguously, from kids' fun days and kite festivals to ethnic-minority fairs and political and religious rallies, all of which could bolster a sense of self-expression, identity and community in any given area. And yet for decades parks had come second to sports centres, as local-authority recreation departments had been steadily infiltrated by, as Worpole puts it, 'young men, and usually men trained at Loughborough in Leisure Management'. All of whom 'wore short-sleeved shirts and ties, chunky jewellery. They looked fit and dynamic and sold politicians on the idea that indoor leisure was the future.'

Their reign was finally tempered in 1995 with the Tory govern-ment's decision, taken on the back of the Demos/Comedia report, to pump millions of pounds from the National Lottery's Heritage Fund into parks and open spaces. This, in Worpole's opinion – and he's far from alone in acknowledging it – 'saved the parks in this country'. In fact, the nation's parks had been blessed with good timing. A month before the report's publication, Lord Rothschild, who chaired the fund, had come under fire for using £12.5 million of lottery money to buy

Winston Churchill's papers for the nation. The National Lottery, only introduced the previous November, was supposed to support 'good causes': the arts, education, environment, heritage, health, sport and charity. However worthy the archive, here the cash had gone to the wartime Prime Minister's grandson, then a serving Tory MP. Critics argued that much of the material was already state property. In a poll conducted for the *Independent* newspaper and published on 2 May 1995, more than half the public felt the Churchill family should have donated the papers in any case. John Major's government, dogged already by financial and sexual scandals, was desperate for something vaguely egalitarian to distract attention from the Churchill payout and any lingering memories of Tim Yeo's love child. A scheme for reviving public parks, therefore, arrived like manna from heaven.

So, at least, runs Worpole's interpretation of events. Whatever the case, the adoption of many of the report's recommendations and the injection of hard cash into parks remain visible across Britain today. For instance, with the granting of Heritage Lottery Fund money came conditions relating to the management and maintenance of each park. The most significant was the reinstatement of permanent skilled gardening and supervisory staff. In addition, there was an insistence on recruiting managers with degrees and training or experience in administration, public relations and marketing to make parks both more 'professional' and more 'people friendly'. The effect, along with the restoration of historic features like pagodas and bandstands and the installation of new ones like outdoor exercise equipment, was to give parks some of their former dignity and prestige, making them safe and desirable places to visit again. The subsequent introduction in 1996 of the Green Flag Award, which did for parks what the Blue Flag did for beaches, dishing out an environmental gong that staff and users could brag about, was another step towards their rehabilitation. Alongside the presence of staff, a revival of horticultural elements other than dull expanses of ineptly mown grass largely claimed by the kickers and throwers of balls, perhaps added to the appeal of some parks to women, with both traditional and contemporary planting helping to add interest.

If Worpole, now a tall sixty-something with white hair and twinkly blue-grey eyes, and smartly casual in corduroy, has a concern about city parks today, it is, he says, the presence of the dead rather than the living. The trend for plaques, the planting of flowering cherry and the scattering of ashes – if accepted as a revival of sorts of the old inner-city burial grounds and memorials after nearly two centuries of suburban interments – has, he thinks, 'got out of hand'. They threaten to give many parks too much of a 'funereal air'.

He also fears that 'the tradition of the English garden is too strong' to allow some of the developments in 'linear parks' to get a proper foothold here. Linear parks were established in Scandinavia as early as the 1930s and have flourished across continental Europe more generally ever since. They are usually a linking series of green spaces, comprising gardens, playgrounds and foot and cycle paths, and often plotted through existing city or town districts. Dispensing with fences and the traditional formal barriers, the boundaries between the park and the area it serves are much more amorphous, and the distinction between the pavement and a lawn or flower bed, say, deliberately hazy.

Yet the English lag behind, despite the valiant strides made in urban gardening by the likes of Manor Fields Park in Sheffield, a 'wildscape' assiduously cultivated on inner-city wasteland that was previously home to the Deep Pitts allotments but eventually became so famed as a dumping ground for burnt-out cars and nefarious activities it was known locally as the 'bandit-lands'. Further south, there is Burgess Park, which runs across roads, canals and vacant factories in post-industrial Southwark. Elsewhere in the capital sits London's rather less acclaimed forerunner to New York's elevated High Line, the Greenway. This garden walk, sown along a defunct railway track, runs from Finsbury Park to Highgate, in contrast to Manhattan's gallery-strewn West Side, and at a more earthbound, ground level. And, on Worpole's last visit at least, it seemingly suffers from much more graffiti and litter than its pristine transatlantic cousin.*

---

* The High Line was refurbished with private money and as the spine of the massive luxury redevelopment of the Meatpacking District, West Chelsea, and the Hudson Yards. Since it opened in 2009 it has also become New York's most popular attraction, pulling in over 6 million visitors a year. Though it does have its detractors. In 2015, the art critic Jerry Saltz confessed to being 'creeped out by its canned, fabricated naturalness'. Railing against the trend for 'ersatz, privatized public spaces built by developers', he wrote that, for him, the High Line was 'the harbinger of a bad pathogen ... transforming public space into fussy, extra-busy, overdesigned, high-maintenance mannered playgrounds, curated experiences, and crowd-pleasing spectacles.'

Back in the mid-1990s global warming was belatedly moving up the political agenda, giving further weight to those arguing for regeneration of the nation's urban parks. Here already were homes for wildlife, trees that would help lower a city's ambient temperature, landscapes capable of water retention and which therefore reduced the risk of flooding.

The question of the environment remains the most pressing issue for contemporary landscape architects; increasingly so in relation to waste. In the last decade and a half, for example, landfill sites have begun to be successfully converted into parks, like the much-loved and aptly named Mount Trashmore near Virginia Beach in the United States. A self-sustaining, low-water-use public park, with a picnic area and a baseball field on a former dump, its centrepiece is a large grassy hill whose core component is compacted trash. Freshkills Park in Staten Island, New York, meanwhile was created on what was once the largest landfill site in the world and it has ambitions to gradually extend itself to three times the size of one-time islander Olmsted's own Central Park by 2036. Closer to home, 120 acres of the old Mucking Marshes refuse tip by the Thames at Thurrock in Essex officially reopened as a nature park in 2013. For more than fifty years it accumulated the waste of five London boroughs, but today its reed beds and grassy banks nourish water voles, barn owls, skylarks and wild orchids.

Equally impressive, the methane gas from the rotting foodstuffs buried deep below is expected to provide electricity for up to 100,000 homes in the decades to come. And at Avondale Park in Kensington, 2013 saw the planting of the world's first floral lawn in a park, a 'pollinator-friendly patchwork' believed to attract 25 per cent more insect life than traditionally managed grass lawns. Worpole himself hoped that all urban 'parks systems' might ultimately prove capable of demonstrating the 'consequences of consumption' and be re-engineered with the aim of 'bringing sewage back into the city'.

But in Britain today – in the new age of austerity – such ideals seem a long way off. Local authorities are having their budgets cut and find themselves under enormous pressure to raise revenue. Increasingly, this means that parks are forced to turn to private events, sponsors and volunteers in order to make up the shortfall. In June 2015 Julian Bell, a councillor in Ealing and chair of London Council's Transport and Environment Committee, was reported as warning that government austerity 'threatened a slide towards privately run parks in the next decade', citing the fact that councils' budgets had been cut by '47 per cent in real terms since 2010'. Spending on 'open spaces' across the London boroughs had fallen by 18 per cent in the previous four years – 'with a drop of more than 10 per cent in 2014/15 alone'. Quoted at length Bell stated that:

London's parks are at a crossroads and we cannot continue as we have in the past – the money simply isn't there. If we pass the tipping point communities risk losing control of parks, along with democratic accountability for the open spaces that they value so much. London boroughs face increasing financial pressure and the strain is showing on the resources available for parks, leisure and sports facilities. The current climate of austerity does not suggest the situation will improve.

A report entitled *The State of UK Public Parks*, published in June 2014 by the Heritage Lottery Fund, had already found that '86% of park managers had seen their revenue cut in the previous three years'.

Staffing levels were, accordingly, falling again and steeply. It argued that, given the projected cuts to budgets, the 'decline in spending on public parks' was 'potentially greater and more rapid than that faced during the late 1970s to early 1990s'. Visiting Derby Arboretum on its 175th birthday in October 2015, the *Telegraph* journalist Harry Wallop saw this decline in full effect, reporting that its staff of full-time rangers had been cut from thirty-three to just thirteen in the last four years. The park was visibly suffering as a result – Wallop found that many of its gates were locked and the public toilets out of order and that the grounds were littered with spent metal nitrous oxide canisters.

The Lottery Fund's report also claimed that 'just under half of all councils' were 'planning to dispose of some of their green space with 19% considering the disposal of parks'. Piecemeal sales of slivers of parks were on the rise, with a plan in Liverpool to sell the Sefton Park Meadows that adjoin Sefton Park to developers to build houses, as a means of clawing back money lost from central government for other essential services. In November 2015, the council in the London Borough of Bexley also approved the sale of three open spaces in the Erith district, as well as the eastern half of the Old Farm Park in Sidcup. This decision was justified on the grounds that the council was suffering 'unprecedented... financial pressures'. Other authorities, aided by an initiative promoted by the charity Nesta, have responded rather more imaginatively. Burnley in Lancashire, for instance, has attempted to make savings by replacing traditional flowerbeds with perennials and turning lawns into hay meadows, which require less maintenance. They have also experimented, if somewhat less successfully, with cultivating commercial crops such as borage in one park.

The effects are being felt beyond local authorities. In 2013, it emerged that 'Royal Parks', officially described as 'an executive agency of the Department for Culture, Media and Sport', were attempting to charge the London Charity Softball League a fee of £600 a summer for playing in Hyde Park. The League, which began when a group of charity workers began playing softball informally in the park over a decade ago, had been taken aback. Their matches, initially quite spontaneous affairs, had never been subject to any fees before and the area of the park they used, known as the 'Old Football Pitches', was an unremarkable stretch of grass by the Albert Memorial open to all parkgoers. The League was informed that if they played without paying the police would be called, and they later discovered that the job of collecting the fee had been outsourced to a private firm – which immediately added (if equally quickly withdrew) an additional administration charge. The charge rule was eventually overturned, but it is a far from unique or uncommon case of part of a public park being turned into a private 'for profit' venue. At Battersea Park, a section of an admittedly slightly run-down but well-used adventure playground was turned over to a private company, Go Ape, to refurbish and run at a profit. When the playground reopened in December 2015, local people protested at the company's new fees. Where the previous facilities were free, Go Ape charges between £18 and £33 per child for climbing sessions. And these sorts of arrangements look certain to increase, especially in London, where the new body set to take over the management of the Royal Parks in the autumn of 2016 is committed to amping up the commercial activities across its estate. In a mission statement, it has specifically pledged to 'generate substantial annual revenue from more events, concessions and licences'.

One 'alternative model of maintaining parks and green spaces without privatisation', and advocated by the London councils, is to transfer them 'to volunteers, community interest companies or trusts' – in the manner of some libraries. But given that some 324 libraries closed under cuts implemented by the Coalition Government between 2010 and 2015, and of those left, '330 fewer are open 10 hours or more a week', it's not a plan to fill anyone with an enormous degree of optimism.

The future of public parks, like that of the public sector as a whole, therefore looks more imperilled than it has done for some time. One ray of hope may lie in a scheme to declare the whole of London a National Park, backed by, among others, the architect Sir Terry Farrell. As '47% of London is green space', making it one of the greenest cities in the world for its size', Daniel Raven-Ellison, the main proposer of the scheme, argues that the status of National Park would further encourage its biodiversity. It would also improve the health of its residents, with the city's ongoing 'densification' accompanied, in effect, by foliation – something already officially backed by the Mayoral All London Green Grid plan, which aims to increase green cover by 5 per cent by 2030. More canal banks and back alleys could be reinvented as public green spaces and urban gardens and allotments, the whole city growing year by year and bud by bud into one all-encompassing wild park. And what, in all honesty, could be better than that?

But this is a world where the Olympic Park in Stratford (now the Queen Elizabeth II Park) finds itself under the stewardship of the London Legacy Development Corporation, raising serious questions about democratic accountability and the status of the 'public' in supposedly 'public parks' these days. After the Olympics it was not handed over to the Lee Valley Regional Park Authority – the local borough, which manages the other parks in the area. Nor, despite its new name, was it handed over to the Royal Parks administration. The London Legacy Development Corporation is instead a London Mayoral development corporation.

With areas around the park ensnared by wire-mesh fencing as building work on new office and apartment blocks continues, Ken Worpole, for one, expresses doubts about the long-term future and scale of public access to the space.

And with central London on the brink of becoming 'Dubai-on-Thames', a city of, for most of us, unaffordable and unoccupied towers, with flats serving as safety deposit boxes in the sky, there's a worrying sense that vast areas of parkscape could quite easily slip into becoming, once again, the great preserves of the rich. And London, of course, is always in the vanguard – what happens there may soon be the case up and down the country. We may find ourselves, in short, with parks of a type that are a little too familiar, recalling the dimmer days of history and those first aristocratic hunting ranges.

Afterword

In the intervening period since the final manuscript of this book was delivered and the preparations for this paperback edition, quite a few things have happened. Not all of them connected to parks, obviously. But the decision of United States National Parks Service employees to go rogue on Twitter following President Trump's inauguration serves to illustrate once again that parks are nothing if not political.

Here in Britain and despite everything else that went on in 2016 (the death of David Bowie, the introduction of plastic fivers, the changing of the shape of Toblerone chocolate bars, etc.), some 322,000 people found the time to sign a petition calling for the protection of parks in Britain. The government was also to receive more than 4,000 emails opposing any privatisation of parks. Each of these grassroots campaigns was initiated following the decision of the House of Commons to convene a select committee inquiry into public parks in the autumn of the year. A year that had already seen sections of parkland sold off in Sidcup, Kent and a charity run by Parkrun near Bristol cancelled over Stoke Gifford Parish Council's demand for fees to help pay for the upkeep and repair of Little Stoke Park after the event.

Reflecting the level of public concern, the committee received close to 400 formal submissions from park managers, user groups and other interested parties. Its open survey, meanwhile, elicited an impressive 13,000 responses. And its official hashtag #myparkmatters, notched up more than 900 tweets. None of them seemingly sent by Donald Trump or

Russian hackers. In addition the committee interviewed twenty-seven witnesses over four formal oral sessions.

Eagerly anticipated and trailed in the preceding months by acres of newsprint on the state of the nation's estimated 27,000 parks, and a forest of similar TV and radio items, most soundtracked by snatches of a certain tune by Blur, their report was finally published on 11 February 2017.

In it the MPs saluted Britain's green spaces as 'treasured assets' which were 'heavily used and much valued', with regular users numbering around 37 million. Parks, they concluded, were 'great value' as both amenities and 'for the contribution which parks make to wider policy objectives including community cohesion, improvement of air quality and biodiversity'. They commended 'the passion [with] which people [had] described their parks' and confessed that they too were 'worried about the potential deterioration or even loss' of parks or the facilities they offered.

But with council budgets shrinking by 27 per cent since 2010/11 under austerity measures – measures that the government seemingly remained intent on continuing, regardless – parks were, as they emphatically stated, 'at a tipping point' of decline. Across the country 92 per cent of all park budgets were found to have been cut to some degree – while in Newcastle the funds for parks were slashed by some 97 per cent. And it was far from the sole example of such extreme pruning of park budgets.

To avoid the 'severe consequences' of such cuts the committee urged local authorities to take into account the 'wider value' of parks when allocating their resources. And it entreated all local authorities to consider alternative models for looking after their parks, from volunteer groups to trusts.

Ruling out privatisation and the reintroduction of entrance fees, the report maintained that parks should remain under local authority ownership and be freely available to all. But those who had wished that the committee might recommend that parks be made a statutory service, or that, at least, a national agency be established to help guide policy on Britain's green spaces, were to be disappointed. And while the composition and the candour of the report were praised, its remedies have been greeted by a rather more muted response from park professionals and councils, with the phrase 'missed opportunity' issuing from several informed quarters. Blunter still was the University of Leicester's Dr Katy Layton-Jones, who told *Horticulture Week* that there was 'nothing in that document' that reassured her 'that parks will be funded properly in the next decade'.

When it was first suggested that I might write an afterword to *A Walk in the Park* to include the findings of the reports and other more recent developments, perhaps even throw in something on the Garden Bridge and the perfidiousness of public funded pseudo-public space, for good measure, I had rather hoped to sweeten the book's original somewhat pessimistic ending. But unfortunately at the time of writing too much remains in the balance to completely overturn my original conclusions. If anything, the future of parks, like almost everything else right now, feels just as uncertain as eighteen months ago.

But the success of campaigns like that led by the local resident and author Virginia Ironside to limit the number of commercial pay-to-play football pitches in Hammersmith Park in West London and the acknowledgement by central government that parks are in trouble, but loved by their users and good for us and the broader environment, are among those things we can take small comfort in at least.

Acknowledgements

Thanks are first due to everyone at Jonathan Cape, but most of all my editor, Alex Bowler, who when greeted with the idea of a book on parks didn't kick it into the long grass and endured its somewhat protracted production. Further thanks are due to my agent, Nicola Barr, and the team at Greene and Heaton, for their efforts on my behalf.

While I was writing this book I had the great privilege to be appointed as Chisenhale Gallery Victoria Park Residency Artist for 2014–5. I'd like to thank Polly Staple, Laura Wilson, Emma Moore, Tommie Introna and Lizzie Hudson at Chisenhale, and Dave Hime; Joelle Copeland, Andrew McIntyre, Marcelo Noveillo and Stephen Harmer at Victoria Park and Tower Hamlet Parks and Open Spaces Department, for making the residency such a pleasurable and stimulating experience. I'd especially like to thank Paul Kelly for giving up his time and considerable talents to direct *The Ace of Clubs*, the short film that emerged out of the residency events, research and writings. At the park, I am also immensely grateful to Norman Lara, Keith Reynolds, Dean Reynolds and Phil Abbott and the other members of the Victoria Park Model Steam Boat Club; Bob, Terry and Mr Jolly from Victoria Park Bowls Club, and Miranda Garret from Croquet East. Also, further thanks to Julius Beltrame, Ivo Gormley, Trenton Oldfield, Clive Bettington and Joe Murray, along with Justin O'Shaughnessy, Nick Perry and the members of the Hackney Society, for their support during the project.

And Cathy Haynes, whose previous residency inspired a thought or ten about time and motion in parks.

This book could probably not have been written (or would have been far, far worse anyway) without Ken Worpole, who generously allowed me to interview him at length and lent me numerous books, articles and reports about public parks. Obviously, I have only myself to blame for these pages and Ken is in no way responsible for what I have made of his words and wisdom or the contents of said books, articles and reports.

I am immensely grateful to the staff at parks up and down the country who endured my tiresome questions and supplied numerous and invaluable leaflets, maps and guides to their facilities. As always, the British Library in St Pancras and the London Library in St James's, the London Archives and the Metropolitan Archives in Clerkenwell, the Local History Library, Southwark, Tower Hamlets Local History Library and Westminster Reference Library provided many of the records, books, newspapers and pamphlets that I pillaged to write this book.

Thanks to Joe Moran for proffering an invitation to John Moore's University that supplied the excuse needed to take a ferry across the Mersey and visit Birkenhead Park, and Sukhdev Sandhu, whose similar invite to New York University justified the expense of the flight required to reacquaint myself with Central Park and explore Staten Island. Thanks also to Colette Bailey and all at METAL for providing a week's Time and Space residency in the grounds of the lovely Chalkwell Park, in Leigh-on-Sea. This not only gave me a chance to bash out some words undisturbed and only a couple of floors away from a display featuring one of Wilko Johnson's guitars, but also a room with a window to observe the 24-hour cycle of the park, with all the early morning comings and late-night goings-on of dog walkers, military fitness fanatics, et al.

Thanks to Paul Willetts for his thoughts on parks in Norwich and putting me in touch with Keiron Pim, who in turn pointed me towards the *Eastern Daily Press*'s archive.

Jonathan Main of the Bookseller Crow in Crystal Palace showed once again the beauty of the human over the algorithm by suggesting I might want to take a look at James Broughton's film *The Pleasure Garden*, DVDs of which can still be purchased in this fine independent bookshop.

Thanks to Lucy Hurst and Beggars Banquet Records for supplying and granting permission to use the sleeve image of *Replicas*. And Alan Denney, Jonathan Plunkett, Derek Tait and Bill Hicks for allowing me to include their amazing photographs in this book.

Nick Rennison kindly read an early draft of the book and made many useful suggestions and corrections.

And now I must simply resort to a list of friends, colleagues, collaborators, previously kindly commissioning editors and souls who have been nice along the way, so... Thanks to Alex Mayor, Helen Gordon, Katrina Dixon, Debsey Wykes, Bob Stanley, Tessa Norton, Pete Wiggs, Martin Kelly, Sarah Cracknell, Cathi Unsworth, Max Décharné, Syd Moore, Michael Meekin, Ann Scanlon, Marc Glendening and all the Sohemians, Ian Sansom, Mark Mason, Mark Pilkington, John Rogers, John Moore, Stephen and Nix Coates, Gordon Kerr, Julian Mash and Idlers everywhere, Will Hodgkinson, Caroline Catz, Gillian Darley, David Collard, Tony Rich, John Flannery, Liz Vater, Pete Brown, Dusty Miller, Kate Manning, Ben Metcalf, Joe Kerr, Emmanuelle Dirix, Charles Holland, David Crowley, Emily LaBarge, Jessica Lee, David Bownes, Laura Lappin, Oliver Craske, Dirk Bennett, Becky Fincham, Anita

Sethi, Neil Denny and the Little Atoms gang, Zena Alkayat, Rebecca Newell at the National Army Museum and Lt Col. John Kendall, Charlie Philips, Marcus Berkmann, David Quantick, Victoria Falconer, Seb Emina and the good people at the *Happy Reader*, David and Sydneyann Shook, Geoff Nicholson, Daniel Rachel, Paul Baggaley, Kris Doyle, Andy Miller, Andrew Martin, Alice Maddicott, Konrad Fredericks, Simon Grant, Guy Sangster-Adams, Lauren Wright, Gail O' Hara, Richard Boon, Deborah Cohen, Dan Carrier, Andrew Holgate, John Doran, Luke Turner, Manish Agarwal, Tim Burrows, Gareth Rees, Kit Caless, Gary Budden, Briony Bax, Frances Morgan, Chris Roberts, Declan Clarke, Catherine Taylor, Michael Knight, Karen Mcleod, Sarah Maguire, Tom Boll, Charles Beckett, Julia Bird, Katherine Pierpoint, Jamie McKendrick, Jeremy Worman, Matt Brown, Sharmaine Lovegrove, Gerry Hopkinson, Raz at the Betsy Trotwood, Roger Burton and friends at the Horse Hospital, Dan Thompson, Louise Oldfield, Jeff Barrett and Robin Turner and the Heavenly Socialists and Caught by the River folk, John Jervis, Robin the Fog, Katie Bilboa, John Boyne, Noel Murphy, Neil Taylor, Dickon Edwards, Christian Flamm, Paul Lawrence, Lora Findlay and Mathew Lees, Harvey Williams, Peter Doggett, Jerome Weatherald, Ella-mai Robey, Andrew Dunn, Lucy Warburton, Tori Dance, Georgia King, Nick Parker, Katy Evans-Bush, Richard Olson and Lucy Evans, Richard Davies, Chiara Ambrosio and Mikey Kirkpatrick, Johnny Trunk, Tom Campbell, Gareth Evans and Ana Sefer, Harry Parker and Sarah-Jane Forder... There are no doubt many more I've forgotten, but finally thanks to my family here and over the pond, and to my wife, Emily Bick, whose brilliant mind and astonishing beauty I am still unbelievably fortunate enough to be blessed with every day.

Illustration Credits

p. 3 Clissold Park, 2014. Photograph by the author.

p. 5 Speaker's Corner, Hyde Park, 2013. Photograph by the author.

p. 28 Postcard of the Le Petit Trianon. From National Library of Congress, Washington, USA.

p. 36 *A High Wind in the Park* by J. Baker, 1819. From National Library of Congress.

p. 45 Illustration by William Gilpin,1794. From his *Three Essays, etc.*

p. 53 Poster for Vauxhall Gardens. From National Library of Congress.

p. 64 Etching of J.C. Loudon. From the frontispiece of *An Encyclopædia of Agriculture*,1844.

p. 106 The Crystal Palace at the Great Exhibition in Hyde Park, 1851. From National Library of Congress.

p. 114 The Staten Island Ferry. From National Library of Congress.

p. 121 Birkenhead Park sign, 2014. Photograph by the author.

p. 138 Olmsted and Vaux's plan for Central Park. From the New York Public Library.

p. 141 Frederick Law Olmsted. From National Library of Congress.

p. 146 View of Central Park. From the New York Public Library.

p. 157 Postcard of a bandstand at Weston-super-Mare. From National Library of Congress.

p. 169 An Alpine-scene illustration by William Robinson. From *Alpine Flowers for English Gardens*.

p. 211 Troops in Battersea Park, 1914. From London Metropolitan Archives, City of London.

p. 218 Taking tea in Hyde Park. From National Library of Congress.

p. 222 Eaton Park. Photograph by George Plunkett. Reproduced with kind permission from his son, Jonathan Plunkett.

p. 226 Eaton Park. Photograph by George Plunkett. Reproduced with kind permission from his son, Jonathan Plunkett.

p. 230 'Fresh Air' by James Henry Dowd, 1924. ©TfL from the London Transport Museum Collection.

p. 234 Tennis players. From National Library of Congress.

p. 238 Swimmers. From National Library of Congress.

p. 243 St Paul's Cathedral in the Blitz. From National Library of Congress.

p. 254 Plymouth Hoe being tilled during the 'Dig for Victory' campaign. Photograph courtesy of Derek Tait.

p. 258 Amorous GI and girl. From National Library of Congress.

p. 290 The Lollards playground. © London Borough of Lambeth. This image was reproduced by kind permission of Lambeth Archives.

p. 300 The crowds at the Stones concert in Hyde Park, 1969. Photograph by Ian Steel. Reproduced by kind permission.

p.305 Rubbish piled in Stoke Newington Common during the so-called Winter of Discontent. Photograph by Alan Denney. Reproduced by kind permission.

p. 306 Cover of the Tubeway Army's *Replicas* LP. Reproduced by kind permission of the Beggars Banquet Group.

p. 320 Rock Against Racism Concert in Victoria Park, 1978. Photograph by Bill Hicks. Reproduced by kind permission.

p. 322 Clissold Park, 2014. Photograph by the author.

p. 328 Clissold Park, 2014. Photograph by the author.

Sources

This book owes an enormous debt to numerous previous books, pamphlets and articles charting the development of public parks, along with novels, films, and even songs featuring parks too. The sources and select bibliography below should hopefully give credit where credit is due and point those who want to know more in the right directions.

Introduction
Robert Walser's views on parks and Sundays appear in *Berlin Stories* (New York: New York Review Books, 2012).

For British monarchs snaffling land and the general historical development of parks throughout the book see:
—*The English Park: Royal, Private & Public*, Susan Lasdun (London: Deutsch, 1991)
—*Regent's Park: a Study of the Development of the Area from 1086 to the Present Day*, Ann Saunders (Newton Abbot: David & Charles, 1969)
—*The Invention of the Park: Recreational Landscapes from the Garden of Eden to Disney's Magic Kingdom*, Karen R. Jones and John Wills (Cambridge: Polity, 2005)
—*People's Parks: the Design and Development of Victorian Parks in Britain*, Hazel Conway (Cambridge: Cambridge University Press, 1991)
—*Public Parks*, Hazel Conway (Princes Risborough: Shire, 1996)
—*The Royal Parks*, Donald Edgar (London: W.H. Allen, 1986)
—*London's Royal Parks: An Appreciation*, Richard Church (London: HMSO, 1993)

—*The Park and the Town: Public Landscape in the 19th and 20th Centuries*, G. F. Chadwick (London: Architectural Press, 1966)

—*Public Parks: The Key to Liveable Communities*, Alexander Garvin (London and New York: Norton 2011)

I was led back to Don DeLillo's *Great Jones Street* (London: Deutsch, 1974) by Iain Sinclair, who quoted from the novel in his own book *London Overground: A Day's Walk Around the Ginger Line* (London: Hamish Hamilton, 2015).

Chapter 1: Killing Fields and Common Lands

The picture of the goatskin appeared on the Facebook page of the Clissold Park User Group. 'Black magic fears as whole animal skin is found in Clissold Park' was the headline of a piece by Alexandra Rucki in the *Evening Standard* on 3 June 2015.

For Gilgamesh and the earliest years of parks see:

—*The Epic of Gilgamesh,* translated by Andrew George (London: Penguin, 2003)

—*The Invention of the Park: Recreational Landscapes from the Garden of Eden to Disney's Magic Kingdom*, Karen R. Jones and John Wills (Cambridge: Polity, 2005)

—*The English Park: Royal, Private & Public*, Susan Lasdun (London: Deutsch, 1991)

For the Anglo-Norman period and legislation on land rights see:

—*Anglo-Saxon England*, Frank M. Stenton (Oxford: Oxford University Press, 2002)

—*The Anglo-Saxon Age: A Very Short Introduction*, John Blair (Oxford: Oxford University Press, 2000)

—*Conquest and Colonisation: The Normans in Britain, 1066–1100*, Dr Brian Golding (Basingstoke: Pan Macmillan, 2013)

—*The Norman Conquest: A Very Short Introduction*, George Garnett (Oxford: Oxford University Press, 2010)

—*1066: A New History of the Norman Conquest*, Peter Rex (Stroud: Amberley, 2010)

—*The Making of the English Landscape*, G. H. Hoskins (London: Penguin, 1970)

—*The Making of the British Landscape: How We Have Transformed the Land, from Prehistory to Today*, Francis Pryor (London: Penguin, 2011)

For the concept of the common land see:

—*Our Common Land: the Law and History of Common Land and Village Greens*, Paul Clayden (Henley-on-Thames: Open Spaces Society, 2003)

—*Commoners: Common Right, Enclosure and Social Change in England: 1700–1820*, J. M. Neeson (Cambridge: Cambridge University Press, 1993)

For hunting see:

—*Hunting in Britain from the Ice Age to the Present*, Barry Lewis (Stroud: The History Press, 2009)

—*Blood Sport: Hunting in Britain since 1066*, Emma Griffin (London: Yale University Press, 2008)

—*Medieval Hunting*, Richard Almond (Stroud: The History Press, 2011)

For Izaak Walton on the pedagogical qualities of hunting see his book, *The Compleat Angler* (Menston: Scolar Press, 1971)

For the legend of Fair Rosamond see:

—(again) *The English Park: Royal, Private & Public*, Susan Lasdun (London: Deutsch, 1991)

—*Medieval Gardens*, Elizabeth MacDougall (Cambridge, Mass.: Harvard University Press, 1986)

—*Medieval England: A Social History and Archaeology from the Conquest to 1600 AD*, Paul E. Szarmach and Teresa M. Tavormina (New York and London: Garland, 1998)

For the Black Death see:

—*The Black Death*, Philip Ziegler (Harmondsworth: Penguin, 1970)

—*Plague: Black Death and Pestilence in Europe*, William Naphy and Andrew Spicer (Stroud: The History Press, 2009)

In the wake of the plague:

—*The Black Death and the World it Made*, Norman F. Cantor (New York: HarperCollins, 2002)

The quote about the rabbit-chasing rights of the aldermen at Bow is taken from:

—*Victoria Park: a Study in the History of East London*, Charles Poulsen (London: Journeyman Press, 1976)

For Henry VIII's prowess as a horseman and interest in gardening (or at least land) see the hunting books above and:

—*Tudor England*, John Guy (Oxford: Oxford University Press, 1988)

—*Henry VIII: The Quest for Fame*, John Guy (London: Penguin, 2014)

—*Henry VIII: King and Court*, Alison Weir (London: Jonathan Cape, 2001)

—*In the Lion's Court*, Derek Wilson (London: Hutchinson, 2001)

—*Henry VIII: Man and Monarch*, exhibition catalogue edited by Susan Doran (London: British Library, 2009)

For Tudor and Elizabethan gardens and parks see general park histories above and:

—*Tudor and Stuart Gardens*, Anne Jennings (London: English Heritage, 2005)

—*The Tudor Garden: 1485–1603*, Twigs Way (Oxford: Shire, 2013)

—*English Homes of the Early Renaissance. Elizabethan and Jacobean Houses and Gardens*, edited by H. A. Tipping (London: Country Life, 1912)

—*The Making of the English Gardener: Plants, Books and Inspiration, 1550–1660*, Margaret Willes (New Haven and London: Yale University Press, 2011)

Chapter 2: Playing in the Park

For the ghostly goings-on at Versailles see:

—*The Ghosts of the Trianon: the Complete 'An Adventure'*, C. A. E. Moberly and E. F. Jourdain; edited by Michael H. Coleman (Wellingborough: Aquarian, 1988)

—*The Trianon Case: a Review of the Evidence*, D. L. Johnston (Ilfracombe: A. H. Stockwell, 1945)

—*The Ghosts of Versailles. Miss Moberly and Miss Jourdain and their adventure: a Critical Study*, Lucille Iremonger (London: White Lion Publishers, 1975)

For the palace and its gardens see:

—*The Sun King's Garden: Louis XIV, André Le Nôtre and the Creation of the Gardens of Versailles*, Ian Thompson (London: Bloomsbury, 2006)

—*The Gardens of Versailles*, Jean-Baptiste Leroux; translated by Alexis Gregory (London: Thames & Hudson, 2002)

—*Versailles Gardens: Sculpture and Mythology*, Jacques Girard (London: Sotheby's Publications, 1985)

—*André Le Nôtre: Gardener to the Sun King*, Érik Orsenna; translated by Moishe Black (New York: George Braziller, 2001)

—*The Sun King*, Nancy Mitford (London: Hamish Hamilton, 1971)

For Charles II's grand ambitions see park histories listed before but especially:

—*The Royal Parks*, Donald Edgar (London: W.H. Allen, 1986)

—*London's Royal Parks: An Appreciation*, Richard Church (London: HMSO, 1993)

—*St James's Park and the Green Park*, Pat Pierce (London: The Royal Parks, 1993)

—*Restoration London*, Liza Picard (London: Weidenfeld & Nicolson, 1997)

For Joseph Addison and gardening see general park histories already listed and:

—'The Pleasure of the Imagination: Joseph Addison's Influence on Early Landscape Gardens', M. Batey, in *Garden History* (vol. 33, number 2, 2005)

—*A Writer's Britain: Landscape in Literature*, Margaret Drabble (London: Thames & Hudson, 1979)

On the emergence of the English landscape park and the Picturesque see:

—*Stowe: The Garden and the Park*, Michael Bevington (Stowe: Capability, 1995)

—*The Work of William Kent: Artist, Painter, Designer and Landscape Gardener*, Margaret Jourdain (Westmead: Country Life, 1948)

—*William Kent: Designing Georgian Britain*, edited by Susan Weber (New Haven and London: Yale University Press, 2013)

—*Capability Brown and the Eighteenth-century English Landscape*, Roger Turner (London: Weidenfeld & Nicolson, 1985)

—*Capability Brown*, Dorothy Stroud (London: Faber, 1975)

—*Capability Brown: The Story of a Master Gardener*, Thomas Hinde (London: Hutchinson, 1986)

—*Capability Brown and Humphry Repton*, Edward Hyams (London: Dent, 1971)

—*Humphry Repton: Landscape Gardening and the Geography of Georgian England*, Stephen Daniels (New Haven, Conn.: Yale University Press, 1999)

—*Humphry Repton*, Laura Mayer (Oxford: Shire, 2014)

—*British Gardens in Time: The Greatest Gardens and the People Who Shaped Them*, Katie Campbell (London: Frances Lincoln, 2014)

—*Aesthetics and the Picturesque, 1795–1840*, edited by Gavin Budge (Bristol: Thoemmes, 2001)

—*Three Essays on Picturesque Beauty*, William Gilpin (Hampshire: Gregg International, 1972)

For Sidley Park's gloomy forest and towering crag see:

—*Arcadia*, Tom Stoppard (London: Faber, 1993)

For Vauxhall and other pleasure gardens see:

—*Vauxhall Gardens: a Chapter in the Social History of England*, James Granville Southworth (New York: Columbia University Press, 1941)

—*Green Retreats: The Story of Vauxhall Gardens, 1661–1859*, Walter Sidney Scott (London: Odhams Press, 1955)

—*Vauxhall Gardens: a History*, David Coke and Alan Borg (New Haven and London: Yale University Press, 2011)

—*Vauxhall: Sex and Entertainment. London's Pioneering Urban Pleasure Garden*, Penelope J. Corfield (London: History & Social Action Publications, 2012)

—*The Pleasure Garden: from Vauxhall to Coney Island*, edited by Jonathan Conlin (Philadelphia: University of Pennsylvania Press, 2013)

—*The London Pleasure Gardens of the Eighteenth Century*, Warwick Wroth, assisted by Arthur Edgar Wroth; with a foreword by A. H. Saxon (London: Macmillan, 1896; 1979 reprint)

—*Ranelagh and its Times*, Cyril FitzGerald (London: Northern Printeries, 1913)

—*The English Pleasure Garden: 1660–1860*, Sarah-Jane Downing (Oxford: Shire, 2009)

Chapter 3: Park Land of Hope and Gloria

For Victoriana see:

—*The Victorian Mind: An Anthology*, edited and selected by Gerald B. Kauvar and Gerald C. Sorensen; with a Preface by Jane Fawcett (London: Cassell, in association with the Victorian Society, 1969)

—*The Victorian Vision: Inventing New Britain*, edited by John M. MacKenzie (London: V&A Publications, 2001)

—*The Making of Victorian Values: Decency and Dissent in Britain, 1789–1837*, Ben Wilson (New York: Penguin Press, 2007)

—*Victorian Cities*, Asa Briggs (Harmondsworth: Penguin, 1971)

—*Victorian Things*, Asa Briggs (Harmondsworth: Penguin, 1990)

—*Victorian People: a Reassessment of Persons and Themes, 1851–67*, Asa Briggs (Harmondsworth: Penguin, 1965)

—*The Victorians*, A. N. Wilson (London: Hutchinson, 2002)

—*Inventing the Victorians*, Matthew Sweet (London: Faber, 2001)

—*The Victorian City: Everyday Life in Dickens' London*, Judith Flanders (London: Atlantic, 2012)

—*London in the Nineteenth Century: 'a human awful wonder of God'*, Jerry White (London: Jonathan Cape, 2007)

For the emergence of the railway age see:

—*The Last Journey of William Huskisson: How a Day of Triumph Became a Day of Despair at the Turn of the Wheel*, Simon Garfield (London: Faber, 2002)

—*Fire & Steam: a New History of the Railways in Britain*, Christian Wolmar (London: Atlantic, 2007)

—*The Victorian Railway*, Jack Simmons (London: Thames & Hudson, 1991)

—*The Victorian Railway and How it Evolved*, P. J. G. Ransom (London: Heinemann, 1990)

—*Nineteenth Century Railway History through The Illustrated London News*, edited by Anthony J. Lambert (Newton Abbot: David & Charles, 1984)

For Royal Victoria Park, Bath see:

—*A Manual for the Park: Or, a Botanical Arrangement and Description of the Trees and Shrubs in the Royal Victoria Park, Bath*, Frederick Hanham (London, printed in Bath, 1857)

—*The Royal Victoria Park*, Robin Whalley: undated but a PDF of his text is available online at the Bath Spa University's website at: https://www.bathspa.ac.uk/Media/CHC%20Images/Vol%2005%20-%2007.%20Whalley%20-%20The%20Royal%20Victoria%20Park.pdf

For Queen Victoria and her unusual name see:

—*Becoming Queen*, Kate Williams (London: Hutchinson, 2008)

—*Victoria: A Life*, A. N. Wilson (London: Atlantic Books, 2014)

For John Claudius Loudon and his steam-powered-plough-imagining wife, Jane, see:

—*Some Nineteenth Century Gardeners*, Geoffrey Taylor (London: Skeffington, 1951)

—*Loudon and the Landscape: from Country Seat to Metropolis, 1783–1843*, Melanie Louise Simo (New Haven and London: Yale University Press, 1988)

—*The Loudons and the Gardening Press: A Victorian Cultural Industry*, Sarah Dewis (Farnham: Burlington: Ashgate, 2014)

—*In Search of English Gardens: the Travels of John Claudius Loudon and his Wife Jane*, edited by Priscilla Boniface (Wheathampstead: Lennard, 1987)

—*Lady with Green Fingers: The Life of Jane Loudon*, by Bea Howe (London: Country Life, 1961)

For Loudon on public parks see various issues of:

—*The Gardener's Magazine: and register of rural & domestic improvement for gardening and gardeners conducted by J. C. Loudon* (London: Longman, Rees, Orme, Brown, and Green, 1826–1843)

For Sir Benjamin Thompson and the Englischer Garten at Munich see:

—*An American in Europe: the Life of Benjamin Thompson, Count Rumford*, Egon Larsen (London and New York, Rider, 1953)

—*Benjamin Thompson, Count Rumford*, Sanborn C. Brown (Cambridge, Mass: MIT Press, 1979)

—*Knight of the White Eagle: a Biography of Sir Benjamin Thompson, Count Rumford (1753–1814)*, W. J. Sparrow (London: Hutchinson, 1964)

For R. A. Slaney's investigations into the health of the poor see:

—*Reports of the House of Commons on the Education* (ordered to be printed 13 July 1838), and *on the Health* (1840) *of the Poorer Classes in large towns; with some suggestions for improvement*, R. A. Slaney (London: C. Knight & Co., 1841)

For more on the creation of the first proper public parks see general park histories listed previously, especially:

—*People's Parks: the Design and Development of Victorian Parks in Britain*, Hazel Conway (Cambridge: Cambridge University Press, 1991)

—*The English Park: Royal, Private & Public*, Susan Lasdun (London: Deutsch, 1991)

—*The Park and the Town: Public Landscape in the 19th and 20th Centuries*, G. F. Chadwick (London: Architectural Press, 1966)

and local park histories:

—*Victoria Park: a Study in the History of East London*, Charles Poulsen (London: Journeyman Press, 1976)

—*Birkenhead Park*, Jean McInniss (Birkenhead: Countyvise, 1984)

—*Parks for the People: Manchester and its Parks, 1846–1926* (Manchester: Manchester City Art Galleries, 1987)

—*Lambeth's Open Spaces: an Historical Account*, Marie P. G. Draper (London: London Borough of Lambeth, 1979)

On the pre-parked Battersea see:

—*Old and New London: a Narrative of its History, its People, and its places*, Walter Thornbury (London: Cassell, 1897)

For Derby and other arboretums see:

—*The Derby Arboretum; Containing a Catalogue of the Trees and Shrubs Included in It; A Description of the Grounds and Directions for Their Management; as It Was Presented to the Town of Derby etc.*, John Claudius Loudon (London: Longman, Rees, Orme, Brown, and Green, 1840)

—*The British Arboretum: Trees, Science and Culture in the Nineteenth Century*, Paul A. Elliott, Charles Watkins and Stephen Daniels (London: Pickering & Chatto, 2011)

For Strutts and their circle see:

—*The Strutts and the Arkwrights, 1758–1830: A Study of the Early Factory System*, R. S. Fitton and A. P. Wadsworth (Cambridge, Mass.: Harvard University Press, 1969)

—*The Lunar Men: the Friends Who Made the Future, 1730–1810*, Jenny Uglow (London: Faber, 2002)

Coleridge's thoughts on Derby appear in *Reminiscences of Samuel Taylor Coleridge and Robert Southey*, Joseph Cottle (Cambridge: Cambridge University Press, 2014 edition). Also see *Unruly Times: Wordsworth and Coleridge in Their Time*, A. S. Byatt (London: Vintage, 1997 edition) for more on Coleridge's tours of the Midlands

For Peel Park in Salford see:

—*Salford: a City and its Past*, edited by Tom Bergin, Dorothy N. Pearce and Stanley Shaw (Salford: City of Salford [Cultural Services Department], 1975)

For James Pennethorne and his London parks see:

—*Sir James Pennethorne and the Making of Victorian London*, Geoffrey Tyack (Cambridge: Cambridge University Press, 1992)

—*Early Victorian Architecture in Britain*, Henry Russell Hitchcock (New Haven and London: Yale University Press; Architectural Press, 1954)

—*Victoria Park: a Study in the History of East London*, Charles Poulsen (London: Journeyman Press, 1976)

—*Lambeth's Open Spaces: an Historical Account*, Marie P. G. Draper (London: London Borough of Lambeth, 1979)

For George Lansbury's reminiscences about Victoria Park and its pagoda see:

—*My Life*, George Lansbury (London: Constable, 1928)

—*The Life of George Lansbury*, Raymond Postgate (London: Longmans, Green, 1951)

SOURCES

For Fanny Price on the green stuff see:

—*Mansfield Park*, Jane Austen (Oxford: Oxford World's Classics, 2008 edition)

For the Chartists see Victorian histories previously listed plus:

—*Chartism*, Asa Briggs (Stroud: Sutton, 1998)

—*Chartism*, Harry Browne (London: Hodder & Stoughton Educational, 1999)

—*Chartism*, Edward Royle (London: Routledge, 1996 edition)

—*Kennington Park: the Birthplace of People's Democracy*, Stefan Szczelkun (London: Past Tense, 2005)

—*1848: the British State and the Chartist Movement*, John Saville (Cambridge: Cambridge University Press, 1987)

For Prince Albert see:

—*Prince Albert and Victorian Taste*, Winslow Ames (London: Chapman & Hall, 1967)

—*Prince Albert, His Life and Work*, Hermione Hobhouse (London: Hamish Hamilton, 1983)

—*King without a Crown: Albert, Prince Consort of England, 1819–61*, Daphne Bennett (London: Pimlico, 1983)

—*Uncrowned King: The Life of Prince Albert*, Stanley Weintraub (London: Simon & Schuster, 1996)

For the Great Exhibition see:

—*The World for a Shilling: How the Great Exhibition of 1851 Shaped a Nation*, Michael Leapman (London: Headline, 2001)

—*The Great Exhibition*, John R. Davis (Stroud: Sutton, 1999)

—*The Great Exhibition of 1851: a Nation on Display*, Jeffrey A. Auerbach (New Haven and London: Yale University Press, 1999)

—*The Crystal Palace and the Great Exhibition: Art, Science, and Productive Industry: a History of the Royal Commission for the Exhibition of 1851*, Hermione Hobhouse (New York: Athlone Press, 2002)

—*1851 and the Crystal Palace: being an Account of the Great Exhibition and its Contents; of Sir Joseph Paxton; and the Erection, the Subsequent History and the Destruction of his Masterpiece*, Christopher Hobhouse, with an introduction by Osbert Lancaster (London: Murray, 1950)

For Joseph Paxton himself see:

—*Paxton and the Bachelor Duke*, Violet R. Markham (London: Hodder & Stoughton, 1935)

—*The Works of Sir Joseph Paxton, 1803–1865*, George F. Chadwick (London: Architectural Press, 1961)

—*A Thing in Disguise: The Visionary Life of Joseph Paxton*, Kate Colquhoun (London: Fourth Estate, 2003)

On his Crystal Palace's new life and death in Sydenham see:

—*The Crystal Palace, 1851–1936: a Portrait of Victorian Enterprise*, Patrick Beaver (London: Hugh Evelyn, 1970)

—*Palace of the People: the Crystal Palace at Sydenham 1854–1936*, J. R. Piggott (London: Hurst, 2004)

—*The Phoenix Suburb: A South London Social History*, Alan R. Warwick (London, 1973; Norwood Society edition, 2008)

—*The Crystal Palace Dinosaurs: The Story of the World's First Prehistoric Sculptures*, Steve McCarthy with Mick Gilbert (London: Crystal Palace Foundation, 1994)

For carpet bedding see:

—*Victorian Gardens*, Brent Elliott (London: Batsford, 1986; 1990 edition)

—*Flora: An Illustrated History of the Garden Flower*, Brent Elliott and W. B. Elliott (London: Scriptum Editions, 2001)

Chapter 4: Central Parking

For Staten Island see:

—*Staten Island: A Blue Guide Travel Monograph*, Carol V. Wright (London: Blue Guides, 2013)

Historic Richmond Town can be found at 441 Clarke Avenue, Staten Island, NY 10306, United States

Their website is: www.historicrichmondtown.org/

Many books on the life and work of Frederick Law Olmsted provided raw material for this chapter but in particular see:

—*F.L.O.: A Biography of Frederick Law Olmsted*, Laura Wood Roper (Baltimore and London: Johns Hopkins University Press, 1973)

—*Park Maker: a life of Frederick Law Olmsted*, Elizabeth Stevenson (New York: Macmillan; London: Collier Macmillan, 1977)

—*Frederick Law Olmsted: the Passion of a Public Artist*, Melvin Kalfus (New York and London: New York University Press, 1990)

—*A Clearing in the Distance: Frederick Law Olmsted and America in the Nineteenth Century*, Witold Rybczynski (New York: Scribner, 1999)

Also see:

—*Frederick Law Olmsted's New York*, Elizabeth Barlow and William Alex (New York: Praeger, in association with the Whitney Museum of American Art, 1972)

For Olmsted's own writing see:

—*Walks and Talks of an American Farmer in England*, Frederick Law Olmsted; with an introduction by Charles C. McLaughlin (Amherst: Library of American Landscape History, University of Massachusetts Press; London: Eurospan, 2002)

—*Frederick Law Olmsted: Essential Texts*, edited by Robert Twombly (New York and London: W. W. Norton, 2010)

—*Writings on Public Parks, Parkways and Park Systems*, Frederick Law Olmsted, edited by Charles E. Beveridge and Carolyn F. Hoffman (Baltimore and London: Johns Hopkins University Press, 1997)

And for Central Park specifically see: *Volume 3: Creating Central Park, 1857–1861*, edited by Charles E. Beveridge and David Schuyler in *The Papers of*

Frederick Law Olmsted (Baltimore and London: Johns Hopkins University Press, 1983)

For Andrew Jackson Downing see:
—*Andrew Jackson Downing: Essential texts*, edited by Robert Twombly (New York and London: W. W. Norton, 2012)
—*Apostle of Taste: Andrew Jackson Downing*, David Schuyler (Baltimore: Johns Hopkins University Press, 1999)

For Central Park and New York see:
—*The Park and the People: a History of Central Park*, Roy Rosenzweig and Elizabeth Blackmar (Ithaca, NY: Cornell University Press, 1992)
—*Central Park: An American Masterpiece*, Sara Cedar Miller (New York: Harry N. Abrams Publishers in association with the Central Park Conservancy, 2003)
—*Creating Central Park*, Morrison H. Heckscher (New Haven and London: Yale University Press, 2008)
—*Gotham: a History of New York City to 1898*, Edwin G. Burrows and Mike Wallace (New York and Oxford: Oxford University Press, 1999)
—*Low Life: Lures and Snares of Old New York*, Luc Sante (London: Granta, 1998)

The quote from *Moby-Dick* is from *Moby-Dick, or The White Whale*, Herman Melville (London: Everyman's Library, 1991 edition) and Melville's own views on New York appear in:
—*Melville: His World and Work*, Andrew Delbanco (London: Picador, 2005)

For Birkenhead Park see:
—*Birkenhead Park*, Jean McInniss (Birkenhead: Countyvise, 1984) and also previously mentioned books on Paxton, especially, *A Thing in Disguise: The Visionary Life of Joseph Paxton*, Kate Colquhoun (London: Fourth Estate, 2003).

Chapter 5: We Are Amused

For Hull's Khyber Pass see:

—*The Story of East Park, Hull*, Mary Fowler (Beverley: Highgate, 2002)

For Queen Victoria's Jubilees see earlier books on the Victorian period listed and:
—'*This Brilliant Year*', *Queen Victoria's Jubilee, 1887*, Jeremy Maas (London: Royal Academy of Arts, 1977)
—*Victoria: a Life*, A. N. Wilson (London: Atlantic Books, 2014)
—*Queen Victoria: A Life of Contradictions*, Matthew Dennison (London: William Collins, 2014)

For Arthur Munby's observations of the work-less in St James's Park see:
—*Munby, Man of Two Worlds: The Life and Diaries of Arthur J. Munby, 1828–1910*, Derek Hudson (London: J. Murray, 1972)

For the Anglo-Afghan wars see:
—*The Savage Frontier: a History of the Anglo-Afghan War*, D. S. Richards (London: Macmillan, 1990)
—*The History of Afghanistan*, Meredith L. Runion (Westport, Conn. and London: Greenwood Press; Oxford: Harcourt Education, 2007)
—*Return of a King: The Battle for Afghanistan*, William Dalrymple (London: Bloomsbury, 2013)

For the Crimean War see:
—*Crimea: The Great Crimean War 1854–1856*, Trevor Royle (London: Little, Brown, 1999)
—*A Brief History of the Crimean War: the Causes and Consequences of a Medieval Conflict Fought in a Modern Age*, Alexis Troubetzkoy (London: Robinson, 2006)
—*The Crimean War*, Clive Ponting (London: Chatto & Windus, 2004)
—*The Crimean War: Queen Victoria's War with the Russian Tsars*, Hugh Small (Stroud: Tempus, 2007)

For the arrival of guns and bandstands in parks see general and individual park history books previously listed, but in particular *People's Parks: the Design and Development of Victorian Parks in Britain*, Hazel Conway (Cambridge: Cambridge University Press, 1991)

The introduction of music in Victoria Park is charted in *Victoria Park: A Study in the History of East London*, Charles Poulsen (London: Journeyman Press, 1976)

For self-improvement and Samuel Smiles see:
—*Samuel Smiles and the Victorian Work Ethic*, Tim Travers (New York and London: Garland, 1987)
—*Samuel Smiles and the Construction of Victorian Values*, Adrian Jarvis (Stroud: Sutton Publishing, 1997)
—'Samuel Smiles: The Gospel of Self-Help', Asa Briggs in *Victorian Values: Personalities and Perspectives in Nineteenth-Century Society*, edited by Gordon Marsden (London: Longman, 1990), which contains other essays that are germane too.

For the rise of organised sport see:
—*Sport and the British: A Modern History*, Richard Holt (Oxford: OUP, 1990)
—*The History of Sport in Britain, 1880–1914*, edited by Martin Polley (London: Routledge, 2004)
—*Muscular Christianity: Embodying the Victorian Age*, edited by Donald E. Hall (Cambridge: Cambridge University Press, 1994)
—*Tom Brown's Schooldays*, Thomas Hughes (London: William Collins, 2013 edition)
—*Tom Brown's Universe: the Development of the Victorian Public School*, J. R. de S. Honey (London: Millington, 1977)
—*A Sport-loving Society: Victorian and Edwardian Middle-class England at Play*, J. A. Mangan (London: Routledge, 2006)
—*Land of Sport and Glory: Sport and British Society, 1887–1910*, Derek Birley (Manchester: Manchester University Press, 1995)

—*A Social History of English Cricket*, Derek Birley (London: Aurum, 2013 edition)

—*The Willow Wand: Some Cricket Myths Explored*, Derek Birley (London: Aurum, 2000)

—*Beyond a Boundary*, C. L. R. James (London: Yellow Jersey Press, 2005)

—*Beastly Fury: The Strange Birth of British Football*, Richard Sanders (London: Bantam, 2010)

—*The People's Game: The History of Football Revisited*, James Walvin (Edinburgh: Mainstream, 1994)

—*Love Game: A History of Tennis, from Victorian Pastime to Global Phenomenon*, Elizabeth Wilson (London: Serpent's Tail, 2014)

For climbing and sudden vogue for alpine-type scenery see:

—*Great Ascents: a Narrative History of Mountaineering*, Eric Newby (Newton Abbot: David & Charles, 1977)

—*How the English Made the Alps*, Jim Ring (London: John Murray, 2000)

—*Mountains of the Mind: a History of a Fascination*, Robert Macfarlane (London: Granta, 2003)

—*Alpine Flowers for English Gardens*, William Robinson (London: John Murray, 1870)

—*The Wild Garden*, William Robinson (London: John Murray, 1870)

For the fake rock of the Pulham family see:

—*Rock Landscapes: the Pulham Legacy: Rock Gardens, Grottoes, Ferneries, Follies, Fountains and Garden Ornaments*, Claude Hitching, with photography by Jenny Lilly (Woodbridge: Garden Art Press, 2012)

Chapter 6: Urbs in Horto

For the development of science fiction see:

—*Trillion Year Spree: the History of Science Fiction*, Brian W. Aldiss with David Wingrove (Thirsk: House of Stratus, 2001)

—*The History of Science Fiction*, Adam Roberts (Basingstoke: Palgrave Macmillan, 2006) and the novels:

—*After London, or, Wild England*, Richard Jefferies with an introduction by John Fowles (Oxford: Oxford University Press, 1980 edition)

—*A Crystal Age*, W. H. Hudson (London: T. Fisher Unwin, 1887)

For William Morris and the Arts and Crafts Movement see:

—*News from Nowhere and Other Writings*, William Morris (London: Penguin, 1993 edition)

—*The Political Writings of William Morris*, edited and introduced by A. L. Morton (London: Lawrence & Wishart, 1984)

—*William Morris: Selected Writings and Designs*, edited with an introduction by Asa Briggs (Harmondsworth: Penguin, 1968)

—*The Collected Letters of William Morris, Volumes 1–4*, edited by Norman Kelvin (Princeton and Guildford: Princeton University Press, 1987–1996)

—*William Morris: a Life for Our Time*, Fiona MacCarthy (London: Faber and Faber, 1994)

—*William Morris: Romantic to Revolutionary*, E. P. Thompson (London: Merlin Press, 1977)

—*William Morris: His Life and Work*, Stephen Coote (Stroud: Alan Sutton, 1996)

—*The Gardens of William Morris*, Jill, Duchess of Hamilton, Penny Hart and John Simmons; foreword by Sir Roy Strong (London: Frances Lincoln, 1998)

—*From William Morris: Building Conservation and the Arts and Crafts Cult of Authenticity, 1877–1939*, Chris Miele (New Haven and London: Yale University Press, 2005)

—*The Arts and Craft Movement*, Rosalind P. Blakesley (London: Phaidon Press, 2009)

—*Gardens of the Arts and Crafts Movement: Reality and Imagination*, Judith B. Tankard (New York: Harry N. Abrams, 2004)

—*A Floral Fantasy in an Old English Garden*, Walter Crane (London: Harper & Bros, 1899)

SOURCES

For more on the cult of the pastoral and the creation of Merrie England also see:

—*Back to the Land: The Pastoral Impulse in Victorian England from 1880 to 1914*, Jan Marsh (London: Quartet Books, 1982)

—*Merrie England*, Robert Blatchford (London: Clarion Press, 1894)

—*The Sorcery Shop: an Impossible Romance*, Robert Blatchford (London: Clarion Press, 1907)

—*Robert Blatchford: Portrait of an Englishman*, Laurence Thompson (London: Victor Gollancz, 1951)

—*Edward Carpenter: A Life of Liberty and Love*, Sheila Rowbotham (London: Verso, 2008)

For Shakespeare Gardens see:

—*The Plant-Lore & Garden-Craft of Shakespeare*, Rev. Henry N. Ellacombe (Exeter: W. Pollard, 1878)

—*The Shakespeare Garden*, Esther Singleton (London: Methuen, 1922)

For J. J. Sexby's Old English Gardens see his own guide:

—*The Municipal Parks, Gardens and Open Spaces of London: Their History and Associations* (London: Elliot Stock, 1898)

For George Shaw-Lefevre and London Metropolitan Board of Works see:

—*The Government of Victorian London: The Metropolitan Board of Works, the Vestries and the City Corporation*, D. Owen (Cambridge, Mass.: Harvard University, Belknap Press, 1982)

—*London's Teeming Streets, 1830–1914*, James Winter (London: Routledge, 1993)

On the fight to save the commons and Octavia Hill see:

—*English Commons and Forests: the Story of the Battle during the Last Thirty Years for Public Rights Over the Commons and Forests of England and Wales*, Rt. Hon. G. Shaw-Lefevre (London: Cassell, 1894)

—*Octavia Hill*, Gillian Darley (London: Constable, 1990)

—*Octavia Hill & Open Spaces*, Christopher Hanson-Smith (Wisbech, Cambridgeshire: Octavia Hill Society & Birthplace Museum Trust, 1996)

For T. H. Mawson see:

—*Life and Work of an English Landscape Architect: An Autobiography,* Thomas H. Mawson (London: Batsford, 1927)

—*Thomas Mawson: Life, Gardens and Landscapes*, Janet Waymark (London: Frances Lincoln, 2009)

—*The Art & Craft of Garden Making*, Thomas H. Mawson, 4th edition (London: B.T. Batsford, 1912)

—*Civic Art: Studies in Town Planning, Parks, Boulevards and Open Spaces*, Thomas H. Mawson (London: B.T. Batsford, 1911)

—*An Imperial Obligation: Industrial Villages for Partially Disabled Soldiers and Sailors*, Thomas H. Mawson (London: Grant Richards, 1917)

For Garden Cities and town planning see:

—*Looking Backward, 2000–1887*, Edward Bellamy (London: G. Routledge & Sons, 1850–1898; 3rd edition, 1890)

—*To-morrow: A Peaceful Path to Real Reform*, Ebenezer Howard with commentary by Peter Hall, Dennis Hardy and Colin Ward (London: Routledge, 2009)

—*Garden Cities of To-morrow: Being the Second Edition of 'To-morrow: A Peaceful Path to Real Reform*, Ebenezer Howard (London: Swan Sonnenschein, 1902)

—*Sir Ebenezer Howard and the Town Planning Movement*, Dugald Macfayden (Manchester: Manchester University Press, 1933)

—*The Garden City Utopia: a Critical Biography of Ebenezer Howard*, Robert Beevers (London: Macmillan, 1988)

—*From Garden City to Green City*, Ed Kermits, C. Parson and David Schuyler (Baltimore and London: Johns Hopkins University Press, 2002)

SOURCES

—*English Garden Cities: an Introduction*, Mervyn Miller (Swindon: English Heritage, 2010)

—*Garden Cities and Suburbs*, Sarah Rutherford (Botley: Shire Publications, 2014)

—*New Jerusalem: the Good City and the Good Society*, Ken Worpole (London: The Swedenborg Society, 2015)

—*Visionaries and Planners: the Garden City Movement and the Modern Community*, Stanley Buder (New York: Oxford University Press, 1990)

For Letchworth see:

—*Letchworth: the Well-planned Beautiful Town* (Letchworth: First Garden City, 1934)

—*Letchworth Garden City*, compiled by Mervyn Miller (Stroud: Chalford, 1995)

—*Letchworth Garden City, 1903–2003: a Centenary Celebration of the World's First Garden City in Picture Postcards*, compiled by Margaret Pierce (Letchworth Garden City: Yesterday's World Publications, 2002)

For parks and life at home during the First World War see:

—*The Enemy in Our Midst: Germans in Britain during the First World War*, Panikos Panayi (New York and Oxford: Berg, 1991)

—*Alexandra Palace Internment Camp in the First World War, 1914–1918*. Compiled from Notes made by R. Rocker the Elder, completed and edited by his son, Rudolf Rocker (privately printed in London, 1918)

—*The First World War on the Home Front*, Terry Charman (London: André Deutsch, 2014)

—*First World War Britain: 1914–1919*, Peter Doyle (Oxford: Shire, 2012)

—*The First Blitz: the German Air Campaign against Britain in the First World War*, Andrew P. Hyde (Barnsley: Leo Cooper, 2002)

—*First Blitz: the Secret German Plan to Raze London to the Ground in 1918*, Neil Hanson (London: Corgi, 2009)

—*Zeppelin Nights: London in the First World War*, Jerry White (London: The Bodley Head, 2014)

—*War Memoirs of David Lloyd George*, David Lloyd George (London: Odhams Press, 1938)

—*At Home and Under Fire: Air Raids and Culture in Britain from the Great War to the Blitz*, Susan R. Grayzel (Cambridge: Cambridge University Press, 2011)

Chapter 7: At Swim Model Boats

For the general picture of Britain after the war see:

—*Interwar Britain: a Social and Economic* History, Sean Glynn and John Oxborrow (London: Allen & Unwin, 1976)

—*Britain Between the Wars 1918–1940*, C. L. Mowat (London: Methuen, 1968, 1978 edition)

—*Unemployment and Non-Employment in Interwar Britain*, Ed Butchart (Oxford: Oxford University Press, 1997)

—*Social Conditions in Britain Between the Wars*, John Stevenson (Harmondsworth: Penguin, 1977)

—*Fit for Heroes: A Scrapbook of Britain Between the Wars*, Lionel Jackson (London: Blackie, 1975)

—*Music for the People: Popular Music and Dance in Interwar Britain*, James J. Nott (Oxford: Oxford University Press, 2002)

—*'We danced all night': A Social History of Britain Between the Wars*, Martin Pugh (London: The Bodley Head, 2008)

For Captain Sandys-Winsch and the Norwich parks see:

—*The Captain and the Norwich Parks*, P. Anderson (Norwich: Norwich Society, 2000)

—*The Parks and Open Spaces of Norwich*, Geoffrey Goreham (1961; unpublished. Held in the Local Studies section of Norwich's Millennium Library)

See various numbers of *Playing Fields Journal* (the journal of the National Playing Fields Association) (London: National Playing Fields Association (Great Britain), 1930–1946).

—'Playing Fields & Town Planning', author unknown, in *The Town Planning Review*, 1 November 1926, Vol. 12 (2): http://www.jstor.org/stable/40101689

For the Victoria Park Model Steam Boat Club see: *Victoria Park: a Study in the History of East London*, Charles Poulsen (London: Journeyman Press, 1976). And my own piece, 'Postcards from Victoria Park: At the Model Boating Lake', for the Chisenhale Gallery, published in May 2015 at http://chisenhale.org.uk/offsite/offsite_event.php?id=36

For more on the extraordinary Horatio Bottomley see:

—*The Rise and Fall of Horatio Bottomley*, Tenax (pseud.) (London: Denis Archer, 1933)

—*Horatio Bottomley*, Julian Symons (London: House of Stratus, 2001, *c*.1955)

—*The Rise and Fall of Horatio Bottomley: the Biography of a Swindler*, Alan Hyman (London: Cassell, 1972)

And also:

—*Wilde's Last Stand: Decadence, Conspiracy and the First World War*, Philip Hoare (London: Duckworth, 1997)

For dancing at Manchester and Hull parks see:

—*City of Manchester: Handbook of the City Parks and Recreation Grounds*, W. W. Pettigrew (Manchester: Council Parks and Cemeteries Committee,1929)

—*The Story of East Park, Hull*, Mary Fowler (Beverley: Highgate, 2002)

For more on women's lives in this period see:

—*Singled Out : How Two Million Women Survived Without Men After the First World War*, Virginia Nicholson (London: Viking, 2007)

—*Women in the 1920s*, Pamela Horn (Stroud, Gloucestershire: Alan Sutton, 1995)

—*Women and the Popular Imagination in the Twenties: Flappers and Nymphs*, Billie Melman (Basingstoke: Macmillan, 1988)

—*The Rise and Fall of the British Nanny*, Jonathan Gathorne-Hardy (London: Hodder & Stoughton, 1972)

—*The Thirties: an Intimate History*, Juliet Gardiner (London: HarperPress, 2010)

And in fiction see: *The Prime of Miss Jean Brodie*, Muriel Spark (London: Macmillan, 1961) and *Evil Under the Sun*, Agatha Christie (London: For the Crime Club by Collins, 1941)

For tennis and Fred Perry see:

—*The Last Champion: the Life of Fred Perry*, Jon Henderson (London: Yellow Jersey, 2009)

—*Love Game: A History of Tennis, from Victorian Pastime to Global Phenomenon*, Elizabeth Wilson (London: Serpent's Tail, 2014)

For the courts in London at the time see:

—*London Parks and Open Spaces: Being One of a Series of Popular Handbooks on the London County Council and what it does for London* (London: Hodder & Stoughton, 1924)

For swimming, lidos and suntans see:

—*Swimwear in Vogue: since 1910*, Christina Probert (London: Thames and Hudson, 1981)

—*Farewell My Lido: a Thirties Society Report*, edited by Alan Powers (London: Thirties Society, 1991)

—*Tooting Bec Lido*, Janet Smith (London: South London Swimming Club, 1996)

—*Liquid Assets: The Lidos and Open Air Swimming Pools of Britain*, Janet Smith (London: English Heritage, 2005)

—*Out of the Blue: a Celebration of Brockwell Park Lido 1937–2007*, Peter Bradley (London: BLU, 2007)

For Oswald Mosley and fascism see:

—*'Hurrah for the blackshirts'! Fascists and Fascism in Britain Between the Wars*, Martin Pugh (London: Jonathan Cape, 2005)

—*Blackshirt: Sir Oswald Mosley and British Fascism*, Stephen Dorril (London: Viking, 2006)

—*The Battle of Cable Street, 4th October 1936: a People's History*, compiled and edited by the Cable Street Group (London: Cable Street Group, 1995)

—*East London for Mosley: the British Union of Fascists in East London and South-west Essex, 1933–40*, Thomas P. Linehan (London: Cass, 1996)

Chapter 8: A Patch of Air

For Elizabeth Bowen see her novels:

—*The Death of the Heart* (London: Gollancz, 1938) and *The Heat of the Day* (London: Jonathan Cape, 1949) and:

—*Love's Civil War: Letters and Diaries, 1941–1973*, Elizabeth Bowen and Charles Ritchie, edited by Victoria Glendinning; with Judith Robertson (London: Simon & Schuster, 2009)

—*Elizabeth Bowen: Portrait of a Writer*, Victoria Glendinning (London: Weidenfeld & Nicolson, 1977)

—*Elizabeth Bowen*, Hermione Lee (revised edition, London: Vintage, 1999)

Also invaluable to this chapter was the wonderful:

—*The Love-Charm of Bombs: Restless Lives in the Second World War*, Lara Feigel (London: Bloomsbury, 2013)

For Orwell's Home Guarding see:

—*The Orwell Diaries*, edited by Peter Davison (London: Penguin, 2010)

—*It was Different at the Time: Impressions of England 1938–41*, Beatrice Inez Lisette Holden (London: John Lane, 1943)

Also:

—*George Orwell: the Authorised Biography*, Michael Shelden (London: Minerva, 1992)

—*George Orwell: a Life*, Bernard Crick (London: Penguin, 1992 edition)

—*George Orwell*, Gordon Bowker (London: Little, Brown, 2003)

—*Orwell in Tribune: 'As I Please' and other writings, 1943–47*, edited by Paul Anderson (London: Methuen, 2008 edition)

For Britain during the Blitz see:

—*London at War, 1939–1945*, Philip Ziegler (London: Sinclair-Stevenson, 1995)

—*The Blitz: the British under Attack*, Juliet Gardiner (London: HarperPress, 2010)

—*The War on Our Doorstep: London's East End and how the Blitz Changed it Forever*, Harriet Salisbury, in association with the Museum of London (London: Ebury Press, 2012)

—*Living Through the Blitz*, Tom Harrisson from Mass Observation Archive (London: Collins, 1976)

—*We are at War: the Remarkable Diaries of Five Ordinary People in Extraordinary Times*, edited from the archives of the Mass Observation Project by Simon Garfield (London: Ebury Press, 2005)

—*Manchester at War, 1939–45: the People's Story*, Graham Phythian (Stroud: The History Press, 2014)

For Coventry and its War Memorial Park see:

—*War Memorial Park: the Second World War*, Trevor Harkin (Coventry: War Memorial Park Publications, 2010)

—*Coventry, April 1941, the Forgotten Air Raids: Casualties, Awards and Accounts*, Trevor Harkin (Coventry: War Memorial Park Publications, 2011)

—*Moonlight Sonata: the Coventry Blitz, 14/15 November 1940*, compiled by Tim Lewis (Coventry: T. Lewis and Coventry City Council, 1990)

For the removal of railings see:

—*Whither the Tired Mechanic Could Resort: a History of Braintree & Bocking Public Gardens*, Michael Bardell (Braintree: Michael Bardell, 2012)

—*Manchester at War*, compiled and written by Clive Hard (Altrincham: First Edition Limited, 2005)

For internment see Second World War histories above and:

—*Britain's Internees in the Second World War*, Miriam Kochan (London: Macmillan, 1983)

For the Dig for Victory campaign see again general Home Front histories above and:

—*War Time Allotments*, under the general editorship of C. H. Middleton (London: Daily Express, 1940)

—*Digging for Victory: Wartime Gardening with Mr Middleton*, by C. H. Middleton (London: Aurum, 2008)

—*Your Garden in War-time*, by C. H. Middleton (London: Aurum, 2010)

—*The Spade as Mighty as the Sword: the Story of the Second World War 'Dig for Victory' Campaign*, Daniel Smith (London: Aurum, 2011)

—*The Wartime Garden: Digging for Victory*, Twigs Way (Oxford: Shire, 2015)

—*How to Keep Well in Wartime* (London: HMSO, 1943; facsimile edition London: Imperial War Museum, 2007)

For the saucier side of things see:

—*An Underworld at War: Spivs, Deserters, Racketeers and Civilians in the Second World War*, Donald Thomas (London: John Murray, 2003)

—*The Secret History of the Blitz: How We Behaved During our Darkest Days and Created Modern Britain*, Joshua Levine (London: Simon & Schuster, 2015)

—*Their Darkest Hour: The Hidden History of the Home Front 1939–45*, Stuart Hylton (Stroud: Sutton, 2003)

—*Over Here: the GIs in Wartime Britain*, Juliet Gardiner (London: Collins & Brown, 1992)

—*Millions Like Us: Women's Lives During the Second World War*, Virginia Nicholson (London: Penguin, 2012)

For Holidays at Home see Home Front histories above and:

—'Holidays at Home in the Second World War', Chris Sladen, *Journal of Contemporary History*, Vol. 37, part 1 (Sage Publications, 2002)

—*'Passed to You, Please': Britain's Red-tape Machine at War*, J. P. W. Mallalieu (London: Left Book Club/Victor Gollancz, 1942)

—*Manchester at War, 1939–45: the People's Story*, Graham Phythian (Stroud: The History Press, 2014)

—*War Memorial Park: the Second World War*, Trevor Harkin (Coventry: War Memorial Park Publications, 2010)

Chapter 9: Post-war Playgrounds

For post-war ideas about parks and memorials see:

—*Bombed Churches as War Memorials*, with a foreword by the Dean of St Paul's (Cheam: Architectural Press, 1945)

—*Post-War Planning and Reconstruction, as Visualised by the Institute of Park Administration* (London: Institute of Park and Recreation Administration, 1943)

For general background on the period see:

—*Post-war Britain: a Political History*, Alan Sked and Chris Cook (London: Penguin, 1993)

—*No Turning Back: the Peacetime Revolutions of Post-war Britain*, Paul Addison (Oxford: Oxford University Press, 2010)

—*Never Again: Britain 1945–51*, Peter Hennessy (London: Jonathan Cape, 1992)

SOURCES

—*Having It So Good: Britain in the Fifties*, Peter Hennessy (London: Allen Lane, 2006)

—*Austerity Britain: 1945–51*, David Kynaston (London: Bloomsbury, 2007)

—*Family Britain: 1951–57*, David Kynaston (London: Bloomsbury, 2010)

—*Modernity Britain: Opening the Box, 1957–59*, David Kynaston (London: Bloomsbury, 2013)

For the Festival of Britain and Battersea's Festival Pleasure Gardens see:

—*The Festival of Britain 1951: The Official Book of the Festival of Britain* (Great Britain: Festival of Britain, 1951)

—*Festival Pleasure Gardens: Battersea Park, London, May–November 3rd 1951* (Great Britain: Festival of Britain, 1951)

—*A Tonic to the Nation: The Festival of Britain 1951*, edited by M. Banham and B. Hillier (London: Thames & Hudson, 1976)

—*Beacon for Change: How the 1951 Festival of Britain Helped to Shape a New Age*, Barry Turner (London: Aurum, 2011)

—*The Festival of Britain: a Land and its People*, Harriet Atkinson (London: I. B. Tauris, 2012)

—*Festival of Britain*, edited by Elain Harwood and Alan Powers (London: Twentieth Century Society, 2001)

—*The Autobiography of a Nation: The 1951 Festival of Britain*, Becky E. Conekin (Manchester: Manchester University Press, 2003)

And last – but by no means least – Michael Frayn's 1963 essay 'Festival', in the equally invaluable *Age of Austerity 1945–1951*, edited by Michael Sissons and Philip French (London: Hodder & Stoughton, 1963)

For television in the new Elizabethan age see post-war books listed above and:

—*Armchair Nation: an Intimate History of Britain in Front of the Television*, Joe Moran (London: Profile Books, 2013)

For transformation of Britain after the war and into the 1960s again see Kynaston et al. and:

—*Building the Post-War World*, Nicholas Bullock (London: Routledge, 2002)

—*A Broken Wave: The Rebuilding of England, 1940–1980*, Lionel Esher (London: Allen Lane, 1981)

—*Concretopia: a Journey around the Rebuilding of Postwar Britain*, John Grindrod (Brecon: Old Street, 2013)

—*Space, Hope and Brutalism: English Architecture, 1945–1975*, Elain Harwood (New Haven: Yale University Press in association with Historic England, 2015)

Also the booklet:

—*Playgrounds for Blocks of Flats* (National Playing Fields Association, Great Britain, 1953)

For sport during the Cold War see earlier listed social histories of sport and the period and:

—*Amateurs and Professionals in Post-war British Sport*, edited by Adrian Smith and Dilwyn Porter (London and Portland, Oreg.: F. Cass, 2000)

—*Sport and National Identity in the Post-war World*, edited by Adrian Smith and Dilwyn Porter (London: Routledge, 2004)

For traffic jams in Victoria Park see again:

—*Victoria Park: a Study in the History of East London*, Charles Poulsen (London: Journeyman Press, 1976)

For adventure playgrounds see:

—*Adventure Playgrounds*, booklet from the National Playing Fields Association (Great Britain, 1960)

—*Adventure Playgrounds*, Lady Allen of Hurtwood (London: Penguin, 1961)

—*Play Parks*, Lady Allen of Hurtwood (London: Housing Centre Trust, 1964)

—*Planning for Play*, Lady Allen of Hurtwood (London: Thames & Hudson, 1968)

—*Memoirs of an Uneducated Lady*, Lady Allen of Hurtwood with Mary Nicholson (London: Thames & Hudson, 1975)

—*Adventure Playgrounds*, Arvid Bengtsson (London: Crosby Lockwood, 1972)

Also worth seeking out (at the time of writing, it is on YouTube) is the Central Office of Information film about Lady Allen of Hurtwood and her work with adventure playgrounds from their Pacemakers series (1969–1971).

For Dennis the Menace's first park-keeper-worrying appearance in the *Beano* comic see:

—*AARGH! it's Dennis the Menace!: 1951–2001* (London: D. C. Thomson & Co. Ltd, 2000)

The Pleasure Garden (1954), directed by James Broughton, was released on DVD by the BFI in 2010. The disc (reference BFIVD831) also includes an additional short film, *The Phoenix Tower* (1957), about the building of BBC Television's Transmission Tower in Crystal Palace Park.

For Paul McCartney on floral clocks and the *Sgt Pepper* LP see:

—*Paul McCartney: Many Years from Now*, Barry Miles and Paul McCartney (London: Secker & Warburg, 1997)

Also see:

—*Shout! The True Story of the Beatles*, Philip Norman (London: Vintage, 2nd edition, 2008)

—*The Beatles: the Only Authorised Biography*, Hunter Davies (London: Jonathan Cape, 1968; 1992 edition)

—*It was Twenty Years Ago Today*, Derek Taylor (London: Bantam, 1987)

For the late 1960s more generally see:

—*Ready, Steady, Go! Swinging London and the Invention of Cool*, Shawn Levy (London: Fourth Estate, 2002)

—*Revolt into Style: the Pop Arts in Britain*, George Melly (Harmondsworth: Penguin, 1972)

—*Hippie*, Barry Miles (London: Cassell Illustrated, 2003)

—*The Sixties*, Jenny Diski (London: Profile Books, 2009)

—*Days in the Life: Voices from the English Underground, 1961–71*, Jonathan Green (London: Pimlico, 1998 edition)

—*All Dressed Up: the Sixties and the Counter Culture*, Jonathan Green (London: Pimlico, 1999)

For the purveyors of Victorian apparel see:

—*Boutique London: A History: King's Road to Carnaby Street*, Richard Lester (London: ACC Editions, 2010)

—*King's Road: The Rise and Fall of the Hippest Street in the World*, by Max Décharné (London: Weidenfeld & Nicolson, 2005)

For rock concerts in Hyde Park and the Rolling Stones see:

—back issues of *International Times*: their archive is online at: http://www.internationaltimes.it/archive/

—*Pink Floyd: The Early Years*, Barry Miles (London: Omnibus, 2006)

—*Margrave of the Marshes*, John Peel and Sheila Ravenscroft (London: Bantam, 2005)

—*The Olivetti Chronicles: Three Decades of Life and Music*, John Peel (London: Corgi, 2009)

—*The Stones: The Acclaimed Biography*, Philip Norman (London: HarperCollins, 2012)

—*Mick Jagger*, Philip Norman (London: HarperCollins, 2012)

—*The Rolling Stones: Fifty Years*, Christopher Sandford (London: Simon & Schuster, 2012) and also:

—*Sympathy for the Devil: the Birth of the Rolling Stones and the Death of Brian Jones,* Paul Trynka (London: Bantam Press, 2014)

—*Let It Bleed: The Rolling Stones, Altamont, and the End of the Sixties,* Ethan A. Russell; with Gerard Van der Leun (New York: Springboard Press, 2009)

The Stones in the Park (1969) documentary, directed by Leslie Woodhead for Granada Television, was released in 2006 on DVD by Network (B000GUK3SI)

Chapter 10: When the Sun Cries Morning

For Gary Numan see:

—Ian Cranna's *Smash Hits* interview with Numan, anthologised in *The Best of Smash Hits: Six Years of Interviews from the Sex Pistols to Frankie Goes to Hollywood,* compiled by Neil Tennant, with an introduction by John Taylor of Duran Duran (London and Scarborough: EMAP/Pinder Press, 1985)

—*Gary Numan: the Authorised Biography*, Ray Coleman (London: Sidgwick & Jackson, 1982)

—*Praying to the Aliens: an Autobiography*, Gary Numan with Steve Malins (London: Deutsch, 1998)

For Central Park in the 1970s see, in particular:

—*The Park and the People: a History of Central Park*, Roy Rosenzweig and Elizabeth Blackmar (Ithaca, NY: Cornell University Press, 1992)

and for the atmosphere of the period perhaps also:

—'My Lost City', Luc Sante, *New York Review of Books*, 6 November 2003

and

—*Ladies and Gentlemen, the Bronx is Burning: 1977, Baseball, Politics, and the Battle for the Soul of a City,* Jonathan Mahler (New York: Farrar, Straus & Giroux, 2005)

For bravura fictionalising the already mythically fictional though not really getting the sartorial mores of 1970s New York punks see the novel:

—*City on Fire*, Garth Risk Hallberg (London: Jonathan Cape, 2015)

There is also, of course, *Death Wish* (1974), directed by Michael Winner, and its fortieth anniversary in 2014 was marked with the release of the film by Warner on Blu-ray DVD. Of similar ilk is the *Rambo*-wannabe 1985 TV movie *The Park is Mine*, based on the novel of the same name by Stephen Peters, in which Tommy Lee Jones plays a disgruntled Vietnam veteran who seizes control of Central Park in a bid to gain greater public support for those who served in the South Asian war.

For Birkenhead Park's own troubles on these shores see *The People's Garden: A History of Crime and Policing in Birkenhead Park*, Robert Lee (Birkenhead: The Friends of Birkenhead Park, 2013) and (again) *Birkenhead Park*, Jean McInniss (Birkenhead: Countyvise, 1984)

Quote from *The Day of the Triffids*, John Wyndham (Harmondsworth: Penguin Books, 1954)

For sport and leisure, local government and the park's decline see:

—*Planning for Sport: Report of a Working Party on Scales of Provision*, Sports Council (Great Britain), (London: Published for the Sports Council by the Central Council of Physical Recreation, 1968)

—*The Bains Report* (London: HMSO, 1972)

And especially:

—*Park Life: Urban Parks and Social Renewal: A Report by Comedia in association with Demos*, Liz Greenhaigh and Ken Worpole (Stroud: Comedia; London: Demos, 1995)

Chapter 11: Things Can Only Get Better

For Donald Simon on parks no longer being thought of as amenities see again: *The Park and the People: a History of Central Park*, Roy Rosenzweig and Elizabeth Blackmar (Ithaca, NY: Cornell University Press, 1992)

For George Orwell as proto-gentrifier see: Jonathan Raban's *Soft City* (London: Picador, 2008 reprint)

For parks as tools of urban regeneration, and urban parks, see:
—*The Granite Garden: Urban Nature and Human Design*, Anne Whiston Spirn (New York: Basic Books, 1984)
—*Cities and Natural Process: A Basis for Sustainability*, Michael Hough (London: Routledge, 2004 edition)
—Again for much in the chapter, *Park Life: Urban Parks and Social Renewal: A Report by Comedia in association with Demos*, Liz Greenhaigh and Ken Worpole (Stroud: Comedia; London: Demos, 1995)
—*The Regeneration of Public Parks*, edited by Jan Woudstra and Ken Fieldhouse (London: E. & F. N. Spon, 2000)
—*Public Parks: The Key to Liveable Communities*, Alexander Garvin (London and New York: Norton, 2011)

Author interview with Ken Worpole conducted on 15 July 2014.

The *Independent* newspaper published a report on the park lottery grant on 21 May 1993 by Michael Durham, under the headline 'Lottery cash to fund city parks clean up: revival plan to drive out vandals'.

For a less grim fictional portrait of park gardening in the early 1990s see Nicola Barker's delightful Palmer's Green-set novel, *Small Holdings* (London: Faber, 1995)

For more on the linear parks see:

—again *Park Life: Urban Parks and Social Renewal: A Report by Comedia in association with Demos*, Liz Greenhaigh and Ken Worpole (Stroud: Comedia; London: Demos, 1995) and, also again:

—*The Park and the Town: Public Landscape in the 19th and 20th Centuries*, G. F. Chadwick (London: Architectural Press, 1966)

—*Park for the Future: A Best Practice Guide for the 21st Century*, Paul Geerts (Ostend: Kristof Beuren, 2014)

The State of UK Public Parks report published by the Heritage Lottery Fund in 2014 can be downloaded at: http://www.hlf.org.uk/state-uk-public-parks

For the state of Derby Arboretum on its 175th birthday see:
'Britain's public parks: 175 years old, but will they survive?', Harry Wallop, *Daily Telegraph*, 3 October 2015

For the sale of Bexley's parks see: 'Bexley council chiefs reveal first four open spaces to be sold off as authority attempts to balance the books', Luke May, *Bexley Times*, 18 November 2015

For the Hyde Park softball kerfuffle see: 'What the Royal Parks is doing to a charity softball league should matter to us all', David Allen Green, *New Statesman*, 8 August 2013

For the commercialisation of the Royal Parks see: 'Royal parks forced to hunt for cash', *Financial Times*, 4 March 2016

For the Queen Elizabeth II Olympic Parks environmental credentials see:
https://queenelizabetholympicpark.co.uk/~/media/lldc/policies/lldc_your_sustainability_guide_to_the_queen_elizabeth_olympic_park2030.pdf

Also, however, see: 'The Incredible Shrinking Park' video blog by John Rogers at: http://thelostbyway.com/2015/09/the-incredible-shrinking-park.html

For the campaign to make London a National Park see: http://www.national-parkcity.london

Afterword

For ParkRun and fees at Little Stoke see:

—'Council votes to charge Parkrun for Little Stoke event' (BBC News online 12 April 2016 http://www.bbc.co.uk/news/uk-england-bristol-36030582)

—'Councils might be desperate for cash, but charging parkrun isn't the solution', Peter Watts, (the *Guardian*, 15 April 2016)

For the Inquiry and responses to it see:

—*Inquiry into Public Parks*, Communities and Local Government Committee, (11 February 2017 online at https://www.publications.parliament.uk/pa/cm201617/cmselect/cmcomloc/45/45.pdf)

—'UK's cash-starved parks at tipping point of decline, MPs warn', Damian Carrington, (the *Guardian*, 11 February 2017)

—'Public parks in danger of falling into neglect, warn MPs', (BBC News Online, 11 February 2017 www.bbc.co.uk/news/uk-politics-38935787)

—'What do the parks inquiry findings offer the sector?', Sarah Cosgrove, (*Horticulture Week*, 17 February 2017)

Index

Page references in *italics* indicate photographs or illustrations

Sebastopol, Siege of (1854–5) 154, 155, 171

Second World War (1939–45) 240, 241–64, *243*, *254*, 311

Sefton Park, Liverpool 326

self-improvement 157–8

sexual activity, public parks and 36, 37, 49, 50–1, 54, 88, 210–12, 255–8, 256n, 267–8, 292–3, 307

Sexby, Lieutenant Colonel J. J. 181, 182

Seymour, Lord 156–7

Shaftsbury, Earl of: *The Characteristicks of Men, Manners, Opinions, Times*, 37

Shakespeare, William 41, 144–5, 176, 176n, 178, 269, 307

Sharp, Joseph Fox 150

Shaw-Lefevre, John 182, 184

Shaw, George Bernard 194, 200

Shirley, James: *Hyde Park* 35–6

Shuttleworth, Joseph 171

Sidney Park, Cleethorpes 190

Simon, Donald 315

Skibo Castle, Sutherland 192

Slade, Felix 166–7

Sladen, Chris 260

Slaney, R. A. 70–3, 71n, 88, 90, 98

Smiles, Samuel: *Self-Help* 158–9

Smith, Albert 168

Smythson, Robert 22

Soane, John 62

social clubs, public park 287

Socialist League 176, 200

Society for Improving the Conditions of the Labouring Classes 100

Society for the Diffusion of Useful Knowledge 70

Sørensen, Carl Theodor 289

South Bank, London 49, 73, 268–9, 270, 273, 275, 276, 277, 278

South Kensington Museum, London 187

Southey, Robert 81

Southwark Park, London 212, 238

Spark, Muriel 232

Spear, John Murray 199

Spectator 37, 42

spies, public parks and 264

spiritualism 193, 194–5, 198, 199

sports centres 282, 283–4, 287, 311, 318, 320

sports, organised 159–66, 163n, *164*, 166n, 168–9, 190, 220, 231–4, *234*, 261, 279, 281, 282–4, 284n, 287, 311, 318, 320, 325 *see also under individual sport name*

Sports Council: *Planning for Sport* report (1968) 311

Spring Gardens, Whitehall, London 49

Spry, Constance 232

St James's Park, London 3, 16, 20, 34–7, 50, 93, 212, 245, 264